Values and Stakeholders in an Era of Social Responsibility

Values and Stakeholders in an Era of Social Responsibility

Cut-Throat Competition?

Paolo D'Anselmi

First published 2011 by
PALGRAVE MACMILLAN

Palgrave Macmillan in the UK is an imprint of Macmillan Publishers Limited, registered in England, company number 785998, of Houndmills, Basingstoke, Hampshire RG21 6XS.

Palgrave Macmillan in the US is a division of St Martin's Press LLC, 175 Fifth Avenue, New York, NY 10010.

Palgrave Macmillan is the global academic imprint of the above companies and has companies and representatives throughout the world.

Palgrave® and Macmillan® are registered trademarks in the United States, the United Kingdom, Europe and other countries.

ISBN 978–0–230–30373–7

This book is printed on paper suitable for recycling and made from fully managed and sustained forest sources. Logging, pulping and manufacturing processes are expected to conform to the environmental regulations of the country of origin.

A catalogue record for this book is available from the British Library.

Library of Congress Cataloging-in-Publication Data
D'Anselmi, Paolo.
Values and stakeholders in an era of social responsibility : cut-throat competition? / Paolo D'Anselmi.
p. cm.
Includes bibliographical references and index.
ISBN 978–0–230–30373–7 (alk. paper)
1. Social responsibility of business.   2. Social responsibility of business—Case studies.   I. Title.
HD60.D264 2011
658.4'08—dc22   2011013742

Printed and bound in Great Britain by
CPI Antony Rowe, Chippenham and Eastbourne

For Stefania, Sara and Sofia

Contents

List of Figures, Tables and Questionnaires

Figures

Tables

Questionnaires

Acknowledgements

Chapters 1, 9, 11, 12, 13, 14, 15 are based on: Paolo D'Anselmi, 'Il barbiere di Stalin – Critica del lavoro (ir)responsabile', preface of Aldo Bonomi, Epilog by Toni Muzi Falconi, Università Bocconi Editore, 2008; and: Paolo D'Anselmi, preface by Aldo Bonomi, Epilog by Toni Muzi Falconi, 'Critica della Social (ir)Responsibility', *Communitas*, 11, October 2006.

Chapters 2, 3, 4, 5, 6, 7, 8 are based on: Paolo D'Anselmi, Giuseppe Frangi, Sebastiano Renna, Simone Morganti, Maria Carmela Basile, Margherita Cappelletto, Alessio Richichi, 'CSR: la forza del contro-esempio', *Communitas*, 39, December 2009.

The case study in Chapter 12 is based on: CNR Report 2003 e 1998 Consiglio Nazionale delle Ricerche, team leader Andrea Lapiccirella; team members: Fabrizio Tuzi, Simone Morganti (co-authors of the case study).

The case study in Chapter 13 is based on: 'Forze dell'ordine. Dar conto del lavoro pubblico', Paolo D'Anselmi and Romina Giannini, Simone Morganti, Riccardo Coratella, Lorena Mazzenca, *Rivista italiana di comunicazione pubblica* pp. 89–106, no. 34, Franco Angeli, 2007 (co-authors of the case study).

The case study in Chapter 14 is based on: 'Posi – Pon Atas', Simone Morganti, Margherita Cappelletto, Alessio Richichi, 2008 (co-authors of the case study).

I am grateful to Giuseppe Ambrosio, to Güler Aras for encouragement from the Social Responsibility Research Network, and to Simona Argentieri, Francesco Baldanza, Giuseppe Berta, Riccardo Bonacina, Giuliana Bonanni, and to Ettore Cambise for early guidance. My thanks go also to Roberta Caterini for checking the numbers of national accounts for Table 15.2, and to Maurizio Carrara, Sergio Casartelli, and Michele Cilli for over twenty years of work together. Thanks to Filippo Colangeli and Giorgio Colangeli, and I welcome also David Crowther's encouragement from the Social Responsibility Research Network. Jacob Dahl Rendtorff, Mario Dal Co, and Guerrino De Luca gave much needed advice and tough criticisms. My gratitude also goes to Massimiliano Di Bitetto and to Dario Di Vico for space on the *Corriere della Sera* website. I am grateful to Stefano D'Orazio and to Alessandro Ferrara for friendly philosophical teachings. Thanks to Gaia Fiertler, Giuseppe Frangi, and Antonella Gargano, as well as to Marco Ghetti for generously given long-run support, and Olivia Golden, Anselm Görres, and to Donato Iannuzzi for a great deal of work. My thanks go to Kristijan Krkac, and Mauro La Noce, and to Andrea Lapiccirella for criticism and inspiration on bureaucracy and democratic government, to Stefania Lenci, Herman Dutch Leonard, and Antonella Magliocco, and to Gianluigi Mariani for long-run editorial advice and mentorship. Thanks to Claire Mays, Nicola

Melideo, and Cristina Merlo, and to Simone Morganti for over ten years of work together. For his mentorship, I thank Toni Muzi Falconi, and I thank Supriya Nayak, Jane Nelson, and Antonio Nunez Martìn. I would also like to express my gratitude to Onyeka Osuji, Vaifra Palanca, Fabio Pagliarini, Paul Parks, and Francesco Perrini, and to Salvatore Pettineo for the great deal of work undertaken. For their work with me at an early stage, I thank Rinaldo Piccolimini and Alberto Quagliata. My gratitude goes also to Christian Rauscher and to Alessio Richichi for the considerable amount of work undertaken on figures and tables. My thanks to Stefano Rolando and to Fabio Savelli of the *Corriere della Sera*, and also to Lisa Shaw and Giorgio Sirilli for exchanges on social issues. I would also like to express my appreciation to Bianca Spadolini, Laura Spizzichino, and Chiara Stangalino for early encouragement, and Tania Strelkoff for translation, editing, and moral support. My thanks to Akshaya Tankha, Antonio Tencati and to Roberto Turi for checking the data in the national accounts in Table 15.2, and Fabrizio Tuzi, Fabio Ventoruzzo, Marilù Vinci, and Armando Zelli, the 'Reportists Anonymous' group of the weekly magazine *VITA* of Milan, as well as the ferpi.it website.

I am indebted to you all.

PAOLO D'ANSELMI

List of Abbreviations

ACS	American Cancer Society
AIDS/HIV	acquired immunodeficiency syndrome/Human Immunodeficiency Virus
BAe	BAe Systems/British Aerospace
BASIC	British American Security Information Council
BMW	Bayerische Motoren Werke
BP	British Petroleum
BVMW	BundesVerband Mittelständische Wirtschaft
CAPEX	capital expenditure
CDA	Communications Decency Act of 1996 (USA)
CDI	Consumer Delight Index (CDI)
CEO	chief executive officer
CESR	Committee of European Securities Regulators
CNH	New Holland Construction
CNR	Consiglio Nazionale delle Ricerche
CNRS	Centre National de la Recherche Scientifique
CR	Corporate responsibility
CSIC	Consejo Superior de Investigación Científica
CSIR	corporate social (ir)responsibility
CSR	corporate social responsibility
DLNA	Digital Living Network Alliance
DSL	Digital Subscriber Line
EBITDA	earnings before interest, tax, depreciation and amortization
ECB	European Central Bank
EDF	Électricité de France
EITI	Extractive Industries Transparency Initiative
EU	European Union
GDP	gross domestic product
GM	General Motors
GRI	Global Reporting Initiative

ICT	information and communication technologies
ILO	International Labor Office
INSERM	Institut National de la Santé et de la Recherche Médicale
IPIECA	International Petroleum Industry Environmental Conservation Association
ISO	International Standards Organization
JCR	journal citation reports
JRS	Jesuit Refugee Service
KPI	key performance indicator
LBG	London Benchmarking Group
MECR	mean expected citation rate
MIT	Massachusetts Institute of Technology
MPG	Max-Planck-Gesellschaft
MSF	Médecins Sans Frontières [Doctors without Borders]
ODA	overseas development aid
OECD	Organisation for Economic Co-operation and Development
OHSAS	Occupational Health and Safety Assessment Series
PIAP	Public Internet Access Program
PR	public relations
SCI	science citation index
SMEs	small and medium sized enterprises
SUV	sports-utility vehicle
SWOT	strengths, weaknesses, opportunities and threats analysis
UMTS	Universal Mobile Telecommunications System
UMW	Unternehmerverband, Mittelständische und Wirtschaft
UPnP	Universal Plug and Play Forum
WICI	World Intellectual Capital Initiative
WIP	work in progress
WTO	World Trade Organization

Introduction

Talking responsibility with my barista

(Ir)responsibility is not always the responsibility of other people. And not everyone needs to know what (ir)responsibility is. Let us start, then, at the very beginning, with the meaning of the words we will be using:

Barista: Good morning, sir. Your usual brew?

Paolo: Yes, please.

Barista: I never asked you before, but what do you do?

Paolo: I draw up balance sheets. Like an accountant. I write books based on company balance sheets (and government accounts). They're my clients. I could even do it for your coffee shop.

Barista: Thanks, but I already have a book-keeper and he isn't cheap.

Paolo: Oh, I wasn't really offering, just mentioned it in passing.

Barista: My book-keeper doesn't write books, though. He just sends in my tax returns.

Paolo: Sure. The shop is a small business. Writing a book about it would be very expensive. Anyway, I do more than draw up balance sheets. I write documents that have a lot more information than that.

To understand what sort of information I gather, just imagine that you want to sell your coffee shop. There's a person who is interested in buying it – let's call him Ahmed, and he wants to see your tax returns, your official balance sheet – the one that shows your minimum earnings. A company would call that your 'turnover.' So, Ahmed comes here and stands with you behind the counter, by the cash register, to check whether the earnings you've declared are real. You might have even told him that you've declared less than you actually earned. This may not be so in your case, but

1

there are places in the world where this is the norm. I should know. I'm an international professional after all. Anyhow, this would be his way of diligently checking the information your book-keeper gave him.

In company jargon, this is called 'due diligence,' and there are people who specialize in going around and trying to find out whether what's reported in company balance sheets is true or false.

Later, at closing time, Ahmed would go with you to check the cash register and count the sales slips from the pastry and coffee sales. This is what's called 'cost accounting,' and it's not shown in your tax returns. This is how Ahmed would find out that you make much more money from selling pastries than coffee, so that $1 taken from the sale of pastries is worth more than $1 from the sale of coffee. Coffee vs. pastries. This is a typical assessment of what companies call 'profitability of action' or 'direct product profitability.'

At this point, Ahmed would probably begin to take note of other things he needs to know. Are the staff polite to customers? Do they work quickly? Are they cheating on the coffee; using too much of it? Are they diligent in the consumption of basic supplies? In other words, are they interested in 'customer care' and 'loyalty' to the business? Ahmed will also want to know whether the customers are passers-by or regulars. Regulars are a sign of satisfaction (customer satisfaction) with the coffee shop and the service. If they come back, it means they're getting exactly what they want.

He might have some questions, too, like whether the vacant lot next door to the coffee shop will be used for new office blocks or a massive multi-story car park, or whether or not the bus stop right in front might be moved a few yards further down. He'll talk to the local police to find out what they're like; whether there'll be hassles should he decide to upgrade the coffee shop to a kebab restaurant or make the shop sign bigger; or the likelihood that they'll grant him a license to put a few tables outside on the sidewalk. He'll probably go to a nearby coffee shop and order something. He'll ask himself whether he can put up with the traffic noise at this intersection, since he'd have to spend most of his waking days there. He'll check the prices of the suppliers compared with those he works with already. This comparison price is called a 'benchmark.' He'll check whether health and hygiene regulations are being applied, examining the toilets and the extractor fan, which seems to be on its last legs. And also what will be done about any unpaid fines.

In other words, Ahmed will weigh the opportunities and the risks to see whether he'll be able to pay the bills of exchange he'll be signing. This is what's called 'creditworthiness,' and it's a useful concept for you, too, because it's no joke to bargain a high selling price for your shop only to find that your buyer can't afford to pay it!

In this way, we've looked at all these people – the local police, the customers and the suppliers – who never figure in your tax returns but who do affect the performance of your shop. In company jargon, they are called 'stakeholders.' Only when he has all this information can Ahmed answer the question: Do I buy this place or not? And if I do buy it, what price should I pay?

So, you see, there's a lot more going on between the lines of what actually ends up in a tax return.

Barista: Now your coffee's cold. Let me make you another one.

The theoretical balance sheet that I've just drawn up whilst standing at the counter having breakfast is called a corporate social responsibility (CSR) report, or a sustainability report. It is a document that 'tells all,' and tries not to leave anything out or hide anything from the reader.

CSR reporting should be leveraged to provide a serious tool of internal and external communication. At present, many major companies publish an annual CSR report, or sustainability report. Many studies are available on CSR, but very few on CSR reporting. CSR reports are written in a heuristic fashion. Standards are observed in a useless way; see, for instance, the table that most companies write at the end of their report to cross-reference the Global Reporting Initiative (GRI) standards. The result is that resources are spent and very little is accomplished: colleagues within the company look at the report as a perfunctory activity, stakeholder representatives go with the flow, journalists shun the reports as 'news-less' propaganda, and top managers – above all – tolerate this good-manners habit.

The sustainability reports of corporations are the empirical basis of this study. The aim is to figure out what its optimal content would be – what information should it provide to perform a worthy job. It is opportune to do this because these reports are an opportunity for awareness on the part of the corporation, as well as for the public to find out what is going on in the economy and in society.

There are many skeptics of sustainability reports who view them as a perfunctory activity of the organization, and this healthy skepticism will be confronted at once.

Sustainability report: balance sheet or bull sheet?

'"Bullsh*t," my CEO would say, if I went in and proposed drawing up a sustainability report for our company.' This was the sour reply of my friend, the assistant of a well-known European manager, when I offered to undertake a sustainability report project for his company. This consideration would have been even more appropriate, since the company was not a real company but some sort of institution – a foundation working on a dictionary of language, enjoying generous government subsidies.

Managerial stallions were very harsh towards CSR. In January 2005, *The Economist* came out with a very critical survey that basically stated that all monies spent on social activities were not only a drain on money from shareholders' pockets, but also a distraction of management time, attention and energy.

Not only the orthodox *Economist*, but also fine intellectuals partial to social issues were – perhaps unawares – feeding a culture of economic machismo. In a well-documented study of Italian corporations in the 1980s and 1990s many utilities were praised as profitable, since ranking was based on profits and stock valuation.

What is the relevance of this to CSR and the sustainability report? I believe the sustainability report is an opportunity to ask oneself (and cultivate a doubt about) whether a utility that is making profits above the market average is perhaps strangling consumers. The sustainability report is not necessarily a window for alms or sponsorship of the performing arts. In a sustainability report, a company can give an account of the competitive context whereby profits are earned. Along this line, one can point out a difference between a company that is subject to international competition, one that has a dominant market position and a utility that is a full-fledged monopoly.

In a sustainability report, a company can extend its view beyond the shareholders, to consumers and society at large. In 2004, in Italy, the antitrust and energy regulators found out that prices of energy products were high while the quality of service was poor. In the sustainability report produced by Fiat, one could read of the so-called voluntary agreements that kept Japanese cars out of Italy for a long time, an account of repeated government subsidies for Fiat investments in the Italian south, and quality checks versus BMW mechanics.

In a sustainability report, one could read about the share of deposits from government agencies in the Italian branch of BNP Paribas, which made up for the key value of that bank when it was acquired by the French giant from the Italian government itself. Maybe all this information is confidential? Well, perhaps it is time that the confidentiality be removed and competition be extended to other areas, benefiting all parties involved.

A sustainability report raises its gaze towards the wider impact of a corporation on the economy and society. It's about the disclosure of information and responsibility. Seen this way, the report appears less perfunctory. It is clear that what is said in it is of equal interest to us as what could have been said. It appears that there are opportunities in sustainability reports that are not currently being taken up. Chapter 1 takes a detailed look at what sustainability reports look like at present.

It is a general finding of communication theory that what is communicated reveals about the communicator something of which the communicator himself may not be aware. Even if the organization is not truthful about itself, the very act of communicating, of writing a report, reveals about the organization something more than the organization itself meant to communicate in the first place. In other words, I contend that by analyzing responsibility reports – provided we reveal what we think ourselves, in our turn – we can also reveal something the organization did not mean to reveal in the first place.

'The reluctance to open up and relay "what is really happening here" is a common experience' (Kakabadse *et al.*, 2007). This is no secret about organizations and individuals; neither does it carry particular stigma on specific subjects at hand. Without resorting to psychoanalysis, the thesis about revealing relationships found normative explication in the two-way model of communication of James Grunig (Grunig *et al.*, 1995), which establishes a symmetrical relationship between the parties involved. Finally, theater was the first form of communication explicitly meant to elicit sentiments and truths out of unaware parties. Shakespeare poetically expressed this circularity and synthesized it in one line, spoken by Hamlet: 'The play's the thing wherein I'll catch the conscience of the king.' Through the representation that organizations give of themselves in sustainability reports, I'll catch their social responsibility.

Preview

A latent energy lies at the heart of many economies of the world: that energy is the positive value of competition by which hundreds of millions of people live their daily occupations. Being subject to competition, they are accountable for their work. Competition is therefore a powerful driver of responsibility. Many other workers in the same economies are less accountable to positive social or economic forces: the workers of regulated industries, monopolies and public administration, or government. However, tapping the energy of competition is a difficult task as competition is a tricky force, despised by those very people who live by it. In public and private discourse, 'competition' is quite often preceded by a scary adjective: 'cut-throat.' Hence cut-throat competition. Thus, economic units subject to competition fail to bring that value to bear in the social and political arena, thereby failing to turn their weakness – being subject to competition – into an opportunity (i.e. asking that all workers be subject to a form of competition or accountability). This predicament delivers a deficit of meritocracy in society, a deficit of effectiveness in governments' action, and lack of efficiency in protected and regulated industries. The end result is an overall weakness in the economies affected by such deficit, a competitive disadvantage. The goal of this book is to show – with cases in capsule form – the differences of accountability in the diverse sectors of the economy, to quantify the potential, to identify the hindrances that prevent the coming of competition as a factor of social and political advance within each country, and, finally, to reveal those economic actors that could benefit from gaining awareness of being subject to competition, thus questioning the negative aura that pervades the value of competition and turning that value into a positive one.

Competition is lived within the narrow limits of vertical industries and international trade debate. Thus, it is only characterized as a constraint. Competition should be brought to bear horizontally, among different economic sectors, within the boundaries of each country and nation, in order to make governments accountable for their actions and regulated industries efficient in their functioning. Governments, infrastructure and monopolies – when accountable, and therefore on their way to being efficient and effective (the governmental equivalent of being subject to competition) – contribute to the competitive advantage of nations. The logic of collective action (i.e. structured self-interest) thus delivers SMEs as a key stakeholder to embrace the value of competition and have it observed by those sectors of the economy and the institutions that do not observe it today. SMEs are too small to be studied, too many to be ignored, too fragmented to be helped. The value of SMEs lies only in their efficiency as a shock absorber in the economy, but this only brings vague statements of principle. Through the force of competition, the representative bodies of SMEs have an opportunity to become a full field stakeholder in the political arena, and to make governments effective and regulated industries efficient.

Starting from CSR, analyzing what CSR is, what it is not, and what I'd like it to be, I extend CSR to all organizations in the economy (private businesses and public institutions). I thus develop the concept of 'accounting for work' as a duty for everybody within society. Such a duty brings to the political and economic foreground the struggle between work subject to competition and work performed under monopoly privilege. Once the political arena is redefined along these lines, SMEs become a protagonist in the debate for the advancement of society. SMEs have a potential benefit to reap here, and all they have to do is become aware of the value of the competition/accountability that they already embody. With no extra effort, they can achieve advancement in society.

What is CSR?

CSR is present when businesses respond positively to society's problems. The invitation to take such responsibility came in the early years following the turn of the millennium from the United Nations Global Compact. The United Nations Global Compact is a strategic policy initiative for businesses that are committed to aligning their operations and strategies with ethical principles. The idea of companies adhering to CSR has spurred the reporting of such behavior, and such reporting has given rise to guidelines for doing so. An example of such guidelines is provided by the GRI.

Because it involves activities done outside the core business of firms, CSR as defined in the preceding paragraph has encountered much skepticism on the part of the managers of corporations. I therefore embarked on analyzing the CSR reports of various corporations and came up with a solution that would hopefully be seen as more relevant to business: a process framework that is also compatible with issue frameworks such as the GRI guidelines. An issue framework consists of guidelines that tell you what data to provide in order to report on CSR. The proposed process framework is formed by four values:

- the unknown stakeholder;
- disclosure;
- implementation; and
- micro-ethics.

This framework is about the 'how' of looking at the core business of firms in order to identify instances of CSR, to manage them and to report on them.

A key element of the proposed process framework is that CSR ought to look at the instances where 'irresponsibility' can be identified within corporate behavior. This is also expressed through the concept of 'think negative,' commonly expressed as 'negative testing'; this is testing aimed at showing that something does not work ('test to fail'). In fact, we believe that the 'positive' reporting of the issue frameworks is subject to the risk of 'anesthetizing' oneself with all the good things that organizations do, thereby missing the point of possible irresponsibility. This point of view makes CSR germane to risk management.

Extending the concept of CSR

I then propose to extend the concept of CSR to all organizations, beyond the private businesses and corporations listed on the stock market. The cogent reason for doing so is that the boundaries between private and public institutions are far from clear-cut. A further reason is that current non-market mechanisms of accountability of public institutions – mostly based on legal control – appear to be inefficient, and need to be extended or modified. Therefore, the general notion of CSR is formulated as 'accounting for work': all work must be accounted for.

Vertical competition

One driver of accountability is vertical competition: this is the struggle experienced by companies engaged within each industry and within the same economic sector. This is the competition to which we are accustomed: the competition that brings producers (but not consumers) unwelcome phenomena such as price cutting, international relocation and imports. Vertical competition is central to the process of accounting for work because vertical competition in and of itself makes work accountable, if not instantly valuable from a social point of view, and at least subject to social scrutiny. Vertical competition certifies accountability. It does not guarantee society that the firm or the organization will behave correctly, but it does guarantee society that – having the opportunity to adopt competing goods and services – it can do without the bad company. Competition does not rule out the need for awareness, management and reporting of CSR.

Horizontal competition

However, not only vertical competition is at work here: horizontal competition is also present. Horizontal competition is the struggle between different industries and sectors of society to appropriate shares of national income. The objective of vertical competition among individual companies is to prevail over competitor companies and win shares of vertical markets. But competition also takes place – less obviously, but having no less impact on income – on an aggregate level, between entire sectors of society: for instance, public administration vs. private companies. Originally, CSR came into being under the pressure of public institutions on private corporations: this pressure was one instance of horizontal competition between different economic sectors (public institutions forcing private businesses to do something for society, and therefore also for the workers in public administration). Once the duty of accountability is extended to all economic sectors (public and private, profit and non-profit), horizontal competition between economic sectors becomes the crucial driver of accountability, and a reverse process can take place: sectors subject to competition (i.e. private companies) can ask accountability from those sectors that are not subject to vertical competition (i.e. the public sector), with the objective of reaping benefit from better and more socially profitable work by the public sector.

The workforce in the economy can therefore be partitioned horizontally between that part of it which is subject to vertical competition and that part of it which is not subject to vertical competition. The notion of 'competitive divide' is thus derived: the work of workers, employees and executives who are not subject to vertical competition enjoys a shelter *vis-à-vis* the work of those who are subject to competition; therefore, those who are not subject to competition must give account of their work through the introduction of vertical competition or through pseudo-market mechanisms, such as CSR reporting and benchmarking. Somehow, the work and the jobs that are not subject to competition must account for the validity of their social contribution – basically through virtual vertical competition (benchmark) and transparency reporting. From an empirical point of view, SMEs and the majority of workers and jobs in the economy are on the competitive side of the competitive divide, while monopolistic sectors (such as the government sector) are on the non-competitive side of the competitive divide.

Reversal of the CSR picture

The CSR picture is reversed at this point: CSR appeared to be a game for large corporations who could afford CSR executives and CSR budgets; people struggled to figure out ways to 'do' CSR in SMEs. Under the auspices of competition, SMEs become a key actor of social responsibility in society. They are of foremost significance to CSR, as they are immersed in vertical competition.

Moving society towards accountability

What is the force that will move society towards accountability? Horizontal competition is the answer. This force will be the self-interest and the collective action of those who are subject to vertical competition *vis-à-vis* those who are not subject to competition. Horizontal competition is the competition between those who are, in their work, subject to vertical competition and those who are not subject to such vertical competition. Horizontal competition is a force more relevant to the economy than the owner–employee, public–private, left–right, labor–capital dialectic. We could also call it 'power struggle.' Vertical competition exists because many want to sell to few; horizontal competition exists because social groups – differing by their position *vis-à-vis* competition – still compete with each other to appropriate shares of national income. For instance, public sector workers' salaries are driven by different mechanisms than those regulating the salaries of private sector workers. Nonetheless, there is a struggle between private sector workers and public sector workers to increase their own salaries, one at the expense of the other. This is horizontal competition.

Why bother?

One question always asked about CSR is: 'Why bother?' My argument answers this question through horizontal competition: all institutions must account for their work because it is in the self-interest of those who are subject to competition that those who are not subject to competition account for their work as well.

Who will be the social actor of horizontal competition?

It is certainly not the individual shopkeeper who will be interested in promoting the social value of competition. The representatives of those who are subject to competition will be the associations of small, medium-sized and micro-enterprises – a micro-enterprise being the self-employed and those small businesses with fewer than 10 employees. The specific incentive for the small business association is tapping the reservoir of social and economic value (being subject to competition) – already embodied in their own fabric – in order to obtain political clout and, starting from a vantage point, to negotiate with public sector representatives and governments.

I have therefore undertaken a project to take to the local representative bodies of nationwide SME associations, the following message: 'You are the embodiment of a positive social and political value: competition. You should make that weigh in your local and national interaction with government and large businesses.'

CSR and its harbinger competition confer legitimacy to SMEs as a key actor in the political arena. Under the auspices of competition, SMEs become a full field stakeholder in the social and political arena. They become interested in seemingly remote fields such as government workers' policy, industrial policy and subsidies, law enforcement and justice. This is not a 'noble' end; it is an argument of equality of citizens and workers *vis-à-vis* work conditions, accountability being a key condition of work.

Are SMEs ready to receive the message?

One preliminary finding is that local SME associations are immersed in vertical competition and, though intrigued, are not ready to act upon the value of horizontal competition. Neither are they very much interested in checking the reality of their own social responsibility – there always being room for improvement. They have practical needs that need to be met in order to serve their members, the small entrepreneurs; these needs are of greater relevance to them than listening to general statements of political intent. They are, however, interested in CSR; and they are interested in developing a consulting formula that allows them to deliver a product or service to their members. Therefore, a CSR concept for SMEs is being developed in partnership with some local associations.

The positive value of competition at the supra-national and trans-national levels

Finally, an effort is also being made to bring the message of competition as a positive value to supra-national and trans-national levels. The notion of competitive divide is applicable to all economies, if not to the entirety of each specific economy; our notions are confined to the developed part of society that is well above the poverty line. Also, the notion of SMEs is a global one, when taking into account the diverse structure and dimensions of SMEs in each economy. Therefore, a move by SMEs towards removing the competitive divide appears to be one that all societies and all economies can entertain and profit from.

Part I
Developing a CSR Process Framework

In this first part, the basic argument is laid out and first conclusions reached. The problem is to find a sense of CSR that is useful and not shunned by corporate executives. The solution is a framework of values consistent with corporate needs and catering to information that is not captured by ordinary financial statements.

Chapter 1 analyzes companies subject to competition. Some 'bon ton' is revealed, like the phony messages based on the rhetoric of business as family, ranging from the words of Bill Gates to those of the Egyptian magnate who addressed his employees as 'Dear Family.' Good responsibility reports are identified as those implying disclosure of data beyond the strict needs of law, such as the case of Nike, which, after some trouble, revealed the list of its suppliers and provided an analysis of its working conditions.

This chapter is made up of 11 cases from companies selected as representative of different industries and prominent on a global scale. This sample appears thus to be universally meaningful for the corporate world.

In Chapter 2 four noble truths of CSR are proposed. From observation of distinctive CSR content – present or omitted in the CSR reports – I derive the four noble truths of CSR and explain why they are noble and why they are truths: (1) CSR always exists, independently of the observer; (2) you can be aware of CSR; (3) you can manage CSR; (4) the CSR report is the vehicle for gaining awareness and management of CSR.

In Chapter 3, equipped with the four noble truths of CSR, I can now check them against the literature. The most encompassing, operational and constructive approach I have seen so far is the *Harvard Business Review* (December 2006) paper by Professors Michael Porter and Mark Kramer. Thus I use the Porter and Kramer paper as the keystone to check my theory by comparing the categories and content I have derived from my cases against Porter's taxonomy (categories and examples).

Chapter 4 asks the question: Is this a heuristic approach? There is such a wealth of notions that it is probably not possible at this time to try to capture CSR into one domain. However, it will be shown later that there is solid cultural background to it. And yet, a framework is needed.

Is there a new model to be proposed? The profession is seeking a model for the CSR report that will not be overwhelmed by the wealth of notions and cacophony of the many points of view in this professional field.

On page 50, I investigate the Figure in the Carpet: deriving a paradigm from the database. I propose four values that summarize the distinctive content identified in the chapters on the database. These are: the Unknown Stakeholder, Disclosure, Implementation and Micro-Ethics (USDIME).

In Chapters 5 through to 8 I elaborate on the four values and illustrate with specific cases. Chapter 9 examines the professional implications of the USDIME framework. This concerns the future of professional reporting culture. The chapter also addresses the issue of the relationship between the Public Relations and the Public Policy Analysis professions.

Thus CSR is a historical opportunity for PR to free itself from the fetters of hidden persuasion. It is a historical opportunity for policy analysts to have their skills probed. The two professions should be allied in this venture. So the USDIME framework moves CSR analysis from communication studies to business and policy analysis.

Applying the USDIME to the 2009 CSR reports of ten big companies in Chapter 10 I find encouraging fragments of what I prescribed should be written in a decent CSR report: Toyota is giving margins (i.e. gross profit) by region of the world, thus providing data about its own Unknown Stakeholder; British Petroleum provides data on reserves' replacement rates, thus providing a quantitative indicator of sustainability (value of Implementation); WalMart provides data on criticized (low) employee salaries – data on production factor resources belong to the stewardship of the Unknown Stakeholder; some bankers timidly mention Lehman Brothers, others pretend it did not even exist; monopolies only whisper they are subject to government regulation (this is the case of a gas duct manager); Unicredit, an important Italian-German bank, discloses data on its own employee infighting (Disclosure).

The relationship of the proposed framework to international standards and other frameworks for corporate analysis is covered. The domains defined by international standards are rather dull – the GRI is a good thing to have but it does not make interesting reading. It is a prerequisite, not the be all and end all of CSR and CSR reporting.

I propose a syncretic approach with the complementary use of other frameworks: value chain and SWOT analysis. There are imperfections in this framework – values are not m.e.c.e. (mutually exclusive and collectively exhaustive.)

A second proof of the quality of the framework is its 'teachability': quality coursework. I enclose here – what I find interesting – observations that my students made on corporate reports after being taught the USDIME framework.

1
The Backstage of Capitalism

Let us now study the social responsibility reports published by those companies subject to greater competition: international organizations. When making comparisons, it is important to keep vast horizons in the forefront; in a nutshell, comparison works best at the international level.

Linux? Microsoft ignores it

We'll begin with a company that, at the turn of the twenty-first century, was a real giant – the archetype of the global company: Microsoft. Microsoft is the producer of the software that makes personal computers go around. It is the author of such partners in our everyday life as *Word*, when we write a letter, and *Excel* when we make a table of numbers.

One by one, the 80 pages of the Microsoft Citizenship Report 2004 slipped agilely out of the printer only to end up virtually unread, mainly thanks to the dreadful preface, co-authored by Bill Gates and Steve Ballmer, which ended with a trite: 'Together we can change the world.' This was a ritual formula, appealing to the people – an entity as abstract as it is inflated. Corporate communication was becoming theoretic and full of generalities, appealing more, it seemed, to the meditators of an ashram than to ordinary human beings who had yet to embark on a spiritual path. Pretentious language haunted much of corporate writing.

However, the report managed to get back on its feet at the table of contents, wherein references to the Global Reporting Initiative (GRI) guidelines were included for each section. The GRI is the global, non-profit organization that elaborates standards for the triple bottom line report (the jargon definition of the corporate social responsibility (CSR) report, owing to the fact that it aims to account for three domains of corporate activity: economic, social and environmental).

How could the Microsoft report have been improved? In subsequent editions, Microsoft should have inserted these references into the body of the text, across the whole report and using the graphic style of the GRI, to allow those who went so far as to want to study the report to be able to evaluate the text's adherence to the standard. Comparability is a key objective of a standard. Comparability should be pursued both within the reports of the same company over time and between reports of different companies. The anarchy of reporting is one element we should keep in mind in our subsequent considerations.

A diligent reader could aim right for Microsoft's weak spots to see whether the report talked about the antitrust cases being filed against the company at that time. Yes, the report talked about them, and even indicated an Internet site for further details, but it would have been useless to dig deeper and ask the report to detail the results of the lawsuits, whether or not Microsoft negotiated a settlement – as in, admitted fault – or whether it had won.

And Linux? Not a word. The open source software system that represented the greatest threat to Microsoft's global supremacy was ignored entirely. Casual reference was made to a computer program capable of doing the same things as the Microsoft programs, with the added advantage of being available for free on the Internet. Linux was the result of collaboration on the part of many programmers and software architects who wanted to contrast Microsoft's pervasive presence on the market, and it would have been correct to mention the existence of similar initiatives in the company's strategic framework. In subsequent years, Microsoft would have done a great job if it had confronted this situation – and even published in its reports large sections of books that analyzed the competitive context in which software is produced, and the economics of cooperative commons.

The Citizenship Report did not have many numbers in it, and this was a wise choice. Being a sustainability report, it could have devoted more space to the core business of the company than the financial statements, which are the accounting counterpart of the sustainability report. It did have a section that was correctly titled, 'Responsible Business Practices,' which was the first in the volume and was dedicated to the disclosure of company affairs – that is, to the revealing and recounting of the company's business activities. This is hardly do-goodery. What was missing, however, was feedback concerning users. Not mentioned, for example, was how many complaints the company received about the pesky *Word* bug that periodically asked users whether they wanted to send an error message to the company.

Better-updated were issues relating to governance. The report confessed to there not being social responsibility among the tasks of top management in the past. It had adapted by inserting it among the tasks of a certain committee (one of many such committees abounding in multinational and domestic companies). It is difficult to evaluate this confounded area of governance, which was so much in fashion all over the world at the time, because one risks demanding ever greater amounts of data. On the other hand, by not demanding it, one runs the risk of accepting lip service – the good intentions that pave our way to Hell. Let's just say that I don't consider issues of governance to be particularly demonstrative of a sense of responsibility.

From the insignificant results gleaned up to this point from Microsoft's report, one is wont to ask whether there are other reasons to disturb the universe with the valuation of Microsoft's social responsibility besides the need for models in life and beyond the previously stated international comparison. Microsoft was paradigmatic. It was successful and couldn't but deal with its various frills and propriety. On the contrary, it could actually talk about its own problems frankly, since it was the first in its class and could handle a B in conduct. So what if Microsoft's Citizenship Report seemed styled vaguely along the lines of a school essay writ big and adjective-heavy, which motivated certain journalists to consider the discussion of CSR just so much bull.

If the only effort on the part of the company entailed paying somebody to write a responsibility report, it means that we are still waiting for someone like Brother Luca Pacioli – who is the man who invented double-entry book-keeping – to invent double-entry social book-keeping. Social balance is not evaluated for brilliant results but for the sharing of certain gems obscured by bureaucracy, misunderstood team spirit or laziness. It is to be evaluated according to the brutality with which things that don't work are admitted to. If Union Carbide wrote about Bhopal, it would have written a great social responsibility report. Writing about social responsibility is like undergoing a cleansing of the conscience, and has to hurt. A cleansing of the conscience that does not hurt is not a cleansing of the conscience.

The external effects of McDonald's

From Microsoft to McDonald's, we still find ourselves in the upper echelons of global enterprises. When Ahmed, our future coffee-shop owner, walked by a McDonald's, his Mediterranean sensibilities were offended by the smell of potatoes fried in vegetable oil that drifted around the entire concourse.

McDonald's was a textbook case of CSR reporting, an updated and politically correct version of the classic example of the undesirable external effects of economic activity – the smoke from the Italian pizzerias that blackened the clothes at the Chinese laundry. If you were curious to know whether the McDonald's moguls talked about filters and smells in their responsibility report, you could download their Corporate Responsibility Report 2004 and check it out. They didn't, but they got real close and convinced the reader.

The McDonald's report was convincing because it did not seek a third position – that is, alternative routes to normal business in addressing responsibility. In fact, the report was laid out as a business plan for making money according to the four Ps of marketing: the product (what is being palmed off on the customers), the place (where the product is distributed – the restaurant), the price and the promotion. In other words, the various formulae with which people are enticed into eating more French fries. To these initial four Ps a fifth was added – people – that is, the employees, their career opportunities and treatment.

The report began with an evaluation of responsibility for the product (those good buns loaded with rich sauces) by undertaking a dietary analysis from which the company conceded that it was not healthy to eat at McDonald's every day and at all hours. After the product, place was considered, and here the network of restaurants was bared in every aspect, from a study of the waste generated – solid and otherwise – to a study of the economic impact of McDonald's restaurants on the local community.

McDonald's had hired a business economics professor – a solid, trustworthy looking gentleman (there was even a picture of him in the report) – who studied a specific geographic area around Chicago (McDonald's had more than 24,000 restaurants in 10 countries around the world in which it was most present). The results of the professor's study showed that over 40% of the proceeds of a single restaurant were absorbed by the territory in which it was located in terms of supplies, employee salaries and profits for the restaurant owners. In fact, McDonald's ownership is apportioned. After the main company, one must keep in mind the many local franchise owners. As for the employees, the professor found that, in that particular geographic area, the staff remained with the company on an average of 18 months, which was double the national average. One should add that Chicago is worth more as an example than as a model.

Mention was also made of the GRI, even though there wasn't a trace of the parameters prescribed by it in the report. But let's go back for a second to the waste. It is curious to note how obsessed the company was with garbage around the restaurants: 'Littering is an individual responsibility in the end but the company exhorts its employees to clean up outside the specific restaurant grounds themselves.' No small detail, this, because CSR is about going beyond what's prescribed – outreach, over-delivery. And as far as the smell goes, there was a form available on the website for customers and readers to fill out to provide feedback. In reality, the site and the company did not appear to want more than to receive input from diverse cultures in order to be able to boast that the company's relationship with its customers was so important that they – the customers – would take time to communicate their opinions.

Finally, there was a table in which every kind of waste produced by the restaurants was analyzed, which demonstrated – contrary to what a distracted reader would have expected – that the majority of the waste produced by the restaurant occurred behind the counter where the staff worked and not in front of it, where the customers stand. Certainly, it was not McDonald's that was the biggest polluter in the world – but it was interesting to see how meticulously certain aspects could be studied, especially of large organizations to which possible research results could be applied on a vast scale.

The results of this study and its publication had both practical and cultural implications. Lifting the curtain from the backstage of capitalism, the responsibility report took the myth away from it, showing its modest import, its stinginess, the miserable day-to-day of it. At the same time, analyzing each activity attributed to each the dignity of honest work. Sometimes it even helped to pacify those people who objected to multinationals *per se*, as public opinion in their regard was rarely the best.

BAe Systems' weapons

From software and French fries let's move on-to a more dramatically burning issue: weapons. Once again, we ask, as Tibullus did: 'Who first invented these horrendous swords?' Let's talk about weapons starting with the ancient poet's question, which always insinuates itself in the responsibility reports of this business. Is it to blame for the murders in today's world, and obviously those of yesterday, as much – if not more – attributable to those who produce weapons than to those who use them? Let's see if and how BAe Systems posed this question.

BAe probably stands for British Aerospace, though the Corporate Responsibility Report 2004 gave no explicit definition. To feel at home anywhere in the world, and extend this feeling to its customers and the public, companies at this time sought post-ethnic anonymity behind imaginative (Accenture) or Latin (Vivendi) names, or in unbelievable exotic languages (the unpronounceable nomenclature of IKEA furnishings) or, finally, in undecipherable acronyms such as BAe. BAe was the British multinational of which the Italian Finmeccanica and the French Thales were competitors. Ninety thousand people throughout the world, and sales equal to €20 billion – a company of the same size as Chrysler or Fiat. A producer of contemporary instruments of war: radar systems, airplanes, avionics, ships, military submarines and smaller submarines for civil use.

BAe Systems knew it was operating in the stigmatized business of the arms exporter and recognized 'the particular responsibility of understanding the worries of others.' The Corporate Responsibility Report 2004 began with a bit of theory on stakeholder engagement – that is, the close relationship with the stakeholders against whom the responsibility of a company was often measured. Client, supplier, local community, shareholder – these are the concrete individuals behind the English noun 'stakeholder.' The report cited the good review in the Dow Jones Sustainability Index Assessment regarding the good rating that BAe Systems got on the New York Stock Exchange from the worldwide point-makers of financial do-gooding, but, on page 10, the report got to the heart of the subject and laid out the first of two critical issues: state subsidies.

Given that orders from the Royal Air Force are suspect as government subsidies, perhaps the British government could spend those monies (the suspected subsidies) better elsewhere. This was the point of view of the British American Security Information Council (BASIC), an independent think-tank with which BAe had initiated a debate on the company's impact on the national British economy. BAe maintained that it was very competitive and that it sold its products at a fair price (otherwise they would not have had clients in 130 countries throughout the world). Also, one should appreciate the gentlemanly way that BASIC views on the subject were given greater prominence on the page than BAe's own rebuttals, using a slightly larger print.

After the economic impact and potential government subsidies, the report went on to illustrate methods of interaction with clients – a delicate way to approach the second critical issue: corruption. In fact, it is never sufficiently clear how weapons are sold. Effusive words were spent in the Responsibility Report to show how committed the company was to applying anti-corruption laws, while pointing out the difficulties for such a company in a world where compliance with law was oftentimes questionable (both in the West and in the East) and in which everybody, at least once in a lifetime, has produced a false invoice in order to evade taxes. There was, however, an original element in the approach proposed. BAe undertook an interesting attempt to introduce compliance indicators in its corruption policy.

In order to come up with indicators, BAe established a support hotline for its employees throughout the world. The indicator was made up of the number of telephone calls to the hotline and the type of problems reported. 'In 2004 it received 42 calls for help; of these, 26 were related to personnel issues, 11 were requests for clarification, 2 concerned cases of suspected corruption and 3 had to do with environmental issues.' Succinct and concise, the report signed off: 'We've had our say, now it's your turn.' The model followed was convincing: 'Our responsibility is expressed first of all in good business practices,' do-goodism comes later. Had the list of country clients, numerous throughout the world, been published, it would have only satisfied the curious and not constituted a further gesture of transparency.

There was no trace in the report of the standards of the GRI and, it must be admitted, these were not missed because the analytical work done by BAe appeared incisive, even without a guide. A curious thing – the dark background of the pages of the Responsibility Report available on the Internet caused no small measure of problems for both printers and readers.

And Tibullus? The report did not pick up the poet's stigmatization of arms producers. The responsibility of the manufacturer was resolved in the relationship with buyers thanks to 'clear warning and deliberate consent,' to borrow the Catholic requirement for mortal sin. Perhaps the answers of the report were sufficient to respond to the critical nature of the issues treated; therefore, let's not ask too much of an instrument – the CSR report – the main task of which consists precisely in initiating and recording a debate. The debate itself is a good enough answer. Tibullus, however, followed up his initial question-accusation with verses much more oriented towards the responsibility of the user: 'Maybe the poor man [the producer] had no fault: it was us who turned against ourselves the instruments he had invented to defend us from terrible beasts.'

Total's Club Med

From arms to oil, more burning issues. The title Total gave its 2002 Report was encouraging: Sharing our Energies. But as the report continued, the authors lost their way. With 111,000 employees and a turnover of €105 billion (a good 5% of Italy's gross domestic product – GDP) the corporation is so huge that it looks more like a large electoral constituency. It was the fourth oil company in a competitive context in which the Italian company ENI is a player. Despite Total's size, the structure of the report reflected the classic, Cartesian, triple bottom line. Total acknowledged its awareness of all the key issues regarding accountability:

1 dissent regarding globalization, 'a social and economic order that is perceived as unfair, a source of instability and untenable in the longer term';
2 the distribution of wealth in the producer countries; and
3 the need to 'Combat corruption and enhance transparency.'

It did, however, recognize, discreetly, that there was an 'unflattering opinion' about its business. 'Image is the Achilles' heel of many large companies and Total is no exception.' While it is debatable whether worries about image should be considered a primary issue, here was justification for explicitly mentioning the importance of image, considering the great frankness with which Total had previously addressed the most urgent and substantive issues, and that it had relegated image to the role of a mere effect – a background element.

Total exhibited a sense of responsibility for the future, even though the previous year's report had revealed that its oil deposits had a 45% greater potential than the amounts extracted; this meant that it had not reduced but had actually increased known available resources. With no ace up its sleeve – a solution that would solve, once and for all, the issue of long-term energy supplies – the corporation was committed to researching alternative energy sources in every direction, such as the hydrogen fuel cell on which trials were being conducted in the Berlin research center (far away from certain autarkic temptations which, from time to time, afflict scientific research) and had cooperated in a number of projects with Renault (in a tribute to its French origins).

With regard to its relations with the producer countries, it spoke frankly about security issues and certain self-serving friendships with such countries as Myanmar (Burma), where it claimed to have 'a positive presence in a controversial country,' providing a list of all the criminal trials currently underway. In June 2003, at the Evian G8, Total had endorsed the Extractive Industries Transparency Initiative (EITI) but the (perhaps naïve) desire to know how much of the oil revenues would remain in the countries from which oil had been extracted was to remain unsatisfied.

Its sense of responsibility was much more thoroughly examined at the local level, where the Report considered the development of the communities in which Total was operating its extraction and production facilities. It ranged from Indonesia to Nigeria, offering actual case studies. It is difficult to judge: Republic of Congo, Canada, Angola, Iran, Syria, Russia, the Philippines, Argentina ... you name it and Total is there. Like BAe, Total is present in 130 different countries worldwide. And then there are its environmental projects, scholarships and all the rest of it. Its aim was to work for tomorrow's economy when there would be no more oil left to extract, at a time when oil reserves were only expected to last for another 12 years.

The report waxed eloquent about local development with the typical French knack for making even bureaucracy look like an adventure, with a *grand projet* – great project – for every community; whatever it might be – political, religious or work – it gave the unaware outsider the warming Club Med feel. The accountability report even printed a photograph of the managers of each sector – each village headman: the *gentil organisateur*.

The style may have been a bit wordy and long-winded, but it did get down to brass tacks and gave as the monetary value of the work it was doing for the benefit of the local communities €77 million – peanuts for a corporation with an operating profit of €16,061 million, and post-tax profits of €9,612. Here there arises a general need to assess accountability, because everything is relative. Any expenses on charitable work need a benchmark value with which to be compared to see whether or not the company is in line with the average.

So, let's take a look at occupational accidents. Total did not lock itself inside its corporate perimeter and reported that, including suppliers, 11 people lost their lives in industrial accidents that year. It's a good thing to take account of suppliers' responsibility in times of widespread outsourcing.

I liked Club Total, even though it ignored the GRI. After all, isn't that the French way?

Nike: disclosure and diversity

Now to go from the delicate issue of oil to the delicate issue of child labor. Social responsibility is not just a pastime for idle enthusiasts of this subject. It is a precept of good public relations. Being honest, conducting research and revealing data works. One gains from being transparent by making a hole in the fog of media congestion.

Exemplary was Nike's bold gesture in 2005 to reveal the list of its Asian suppliers and publish the results of research carried out on their labor conditions.

To tell the truth, Nike made this decision after heavy pressure from the international community. In fact, in previous years the company had been the target of a campaign denouncing the exploitation of child labor on the part of its primary suppliers – those in Asia. Photographs were circulated of children sewing shoes with the company logo in clear view. Once the responsibility report was published, the media diffused this news and, in a short period of time, a great deal was said, good and bad, concerning Nike operations.

Let me add a bit of shop talk here to complete the picture. The first point is that when an evaluation of social responsibility is serious, it reduces the reviewer's room to maneuver because it acquires relevance with journalists. Those who aspire to undertake social evaluations, not just to study them, must always keep in mind that disclosure, the revealing of inside company information, is the central idea of the concept of social responsibility.

With regards to Nike, the first objection to be raised will be: 'Finally! The press has been making life difficult over those poor kids forced to work in pitiful circumstances,' and this is true. But, to give a much lighter example from Italy, for how many years have Italians been hearing dreadful stories about the one-sided conditions that Fiat imposed on its suppliers? Have they ever seen a report about that? And let's not forget the well-known memo from Ingegnere Carlo De Benedetti on the brink of the 1992–94 recession: suppliers paid after 180 to 210 days. At the time, De Benedetti was the owner of Olivetti, a company from the Piedmont region that produced personal computers – once a famous brand of typewriters and teleprinters.

Second, it must be clear that the more you open up, the more you reveal, the more you can be criticized. This is a general principle of reporting. A well-made report offers occasions for the reader to ask for even more information, because it opens new horizons for the company as well as for its readers. Nike's responsibility report got to the heart of the issue in a table that went far beyond the list of suppliers being focused on by the media and by describing the working conditions in each of its 569 factories. A group of inspectors had been sent out to evaluate each place and had meticulously compiled the results of the inspections. Conditions in the factories were deplorable, but hardly amounted to slavery. In the table, the line corresponding to slavery was the only one not filled in, thus guaranteeing that no cases were found.

If this information, far from making us feel outraged, led us to conclude that knowing is, in any case, better than not knowing, and that this is the reality of the world where working for Nike can be an objective for a malnourished child – if we accepted that, then we were dealing with the fact that the parameters we apply at home are far different from those applied elsewhere. This meant we were talking about diversity, and diversity is accepting something negative. We accept something that we regard as negative on the grounds that its context, for instance, might be different from the context in which we evaluate the negative thing. Diversity does not apply when we accept something just because it does not affect us.

It's not that everyone went crazy at Nike and forgot about profits and competition (Adidas and Puma, for example). The last point in the report, in fact, threw out a challenge: We want to jump-start the disclosure of data and collaboration with the entire industry in which we operate. By 'industry' they meant all the competing companies in the strictest economic sense. Not surprisingly, a little further on the report spurs its adversaries: 'We have disclosed our data, now it is the turn of our competitors to do the same. If they do not, we will do it for them.'

Nike counted on starting a contest on labor conditions, thus the competition got fiercer and reached a new level. Beyond the minimum cost of production, it aimed at extending to suppliers the perimeters of perceived quality. This promise helped the public, at least in part, to accept the harsh diversity described previously. And yet, one can object that this doesn't work because we are talking here about confidential company information related to competitive advantages. Were that it was so simple, that all you need is information to gain an advantage. We have seen companies obtaining knowledge step by step about the advantages enjoyed by competitors concerning prices, or how things are done, and still remaining at the starting gate, stupefied by all that information.

Competition is also played by being, not only by knowing. Corporate intelligence, as fascinating as it might be as a subject for Hollywood movies, doesn't seem to appear much in the recipes for organizational excellence. It's the other things that make companies tick: disclosure and self-examination.

The yoke of Fiat

Concerning Fiat's social responsibility, I imagine a note to the managing director, Sergio Marchionne, from the consultant who wrote the report. This note and the report relate to a difficult period in the company accounts – much improved in the months following the document I envisage below, though no causality is identifiable between the delivery of the report and the improvement of corporate accounts:

> Dear Sergio, I enclose herewith the draft of the Responsibility Report 2005, taking this occasion to detail the work undertaken and to transmit some confidential considerations. The report analyzes the company according to the triple bottom line formula. In 110 dense pages, we have detailed a non-evident vision of the company like, for example, the non-automobile component, notwithstanding that your automobile public image, industrial Iveco vehicles and CNH tractors make up nearly half of all sales.
>
> We have developed the indicators proposed by the Global Reporting Initiative and by the Italian Social Policy Ministry, confining them to the end of the text even though this does not satisfy the criteria by

which discussion should be had around them. I hereby note a point to be advertised widely: only one fatal on-the-job accident – no small thing considering the total Italian number of 1,500.

In the past months, in order to produce this report, we have undertaken activities of internal communication that have been creating cohesion within the Fiat Group at a global level. This is a return on internal expenses and energy devoted to the report. In this way, the report loses its taint of 'just one more thing to do' and becomes a productive activity; but the greatest benefit, when analysis is undertaken, is in what is found that wasn't sought. This has to do with information that is not provided, as yet, to the public but that consists of elements of institutional awareness that contribute to company strategy and future decision-making.

We have not side-stepped a single obstacle. All issues have been dealt with but their boldest treatment rests in your hands. It is proper that the evaluation of social responsibility be in the hands of the public relations men, but it is the top management that gives it its soul. Below are my considerations.

Regarding car and transportation safety, we confined its definition to the strictly technological without touching the issue of the responsible use of automobiles. Considering that even brewers worry about our youth (enjoy-heineken-responsibly.com), you might wish to consider shredding the hypocrisy that dominates this sector and talking clearly about the 6,000 automobile deaths in Italy every year, as well as in the other countries of the world.

We have skirted the issue of competition (in the report it's as if Volkswagen and Nissan do not exist), but our hearts are filled with admiration for the solid thunk made by BMW car doors – an intangible benefit guiding the Italian consumers who don't buy national brands.

Concerning traffic congestion, we cannot deny that your sustainable mobility projects are being realized in Stockholm, while in Italy reliance is on alternate license plate days, so one day cars with plates that end with an odd number can circulate and the following day even number car plates can drive around. Concerning the environmental damage to historic city centers, it may be necessary to jump into the fray and lobby for closing historic city centers to cars.

However, the issue that concerns us the most is future commitment – increased company value and competitiveness. We have mentioned the General Motors case but not said why General Motors preferred to pay several billion Euros in order not to have anything to do with Fiat any longer. We said that Fiat has accompanied Italy's development during the twentieth century and have compressed into one-third of a page its role in the Italian state. Five lines have been given to the 40,000 man march in 1980 and two to the burning autumn of 1969, key events in the social history of the country.

We have dealt with the money received from the state in order to spur employment in the south of the country, but the choice to be made now is whether it is beneficial to waste time with this situation any longer, as it traps us in a domestic mind-set. Your president was recently concerned about there being too many Daimler Smart For Two driving around the city of Rome – a very minor and provincial issue. Despite the fact that sales have increased in Italy in 2004, our vision is that Fiat should look to its future outside this nation and take its historic yoke off its shoulders.

Holcim's breathing cement

'Little houses on the hillsides, little houses made of ticky-tacky, little houses on the hillsides, little houses all the same ...' There was a song in the 1960s that lamented poorly constructed city sprawl. Many decades have passed since that song was heard daily, but cement production hasn't suffered. It is a typical 'glocal' business, tied both to local conditions of supply and demand, and to global technologies. Supply was the availability of materials – basically soil – for the layman, too poor to be worth transporting. Demand was the presence of a construction industry engaged in the development of real estate and infrastructure building.

These are the reasons I now consider the CSR report of an international company, Holcim, in one of its local specifications: Holcim of Italy. This was their first responsibility report and it embraced the triennium 2002–04. Considering its long-term perspective, this report started off on the right foot since, having a view longer than a single solar year, as in financial statements, was one of the interesting attributes of the CSR report.

Holcim was present in 170 countries, had reached sales of €259 million in Italy in 2004 and had a pretty healthy cash flow – 40% of turnover. A good several million tonnes of cement were produced; slightly less than one million cubic meters of concrete – enough to build a city, even though no reference was made to market value. The chapter on antitrust talked about an agreement made between competing companies to the detriment of their customers, about the penalty inflicted by antitrust authorities and its overturning by the court.

The report talked about the core business of the company and demonstrated with a clear diagram that the lacerations visible on the hillsides from strip mining supplied necessary raw materials for construction and could be subsequently recuperated. In its initial summary, the report drew a tree with many branches to articulate environmental performance – an exhaustive diagram of the various aspects of the company's impact on the environment: the use of raw materials, energy consumption, water use, emissions, waste, noise pollution, site recuperation, transportation and investments.

It was instructive *per se* because it attempted to identify and understand realities that are often difficult to perceive and define. That attempt symbolized the fascinating implications of responsibility reporting, the challenge that every operational evaluation poses to those who undertake it, the report writer, and those who read it. The report was educational until it got to the numbers and things got complicated – not to confuse people, it would seem, but because it had to do with very technical business.

Substituting raw materials with recycled materials is the key to sustainable production. In 2004, 6.8% of recycled materials to the total of raw materials was the 'technical-economic break-even point.' In particular, clinker was what made cement strong, like nickel in stainless steel. Its use was energy intensive because, to undergo fusion, it required fuel; and it damaged the environment because it came from the strip mines. Holcim demonstrated that, despite the fact that the production of cement had increased, the use of clinker had increased less than proportionally thanks to the company's efforts to substitute clinker with less costly materials. It was thus an example of synergy between economic activity and respect for the environment – a value shared by both company and society.

I would have appreciated a table of the total number of facilities, and a map of those facilities. This would have helped me give the correct weight to the summaries concerning the sites located in the small towns of Merone and Ternate, of which it was otherwise difficult to understand the importance. It is necessary to supply complete references (I would call them, in engineering jargon, the 'denominators') in order to make the reader understand the importance of the measures described.

The Internet site also talked about a Holcim foundation for sustainable construction. This gave rise to a spontaneous proposal on my part: to give out grants to centers of study on housing and real estate in order to consider and propose to the public the demolition of much housing built piecemeal, in a *favela*-like fashion. This would be followed by the undertaking of reconstruction by rehabilitating skyscrapers, making them socially acceptable, in order to ease the century-old problem of the 'high antropic concentration' in Italy, to use the euphemism of the Minister of Industry, Pierluigi Bersani, in *Il Messaggero*, in 2006. The Minister said more: 'When things are done, costs are inevitable,' meaning 'you cannot make an omelette without breaking eggs.' The French provide a good example of such a pragmatic attitude. Despite their fame for being stuck-up, they had no qualms about situating their much-vaunted Parisian architectural feat of *La Défense* in the backyard of the Neuilly cemetery. See it to believe it, on Google Earth.

Monnalisa's caring for China

Monnalisa brand name children's tee-shirts and shorts would seem to have nothing to do with corporate responsibility or socio-operational issues, but that was not the case. The highlight was a graph in the 2006 sustainability report where it noted that, as far as suppliers were concerned, foreign (Chinese) suppliers were growing and domestic (Italian) suppliers were down.

At that time, the commercial balance of the company was still in Italy's favor, in the sense that the difference between Italy and abroad in terms of purchases was still lower compared with the difference between Italy and abroad in terms of sales, but the small increases compared with previous years symbolized the growing Asian threat. Procurement from China was partial, marginal – yet, in this seemingly unimportant aspect lay the crux of the competitive battle between China and Italy.

The domestic clothing manufacturers that were the main suppliers of Monnalisa requested defensive action, worried about that negative trend. The manufacturers were those who cut, sewed and prepared the clothes, while Monnalisa orchestrated the whole thing as a systems integrator – a small joint: 60 employees max. Clever.

Monnalisa appeased its domestic manufacturers by instituting a focus group, a practice designed by marketing consultants aimed at considering issues in a systematic fashion and, perhaps, coming up with some good ideas to face the Asian threat. What this focus group came up with – hardly original – was that it was the fault of others (the Chinese), and Monnalisa pledged to 'make consumers appreciate' the value of products made in Italy so that people would no longer want to buy goods from China (or so the domestic manufacturers hoped). They – the manufacturers – also wanted to end the practice of piecework, so Monnalisa pledged that it would 'train' them to become real entrepreneurs themselves. The usual things, in other words. This was the dynamic, and Monnalisa's report just told the story about it.

Therefore, the results of a survey on the importance for consumers of products made in Italy were provided: 'Do you, the consumer, excluding the brand name of a product, attribute value to where the product is made?' How did Italians respond? 'Always,' 25%; 'Often,' 45%; 'Sometimes,' 25%; and 'Never,' 5%. These numbers provided a quantitative map of consumer preferences about globalization, but the results of the survey – worthless *per se* with regard to consumer purchasing decisions, which one would hypothesize would be biased towards lower prices – seem hardly unanimous in favor of the domestic provenance of a product. One could conclude that the Italian consumer did not much care where a product came from.

The lack of continuity among the suppliers under the 'commercialized' product category was still to be linked to imports from China. In fact, 'commercialized' was a euphemism for 'products entirely produced abroad' but still sporting the Monnalisa brand because it was a Monnalisa design, brand, look and style. Monnalisa neither made a pretence nor acted as if it were above these things but gave its disclosure with a table: the total number of suppliers in relation to the number of suppliers that had been used at least twice in the last four years. Big difference. People came and people went but Monnalisa controlled them all, undertaking to visit them and report on their activities.

This could have been an occasion for development had the working conditions at the various suppliers' sites been evaluated, as Nike had done. Improving those working conditions could have been a means to the ends espoused by the right in the vigorous debate about immigration from the developing countries – let's help them in their countries. Let's help them stay at home. There is an ambiguity in the status of a developing country as perceived by the public in a developed country. People feel compassion as long as miserable living conditions exist and the country in question begs for help. As soon as a developing country actually 'develops', it becomes able to compete and earn its living on the international market. It becomes a commercial threat and the loss of business to that country is no longer listed under the heading of 'development aid.'

The table of Monnalisa stakeholders – weighted by their added value on a double page of the responsibility report – represented a 'galaxy of added value,' which alone compensated the reader for the effort of analyzing Monnalisa's report: 111 pages within which were the financial statements and CSR report, rich with numbers and tables to illustrate concepts and assist the reader. Amid illustrations of roses and violets *à la Seurat*, Monnalisa demonstrated great management savvy.

Novartis and Médecins Sans Frontières

In March 2007, even *Sans logis* – the magazine produced by Parisian *clochards* – published news regarding a petition circulated by Médecins Sans Frontières (MSF) (Doctors without Borders) against Novartis, asking that it desist from carrying out its lawsuit against the Indian government for a law in that country that protected the status of the manufacturers of generic drugs for the use of the poor. In fact, historically, India did not recognize the patents in force in the West and, after having been invited by the World Trade Organization (WTO) to do so, passed a law in 2005 that stated that 'no patent should be granted on a merely minor adjustment of an existing drug.'

The lawsuit concerned Glivec, a drug used to cure a rare form of cancer. MSF said that 84% of the drugs that it acquired to provide relief throughout the world were generic Indian drugs. Novartis countered that 99% of Indian patients that needed Glivec would have received it for free. That data related to different aspects. The confrontation between MSF and Novartis was somewhat difficult to follow. MSF was providing data only about its own consumption of Glivec equivalent drugs, while Novartis was not talking about exports of Indian drugs and only giving data about the Indian population.

The real issue for India appeared to be its own drug industry, not the sick; and it feared that patenting threatened its industrial position in the long term. Novartis' margin in the developing world was not significant, so the issue for the company was not to obtain profit in the medium term. It, too, was looking to the far future when India and China would have substantial income and would become profitable markets capable of providing a profitability comparable with the Western markets.

Besides, the idea of 'merely minor adjustments' meant that an effective generic drug was already available to the public, and this weakened the position of the petitioners. The poor could be treated with the good-enough existing drug, while the rich would be treated with the new drug, which had undergone merely minor adjustments. Calling the results of scientific research 'minor adjustments' appears a rather shaky criterion that requires some more specific information. A media campaign conducted on the basis of such a statement is very prone to the risk of ideology, thus jeopardizing the credibility of the protesters.

It is interesting, however, to note that the mechanism is sort of self-balancing. If it is just a minor adjustment, why fight it? Judging a discovery as minor or not is unacceptable from the logical point of view, and serves only to allow the granting authorities a margin of discretion. It is true that a patent is hardly an optimal solution as compared with the complete freedom to work on discoveries, but the human race has so far devised no other means by which to get private industry (also made up of human beings) to support scientific research. Where collective benefit is recognized, governments and populations should finance scientific drug research instead of developing atomic weapons.

This discussion can be widened. People earning a living from legal dramas or from the amount of time citizens spend sitting in their cars are not stigmatized, while those who earn a living curing the sick – including drug researchers and manufacturers – are considered exploiters. It is certainly curious, this scale of responsibility that people apply when considering gut-level judgments. And yet, there are probably far more doctors riding around in Porsches than there are pharmacists. The truth here, too, lies somewhere in the middle and, before the greatly feared long term arrived, there were other initiatives by the WTO, and other attempts to find an agreement – with Sanofi Aventis, for example, an agreement was apparently reached to make a drug against HIV/AIDS available in Africa.

Sanofi Aventis for Africa?

Contrary to what I was expecting, there appeared to be little emphasis in the work of Sanofi Aventis on the problem of AIDS in Africa. Sanofi Aventis produced drugs to cure those illnesses most common among AIDS sufferers: tuberculosis, malaria and others. It made these drugs available on a two-tier price basis (for higher-income and lower-income people) and was involved in settling the distribution problems. The issue, in fact, was not so much the price to the public but, rather, the existence of a distribution network for the drugs. Making the physical availability and delivery of drugs a sustained reality was an objective, rather than a starting point.

Sanofi Aventis maintained control over the ownership, the production and the distribution of drugs – healthy, paternalistic capitalism, in other words – as was the case in Europe during the 1950s when pharmaceutical companies were involved in profit sharing with pharmacies. That was also one way to make drugs available at the stores, but perhaps discouraged certain wholesalers from getting into the market. A day will come when developing countries will have grown and other pharmaceutical companies will denounce this set-up as uncompetitive; nonetheless, for that day to arrive, today it is essential to stay alive so SA attention to the delivery of drugs was welcome.

The countries being served by Sanofi Aventis in Africa were those in which the company enjoyed certain productive privileges, but we don't know the scope of its reach throughout Africa. Could it have been making things easier for the Francophone countries while leaving the rest in the dust? The devil is in the detail.

The state of the pharmaceutical industry was effectively summarized in the words of a former official of the European Patent Office, Claudio Germinario: 'Small and medium-size enterprise does not innovate and does not patent' (Associazione Liberinsieme, 2007). All this talk about large pharmaceutical enterprises could lead to thinking about some sort of operation that those who oppose the industry could deploy, like Linux freeware overcame, to some extent, the Microsoft monopoly. So, can one imagine an exchange on the part of pharmacological researchers to create a pharmaceutical commons? This would be, as Linux was, an initiative of do-goodery by technicians, motivated by intellectual challenge and anti-establishment leanings more than by the heart and philanthropic feelings.

The ethics governance of Siemens

Between November 2006 and April 2007, an important aspect of the CSR drama was enacted. Slush funds were found in the Siemens books to the value of €420 million, spent between 1994 and 2006 in different countries around the world, such as Saudi Arabia, Greece, in Germany for the unions and in Italy for Enel and Italtel. Let's first take a look at the proportions. Siemens is noted for its size and technology: 475,000 people in 190 countries, an €87 billion turnover in 2006, which can be compared with the €1,500 billion Italian GDP. Profits of €3 billion can be compared with a small government budget. The company's sectors range from electro-mechanics to medical equipment, computers and telecommunications, including such brands as Bosch, Fujitsu and Osram. The scandal forced the 'sad goodbye' of Heinrich Von Pierer, president of the oversight committee and former CEO of the group from 1992 to 2005.

If even Siemens is corrupt, it means that corruption is commonplace. Codes of practice are only words and good for little except an ethical summary. I can point out that the phenomenon in Siemens has very small proportions: €420 million spread over more than 10 years ends up being 40 million a year – a small amount considering the €3 billion profit, and minuscule compared with turnover.

The ubiquity of corruption offers the opportunity to explain a disease that is found in many countries. When corruption is found and the judiciary is in action, those who are accused usually say there is a plot against them, a coup by a group of judges. The public, however, projects its own personal experience on to it. The public sees a light at the end of the tunnel of pervasive corruption and supports the judges, knowing that the boards of directors of government-owned companies are basically committees on behalf of political parties.

Political observers insist in their commentaries on two opposite sides: 'judicialism' or 'guaranteeism.' Judicialism implies that the support by the public of the judges' actions is a revival of the *Terreur* (terror) phase of the French Revolution. The public is blood-thirsty and supports any sort of terrorism through judicial action. Guaranteeism insists that those who are accused should be protected no matter what, even in the face of evident fault. Polito-logical analysis does not deepen its analysis of the economic and social reality, and lacks all culture of implementation. We live amidst corruption – 'Thus Do They All' – but, when the time to change comes and corruption is brought to light, it won't be judicialism to spur public support; neither will guaranteeism stop things.

Stealing on behalf of a political party is worse than stealing for oneself. Stealing for oneself means you are a thief, and society knows how to defend itself from thieves. Instead, he who steals on behalf of a powerful organization implicitly attempts to change the rules of society and the very game that is being played. The strong 'understandings,' shall we say, between political parties and companies smother the economy because bribery isn't just a straight cost. It is not capitalism and, when someone says that things used to get done with bribery but now bribes no longer exist and the economy is stagnant, he reveals an approach that is very provincial and backward.

Siemens' corruption policy in this context appears to be very linear. When a top manager is made responsible to supervise the deeds of his successor and the company's ethics, he becomes the scapegoat for any dirty business that is revealed. This is a good way to stretch, as much as possible, the permanence of a top manager in a responsible position. Knowing that he will be there for a long time to come after he's left office, the top manager is tempered in his temptation to act unlawfully. If we have to live with corruption, the Siemens' case tells us that their way to govern it may very well limit its damages.

Conclusion

In this chapter, we have reviewed mostly large companies subject to international competition that we often hurriedly – and not without disdain – wrote off as multinationals. And yet, a review of their work demonstrates that they reach moments of peak behavior when they open their hearts and supply information that nobody asked for, at least not directly. Nonetheless, moments of retentiveness and good manners are not lacking, along with formalities and ritual. I have demonstrated how responsibility brings us to a pervasive picture of a company. With the use of the picklock represented by the analysis of social responsibility, we can open companies' black boxes and illustrate their activities, dedicating particular care and attention to the work they carry out.

The examples have demonstrated that it is the details that reveal the essence of the work done: McDonald's list of garbage, the table delineating the working conditions in Nike factories, Fiat car doors, the debts of small entrepreneurs, the supply network of Monnalisa and the 'minor adjustments' of Novartis drugs. The stories I have narrated appear to be random samples of good and bad behavior on the part of companies and businesses. Yet, they share common traits that I now briefly summarize:

- they are mostly based on information provided by the companies themselves in their CSR reports;
- they show a criticism of what was said by the companies, as well as expectations on content that the companies do not provide; and
- they implicitly show some nature of CSR.

In Chapter 2, I try to draw some generalizations from the observations that I have interspersed in the stories of the companies considered thus far.

2
CSR Is Who You Are (It's Not What You Do)

What have I been talking about so far? What have I been looking for in the companies' reports? In this chapter, I am going to be asking myself what sorts of observations I've been making about corporations so far, the nature of those observations, whether I can draw generalizations from them and what their relationship is to the rest of the corporate world.

I start by drawing some generalizations from the criticisms I have expressed in Chapter 1, in which I told a series of stories. These stories appear idiosyncratic: I did not examine a whole industrial sector systematically; neither did I adopt any other evident methodology. I just picked some noteworthy stories from CSR reports and personal experience. Moreover, the criticism I expressed is apparently *ad hoc* under the circumstances. I now embark on giving a framework to my story. I try to make a novel out of short stories – I am in search of the figure in the carpet, a possible meaningful pattern that appears from chaos when you study it carefully.

CSR is not philanthropy

> And if I give all my possessions to feed the poor ... but do not have love, it profits me nothing ... Love never fails.

I can't help but go back to St. Paul's first letter to the Corinthians, every time that CSR is confused with philanthropy, and organizational responsibility is confused with support to the non-profit sector. It is a trite example to recall that Lehman Brothers were very munificent but irresponsible business-wise and therefore – I contend – showed little CSR. Lehman is just a global example that everybody knows, but any one of us can come up with the name of a company sporting a code of ethics while filing for Chapter 11 under the US Bankruptcy Code.

As one prominent scholar put it, 'corporations that seek recognition as being socially responsible are usually seeking some regulatory favor.'

Living on the margins

Once more, I have to go back and differentiate between giving money and respect for business. Let's separate 'giving' from CSR. CSR is the attempt to capture the 'spirit of love' within an organized environment. More for the layman, CSR is a genuine intention, honesty towards society. In a nutshell, all businesses and public organizations live on the margins of unlawfulness and good management. They struggle to survive in the short and in the long run. They muddle through.

There was no need for the financial crisis of 2008 to prove this definitively. Any tax accountant or administrative officer for an organization of any size could tell you this. And I am taking an international view here, not only the nice OECD developed democracies of more or less Anglo-Saxon origin and mores, ethical and organizational traditions. I am talking of Mediterranean countries, of South American countries, of countries in the East and Far East.

If this is the agreed upon perception of the state of this world, then it is not abstruse to think that it is beneficial for us to think of CSR as something different from its current understanding. CSR is not philanthropy; it is neither cause-related marketing nor welfare capitalism.

CSR means to become aware of this state of the world and the organization in it, and make an effort, at least, to tell the story of what is going on, if not to make amends.

CSR is to be found in the complex world of things that are done while doing business that have an impact on society and are not revealed in the financial statements. CSR is always there and for everybody: businesses, government institutions, non-profit organizations. Work on CSR must be undertaken as part of the core organizational activities, not outside them.

Like the apostle Paul, who struggled to reach the intimacy of the individual being as his own, so CSR is something you are while you go about your business. You do not 'do CSR' as something added on top of your business.

Organizational responsibility is, therefore, to be proved in the current business of the organization. CSR is who you are (it's not what you do). This is an aphorism that is perhaps worth clarifying. It may be true; it may be false. When the aphorism is true, it withstands probing. CSR is not philanthropy. It is not volunteer work done outside the office in association with co-workers.

Robert Eccles and Michael Krzus (2010) say it politely: in most cases there is 'very little linkage between the information published' in corporate social statements and the information published in corporate financial statements. They say one report should be done. I say the need for preparing one report is a consequence of CSR being sought in the core business of the firm. I think we emphasize different aspects of the same thing.

Philanthropy is something you do outside your earn-a-living work. Philanthropy is fine, but it does not need the conceptual and defensive apparatus of CSR to sustain and justify itself in the world. Worse, if philanthropy cloaks itself in CSR robes, it entails a risk for the philanthropic organization because philanthropy disguised as CSR implies adherence of the philanthropist to the sponsoring company's mission, objective and behavior. If the sponsoring company then happens to be involved in questionable activities, the sponsored organization may be called to answer for the consistency of the sponsor's behavior to the sponsored ideals.

Philanthropy implies no adherence of the benefited to the benefactor's behavior. Thus, we have the Giotto paintings, paid for with money made by money lending when money lending was not a socially respected activity. Indeed, the paintings were made to gain goodwill, to make up for the 'bad will' generated by money lending.

Let's now look at corporate examples of doing things within the core and outside the core of a business.

When an oil company supports the local communities that surround the locations of its production sites, be it oil fields where oil is extracted or plants where it is refined, it ends up being very good and beneficial for the company as well. We saw an example of this when we read Total's CSR report in Chapter 1. However, these kinds of actions – and their recounting – are tainted with an 'aftertaste' of an optional activity, something additional and not intrinsic to the core business of the enterprise. No wrong would be done if you did not do it.

That core of a business is not difficult to identify, since the important variables that keep the business going are easily recognized, and one of them is the sharing of proceeds from the oil fields between the company and the country where those fields are located. Therefore, a key step in CSR is the moment the company tells us what that share amounts to today.

When people are provided with this kind of information – something that is clearly intrinsic to the core business of an organization – they have the feeling that the house is in order. It is at this time that they know that the ground floor of profits is in touch with the attic of communication, the diverse departments of the international company talk to each other and there is genuine reporting to stakeholders. CSR is there.

It is clear at this point that the company's behavior in terms of profit-sharing with the country of its location is that company's intrinsic way of being – that is, the CSR the company 'was being.' The moment the company is aware of that, manages that variable and engages in communicating it, this is CSR in action. At this point, CSR is something you do.

The four noble truths of CSR

Now, a model begins to materialize. When they meet in Davos, Switzerland, in Aspen, Colorado, and other fancy places, politicians and corporate leaders say fancy things about their responsibility and that of the organizations they lead. It is not uncommon to hear phrases such as: 'It is a task of the corporate world to tutor/monitor/pursue the interests of the country.' CSR lies beyond the narrow boundaries of the company, but this seems to be stretching the concept a little too far. I think there is a society within and beyond the organization. The boundaries of an organization are certainly defined by a grey area, but I do not think an organization should feel responsible for the country.

There are four observations that we have used so far about CSR. To draw those boundaries correctly, it is perhaps useful to make those observations explicit and connect them to each other. These, then, are the four noble truths of CSR.

The first noble truth: CSR is always there, no matter what

I define CSR as the impact of the organization on society – especially through intangibles and externalities, which are as pervasive as dust. As I have said, CSR is in the complex world of things that are done while doing business that have an impact on society and are not revealed in the financial statements. CSR is always there and for everybody.

CSR always exists because there are always externalities in economic activities – that is, benefits or costs for consumers and other groups of stakeholders and citizens that are bound by the prices and regulations of goods and services.

There are also intangibles, which are effects or phenomena that are difficult to quantify and manage through the market. These effects may be actual or possible: even the omission of an action is to be included in CSR. To be stagnant and to not produce innovation is a negative thing and should count on the negative side of a CSR account.

Among the possibilities of corporate action, I think that brands have an influence. Think of what would happen if street billboards with the Vodafone logo had encouraging exhortations like: 'Tonight when you go home, kiss your children.' Maybe a little less violence would be vented.

Everything has an impact beyond its immediate scope. Words have an influence: there was a time in the 1980s when we used to speak of the fallout of research in positive terms, and that locution came directly from the World War II nuclear experience.

CSR is like the air. It exists whether the organization knows it or not. CSR exists because we exist; people exist and are responsible, like any home owner is responsible for the threat that is posed by a flower box on a window sill to those who pass by on the sidewalk.

The second noble truth: it is possible to acquire awareness of organizational CSR

If I want to, I can map, I can measure, I can make an inventory, compare, benchmark the externalities and 'internalities' (the well-known secrets of the house). And, if a company does this, the managers that say that it is a task of the corporate world to tutor/monitor/pursue the interests of the country would probably find that it is a great enough job to make their companies tick at this pace and would spare us lip service to the 'interests of the country.'

The third noble truth: CSR can be managed

Once awareness is acquired of the organization's CSR, the organization can do new things or change old things for better or for worse (maybe awareness makes you realize you are too good). Following the example of the flower box on the window sill, once I realize I run that risk I can buy insurance, I can take the box down and put it on the floor of the balcony, or I can leave it as it was.

The fourth noble truth: CSR can be accounted for in a document called a CSR report or sustainability report, or a report with a similar name

Sometimes, we run the risk of thinking that the CSR report is the only CSR activity an organization can perform. Being the fourth step on the path of CSR, the report is often spoken of as CSR *per se* – the report standing for the whole process.

Why are these truths? I call these 'truths' because they are very general statements that one recognizes only after many examples and much practice. They are very basic and are implicit in much of what I have provided in the case histories of corporations. The same can be done for governmental organizations.

Why are these truths noble? They are noble because they are very beneficial to those who recognize them. They help the organization to be honest and to avoid disinformation. They help the organization avoid trouble. They provide a breath of fresh air to those who work in the organization or around it.

On the point of avoiding trouble, for instance, the first truth is very helpful. The first truth says that CSR is always there, whether you know it or not, whether you recognize it or not. This implies that wrongdoings are, sooner or later, found out. Every once in a while, we hear stories emerging from the ill-forgotten past: corruption or monopolistic practices. Investigators may not be very efficient, but they have a long memory.

The first truth of CSR also provides a clear understanding of the disregard journalists have for CSR reports. They realize that those reports do not tell the whole story; they know there is an untold one. This is also a proof of the existence of the first truth: journalists know there is much more to an organization than is told in its glossy, untruthful reports. This time they – the journalists – are right.

Topology of responsibility

CSR is always there. On the other hand, CSR is only a part of organizational behavior. It is, therefore, interesting to gain a better understanding of the universe that encompasses all organizational behavior. (This might be beneficial for the 'reportist' – that is, the person who is called to draft a CSR report for CEO and Board approval.)

My intent is to isolate the germ of CSR, like a biologist in a laboratory isolates the virus of a new influenza. By 'isolate', I mean giving CSR a separate identity from other organizational behavior.

Let me propose that organizational behavior can be placed in three separate categories:

1 observance of the public interest (i.e. lawful behavior);
2 good management; and
3 social responsibility.

I contend that these three domains exist, are different from one another, and are sequential and propaedeutical to each other according to the listed order. Lawful behavior is a necessary but not sufficient condition for good management. Good management is necessary but not sufficient for CSR. It doesn't make much sense, within the limits of this discourse, to make profits by not abiding by the law. It makes no sense to speak of CSR for drug dealers. By the same token, it doesn't make much sense to worry about CSR if we are not making a profit because, if we aren't making a profit, we're not fulfilling the task of good management.

The set of lawful behavior of a government or business organization is included within the set of good managerial behavior: there are things that are done or not done in a company that law has nothing to do with, whereas management does. For instance, I can run or not run a given advertising campaign and no lawyer or judge will be interested in it. On the other hand, management and the owners of the company will be. If I do not run the campaign, sales will probably fall. If I run it, I may be spending too much and not getting an adequate return on my investment. From a legal point of view, nobody can criticize expenditure of a campaign, but from a managerial point of view, positive or negative criticism might very well be in order.

It has happened in the government sector that a manager has been indicted for a managerial crime (such as bad use of government funds), but his or her supervisor or the politician responsible don't take a stance since no verdict has yet been provided. I think this is a case where the politician is hiding behind the law and not fulfilling his or her executive position. Fulfilling it would require taking a managerial stance independent of the judicial verdict.

In turn, the set of good managerial behavior is contained within the set of socially responsible behavior: there are things I can do or not do, and I can be criticized only from a social responsibility point of view. If I hire a disabled person, it is a good thing from the CSR perspective. It is a neutral thing from a managerial point of view. If I reveal data about my suppliers, as Nike did, that may have been an expenditure and a complex program to manage; it may be beneficial for the company from now on, but it was introduced only because of social pressures and was deemed necessary only because it invested externalities of corporate activity – something that was not considered in the domain of management. It is also clear that from now on it will be considered part of management and, in this sense, CSR is something you do after you have acquired awareness of your CSR (the second noble truth), found out you can do something about it and manage it (the third noble truth).

At this point, we can look for the place of CSR *vis-à-vis* the rest of organizational behavior with the help of a Venn diagram (named after John Venn, the British philosopher of the nineteenth century). Figure 2.1 is composed of three sets nested one in the other.

The innermost circle represents the set of all actions undertaken by the organization to abide by the law: provide regular contracts to employees, satisfy regulations on product safety, apply generally agreed upon accounting standards and so on.

The second circle is the set of all good management actions: application of manufacturing skills, customer care and so on – all actions that no law requires me to undertake but that are, nevertheless, necessary for my business.

The third circle represents the set of actions that I have been lauding when undertaken and pointing out as missing when not undertaken by the companies mentioned in Chapter 1 – things that are not necessary but, nevertheless, acknowledge that there is more to business than meets the eye. Such was the McDonald's study on its economic impact on local communities. Such is not the lack of information on the value at risk that we do not find in the sustainability reports of many financial institutions in 2009, following the financial crisis of 2008.

Watch out: the sets are only the pseudo-circular crowns around one another: good management is only what is there after abiding by the law and does not include being law-abiding. CSR comes after good management

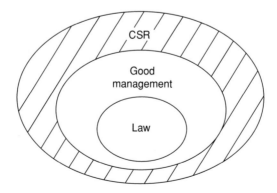

Figure 2.1   The onion rings of organizational behavior

and does not include good management. The sets, in a way, form the 'onion rings' of organizational behavior.

On the other hand, it would not be correct to represent the sets as three separate circles, one next to the other, because there is no CSR if there is no good management to begin with. There is no good management if there is no abidance by the law. Each preceding (inner) value (set) is a necessary but not sufficient condition for the next (outer) set to be actual.

We have thus obtained a topology of CSR.

The Venn diagram is not much different from Carroll's pyramid (1991): very similar. However, I think it is more powerful in depicting and understanding different situations, as it will be shown shortly.

It may be interesting to notice that this model has a dual point of view when the stakeholders are considered: moving from the center of the diagram towards the outer boundary, we find the sequence of the organization's stakeholders. In abidance by the law, we find the general public interest; in good management, we find the shareholders; and in CSR, we find the complete set of stakeholders: customers and those stakeholders who are neither protected by the law nor necessary to management.

Not against thieves

Many authors think that CSR is created to prevent theft. These authors mention the Enron case (early 2000) and the Madoff case (2008). I contend that CSR has nothing, or little, to do with the prevention of crime. Crime is a different thing. This concerns the broad area of management. We are talking and listening to those who are interested in doing well.

Muddling through

Reality is more intricate, however, and not as sequential as we have described. Actions taken to abide by the law become integrated and are part of the same actions taken to manage a corporation. The model is given only to illustrate some conceptual differences. Along this line, let's now consider one complication that I mentioned in Chapter 1.

So far, I have excluded negative behavior; for instance, in the domain of law abidance. Any accountant, however, would tell us that companies display borderline abidance by the law. If our professional experience were not enough, the financial crisis of 2008 should be definitive proof. Misbehavior and greed are everywhere in the economy. The enemy is us. This is different from theft. Less criminal, maybe not criminal – but much more pervasive. Every one of us is like Stalin's barber – not the Devil in person, but serving him with greasy devotion.

Nike's corporate behavior was like Stalin's barber before it took responsibility for its suppliers, undertaking research, providing data on their suppliers' working conditions and (perhaps) taking action to improve some of them. It certainly corresponds with Total providing data on work casualties and BAe Systems commissioning a study on the fairness of their pricing to the British government procurement system in order to respond to arguments that would have it a monopolist at home.

This is an opportunity to refine our model and our diagram: it is CSR if companies and government bodies merely give information about their law abidance. Law abidance is so difficult and complicated that simply doing so, and showing you are doing so, is a socially responsible action. Disclosure about organizational processes and functions is a socially responsible act. Any bank clerk can tell you that, when it comes to sales budgets of savings products, their bosses tell them that they have to sell such and such amount by the end of the quarter 'and I don't care who you sell it to.'

Difficult and complicated laws and managerial inputs do not mean that laws are ill-written or ill-conceived. It is complicated because of the nature of reality: always more demanding than we can handle. Cultural limits also play a great role. Bounded rationality and X-efficiency do the rest.

There are different ways to abide by the law, different degrees. This was true long before 2008. The Sarbanes–Oxley Act is dated 2002 and was enacted after the Enron case. It forces corporations to perform a series of tasks and to provide a series of data to certify the truthfulness of financial reports. It is a real pain in the neck and yet, while corporations strive to implement it, some of them have taken the opportunity to make it an instrument for internal review: voluntary abidance is a very good example of CSR.

At this point, we can revise our topology of CSR: the CSR circle is no longer around the two inner circles but, rather, cuts across them. CSR is the whole set, meaning that there is a part of CSR that is made of law-abiding that would not be there but for a special and voluntary effort of management.

Let's do this with the help of the Gulf of Mexico mess and let's take a step back.

Like others in this field, I feel the need to reframe CSR so that I can understand what it is, analyze it, appreciate it, and preach it. So, I pursue my essence of CSR. I look for a specific realm of CSR: 'a distinct and recognizable subject.' Approaching ethical problems with a beginner's mind leads us to specific solutions anyway, as we ask ourselves very basic questions: 'How to implement CSR?' Definition: CSR behavior is taking into account the wider impact of company core business; that is, everything that does not go into the financial statements – such as intangibles and externalities. Often, CSR may be something you do on top of other things; it may look like a doing 'outside,' a retrofit to business practice. Let me illustrate this by showing a 'philanthropy point,' and let me show this is not what I regard as CSR by crossing out the external circle I drew in Figure 2.1. I thus obtain Figure 2.2, which at this point shows no more CSR.

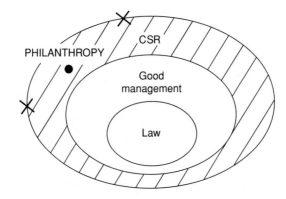

Figure 2.2 Crossing out CSR outside the core business of the enterprise

Let us then come to the question of where CSR comes into the Gulf of Mexico disaster.

I do not think that is particularly relevant to CSR. The lion's share in it is covered by other disciplines: law, regulation, environmental law, and good or bad management practice. Organizational behavior, disaster recovery, crisis management, technical expertise, micro-economics are all areas of activity that come into play before CSR. CSR is the newcomer, so it must squeeze in between these, or indicate a specific use of these methodologies.

So, Enron is out as well, insofar as the Enron case was a breaching of the law. CSR will not free us from the thieves.

Coming to British Petroleum (BP), let's take a moment here: I liked its 2008 CSR report because it was the only one in the industry that allowed competitors to come into the picture; that's what I call the 'unknown stakeholder.'

Let me give two examples of how CSR can play a role in this.

Abiding by the law is not a narrow route; there is no one particular way to abide by the law: you can abide by the law to the letter (point A in the 'law' set in Figure 2.3), or by its spirit. One expert said BP's problems in the Gulf of Mexico in April 2010 would not have happened in Europe, where regulations are stricter on the blowout preventer and other technical features: a company would know technical things that are not yet embodied in regulation and abide by those no matter what the regulations say (point B in the 'law' set in Figure 2.3). (There are real world examples of this kind of behavior in the domain of thin powders coming from car brakes.) This way of thinking leads to the value of implementation.

Management behavior must boil down to personal responsibility as an individual: BP executive Lamar McKay was questioned by a US Congress committee (June 15, 2010). He had to be asked three times by the committee president to apologize for what had happened; he kept resorting to process statements, such as 'we did make the camera materials and videos available to the authorities' (point A in the 'management' set in Figure 2.3). In the end, McKay made an apology and said: 'we are sorry.' Ultimately, he had to recognize that responsibility boils down to a 'yes' or 'no' answer, not a process statement; this is in the realm of personal, individual, human responsibility (point B in the 'management' set in Figure 2.3). This leads to the value of micro-ethics – not big E Ethics, the Ethics of dilemmas.

So, CSR is a specific way of discriminating between ordinary, core business behavior (Figure 2.4); CSR is the knife, it is not the onion. I see CSR as a way to dissect what is there to do: a means of discovering the possibilities of the core business, of expanding the set of feasible core business action.

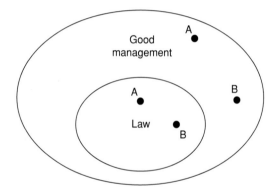

Figure 2.3   Mapping and expanding the set of feasible behavior

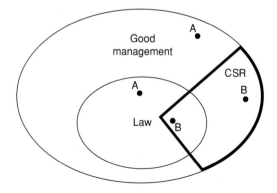

Figure 2.4   CSR is the knife, not the onion

Following the issue, in creating frameworks that prescribe many indicators, we run the risk of anesthetizing ourselves. We must identify only a few issues of potential negative behavior: disclosure value.

The upshot of all this is that I derived a four-value process framework that is useful to manage CSR in a corporation, to write a CSR report, and to evaluate somebody else's CSR report. So, the essence of CSR is: Ain't Misbehaving!

A 'weak' theory of CSR

What I have developed so far is a 'weak' theory of CSR. I call this a weak theory since I am influenced by the philosophy of 'weak thinking' conceptualized by Professor Gianni Vattimo.

Building on his experiences as a politician, Vattimo asks whether it is still possible to speak of moral imperatives, individual rights and political freedom. Acknowledging the force of Nietzsche's 'God is dead,' Vattimo argues for a philosophy of *'pensiero debole'* (weak thinking) that shows how moral values can exist without being guaranteed by an external authority. His secularizing interpretation stresses anti-metaphysical elements and puts philosophy into a relationship with postmodern culture.

My theory of CSR is not necessarily good everywhere and forever. It is sufficient to me that it works here and now, and that it helps us improve communication and organizational awareness; that it helps develop the government sector and competition in monopolies; that it helps protect the consumer from abuse and bad service. On the positive side, it is sufficient to me that it helps companies gain awareness of themselves, and record and improve their performance. Along the lines of Bruno Bettelheim, the author of the famous book on child rearing, *A Good Enough Parent* (Bettelheim, 1987), we do not need a perfect CSR; we need a 'good enough CSR.'

This 'weak theory' kind of approach to CSR is of considerable help when one is confronted with current debate (Karnani, August 23, 2010). According to Karnani, Professor of Strategy at the University of Michigan, the concept of CSR is delusory and potentially dangerous. Stephen Young, Global Executive Director of the Caux Round Table, replied quickly to Karnani (Young, August 27, 2010). According to Young, the case for CSR is very simple: 'it makes firms more valuable.'

I do not want to bypass such discussions, but the idea I am putting forth here is one that can run parallel to the standard 'extra effort' view of CSR. It is an idea that is useful, because it is in the core business of the enterprise and it does not need strong demonstrations of utility, such as that put forth by Young. It is certainly possible to argue for CSR on the basis of value added, but such an argument will always be subject to empirical demonstration, and it frames CSR as one more strategic tool of management. However, our concept of CSR frames it as a responsibility issue, one that is always there, no matter what, as I have argued in the four noble truths of CSR.

3
Think Negative

In this chapter, I want to get inside the individual elements of CSR as described in Chapters 1 and 2. I am going to be asking myself whether the observations I have been making about corporations in Chapter 1 and the model described in Chapter 2 can be derived from some existing model of CSR.

To do this, I am going to tell another story about CSR and analyze it with the instruments provided by the Porter and Kramer model (2006). This story concerns a passenger's experience in the subway system of a major city.

Subway blues

'We're bombarded with advertising and by the media' is a phrase used to make excuses for the personal (ir)responsibility that is thus attributed to the fault of others: someone else is bombarding us; we are not responsible if we then act according to that bombardment's aim. Truthfully, however, access to the media and advertising is a voluntary gesture on the part of an individual. The television set does not turn on by itself; the radio, too, isn't self-starting; the Internet even less so. As far as newspapers are concerned, it's said we do not read them. Books are subject to voluntary perusal. Billboards remain, but you can look away from those as well.

Nonetheless, there are places of coercion where media access is not chosen by the individual but, rather, by the managers of a monopolistic service: proliferating on the subway platforms in Rome is Roma Radio Stereo by means of high-volume loudspeakers and screens that cause everyone to crane their necks upward. In Milan, the screens are eye-level and they go off when the trains enter the station to avoid anybody being so caught up in thought as to pass the yellow line and fall onto the tracks.

Thus, there is an aspect of CSR that monopolies ought to have to observe – the audio health and attention of the audience. Getting a person's attention should be done whilst allowing for the freedom to choose; otherwise it's called 'soliciting' or 'coercion'. Audio is more penetrating than visual;

you can look away from something but it is not safe to plug your ears. You can't escape audio.

This presents disturbing implications when we see that these activities, which are harmful to the citizen, constitute elements of profit for the government or private companies that have an opportunity to capture the attention of said citizen. Without a doubt, the salespeople of subway platform advertising provide their clients with the numbers of travelers who pass through these platforms every day. This does not seem acceptable with regard to the public and is more than reminiscent of duty free in-flight infomercials; the practice brings to mind marketing carried out through low-cost bus excursions to the Lourdes sanctuary with forced stops at household appliance shops.

Is there CSR outside Porter and Kramer?

I would now like to put my critique of the subway company to the Porter and Kramer test in order to prove that I have highlighted something that is specific to my approach and not captured by the Porter and Kramer paradigm of shared value.

My understanding of Michael Porter and Robert Kramer's article 'Strategy and Society' (2006) is that elements of CSR should respond to the criterion of shared value; that is, CSR is something made up of positive actions aimed at benefiting both the company and society. Conversely, there is no CSR if there is no value for the company. From a micro-economic point of view, shared value seems to me to be a positive external effect.

I would like to conduct this test on the piece about the 'subway blues', using the following procedure:

* highlight the specific CSR elements, or lack thereof, that the piece demonstrates – let's say, for now, that I have obtained these elements by means of an heuristic method, a little less than casual;
* insert these elements into the framework proposed by Porter and Kramer to see whether they are compatible with the framework and whether they can be derived from it.

Should we find that the specific elements of CSR that I have identified do not fit into the Porter and Kramer framework, it is for one of two reasons: either I'm not talking about CSR, or there's CSR outside Porter and Kramer. Should it happily be the second of the two, it would mean that instead of hitting on a fragment, I've hit on a useful whole.

Let's proceed with an outline of the distinctive elements of CSR. In the piece on subway blues, there is a theme characteristic of CSR – or 'social issue,' to use the Porter and Kramer nomenclature. The social issue is the absence of respect for the client on the part of the suppliers of public and private transport, and the use of clients for profit on the part of the suppliers of transport.

We find ourselves facing an invasion of the privacy of clients (that is, those using the subway) ostensibly to keep them informed but, in reality, for economic gain. This, then, is the social issue that we have identified in this instance. For simplicity's sake, let's call this 'exploitation of clients'.

The exploitation of clients concerns a company activity situated along the value chain produced by the transport company, both in its operations (as it transports your physical body while exploiting your mental attention span to its own advantage) and in its post-sale services (among which Porter and Kramer list 'respect for client privacy' – privacy invaded, in this case). Up to this point, we are in agreement with Porter and Kramer – it's hard to escape the all-encompassing value chain.

My interpretation continues along these lines: if it described its 'platform information program' in its sustainability report, the transportation company would enter this social issue under 'Strategic CSR', where Porter and Kramer list the heading 'Transform value chain activities to benefit society while, at the same time, reinforcing strategy.'

Seen from the side of the user, however, the 'platform information' issue would be better slotted under 'Responsive CSR': mitigate harm from value chain activities, since it deals with a negative thing from the stakeholder's point of view. In fact, this point of view goes back to a short-term vision – the company behavior under examination isn't strategic at all.

As for fitting into the competitive Porter and Kramer context, this social issue is to be found under local demand conditions and, in particular, refers to the affability of the travelers who accept as good whatever the government gives them. However, the fact that the public independently perforates its own eardrums with car stereos and home televisions does not authorize the authorities to torture said public. Voluntary submission to the media does not warrant a Ludwig's cure *à la A Clockwork Orange* (the Stanley Kubrick movie) to which travelers are subject.

At every step of this procedure, we have found a slot in Porter and Kramer's paradigm into which the social issue being examined can be inserted. Different from Porter and Kramer is that the issue we have identified is a circumstance in which CSR is absent; that is, social (ir)responsibility on the part of suppliers. This is not a shared value – doing good for you and for me – but harassment of the client: doing bad to you to do good for me.

CSR doppelgänger: irresponsibility

There is a peculiarity to the examples I have made: they are examples of what could have been, but was not. CSR is about 'not being irresponsible.' The concept of irresponsibility comes out also in the writings of Sanija Weber (2010), teacher of business psychology and ethics at the London

Metropolitan University. CSR must be tuned in with potential negative behavior; that is, where the think negative prescription comes into play, there is more value added in preventing a negative behavior than in doing one more good thing. This is a utility theory truth.

Cases of social (ir)responsibility are identified thanks to an upside-down view of Porter and Kramer's paradigm – it is not the company that 'creates an explicit and proactive social responsibility agenda' but the external observer who observes company behavior; it is the stakeholder who engages the company, the society that describes the company.

Porter and Kramer's CSR is something you do outside the ordinary workings of managerial duties illustrated in Figure 2.1. Irresponsibility is the CSR that the company undertakes during ordinary corporate life, illustrated in Figure 2.2.

What was not stated – and could or should have been stated – is the measure of corporate social irresponsibility (CSIR). It is important to check whether McDonald's worries about the smell from the kitchens of its restaurants. It is important to check whether BAe Systems worries about the stigma that the public places on arms manufacturing.

Kristijan Krkac's concept of 'Lying by Default'

It is society that reads the company black box. It is always like this when you've got a critical stakeholder, the one that is not represented in the bodies of consultation but who does exist and puts forth his own reasoning. It's always like this when a stakeholder complains about negative company behavior and takes on the role of the self-appointed scorekeeper (according to Porter and Kramer's ironic phrase). This process transforms CSR into its doppelgänger – CSIR, less panegyric and more substantial.

There is an asymmetry here: CSIR is not simply the negative side of a phenomenon of which Porter and Kramer consider the positive side. CSIR has its own specificity from the point of view of economic utility theory – all else being equal, you get better social results from reforming negative behavior than you do from affirming positive behavior (Popper, in Galluccio, 2009). Human psychology is not linear, it is logarithmic: a euro lost is more valuable than a euro earned.

Using CSR methodology to benefit consumers and taxpayers leads to the identification of dirty economic corners and underhand behavior on the part of companies and institutions – not just environmental congestion or adversarial behavior towards citizens, but also cases of more subtle abuse – such as the absence of a long-term social memory (how much of government subsidies went to pseudo-farmers in the European Union?), or the absence of an historical account when plans are made for the future (have we ever seen detailed accounts of the outcome of the European Union seven-year plan?). To be even-handed, we also find cases of better responsibility: the widening of the perimeter of company responsibility that is implicit in the Total account of its work safety data from its suppliers, or the freeway authorities keeping data on the deaths occurring on company asphalt.

Porter and Kramer take on the view of corporate management. However, I do not take an anti-business stance at all, and use my critique to identify recommendations for service development: supplying information to citizens as they wait for their train on the platform has some social usefulness, but must be done in an unobtrusive way – using mute screens, for example. Wait times to the next train could be extended to all platforms. Information could be provided concerning other connecting transport, or anticipated timings could be displayed for those who are not using public transportation – just as a benchmark.

These proposals, however, do not appear to correspond to Porter and Kramer's shared value criterion because they benefit the client but don't increase profits for the company. The only thing the company gets out of it is knowledge; what a public office gains from this is institutional awareness and information concerning the effectiveness of its service. As for advertising monies that would be lost if the Subway Blues was discontinued, that should be replaced by other possible, less intrusive kinds of concession.

Thus, we have found things that do not verify Porter and Kramer's criterion – there is no benefit for the company in giving data, but there is a benefit for society in having it. There would be social benefits from knowing how much public financing has gone to Alitalia over the decades. It would be useful for consumers to know the exact total to be paid to Ryanair before their having been paid.

On a macro-economic level, the doppelgänger of irresponsibility is vulnerability of societies. This is the useful notion put forth by census bureaus in order to connect micro and macro indicators (Giovannini, 2010).

The anesthetic of positive reporting

The asymmetry between reforming negative behavior and affirming positive behavior is very much evident in self-assessment and reporting: you can write many pages about the innumerable positive actions that a company engages in during the course of its ordinary business, but you can fail to mention the one important issue – the relevant touchy piece of information. In trying to account for all the positive actions of CSR, one runs the risk of anesthetizing oneself and failing to notice a key issue when it presents itself. Therefore, it is useful to take the opposite view of CSR; that is, to prove that the organization is not irresponsible. Thus, we draw the best elements of CSR. These show us that CSR is not something you do but something that you are. CSR exists always. CSR is a discovery, not an invention. The problem is finding it. In Chapter 4, I try to identify a framework that helps us find irresponsibility.

4
The USDIME Framework

Irresponsibility is important

In Chapter 3, I concluded that it is good that an organization prove itself 'not irresponsible': but how to prove that operationally? An organization performs many activities. If we wanted to describe them all, we could fill libraries and still miss the objective, which is to identify problem areas and try to amend them. Focusing on good management and law abidance, we run the risk of anesthetizing ourselves: we must take a different path. Let's turn our argument upside-down and approach the organization with the opposite intent: to prove that it is irresponsible.

The theme is irresponsibility and disclosure: to speak about what is not good is much more relevant because, when you speak about yourself, it is safer to say the things you think are not good: let other people say good things about the organization.

As I said in Chapter 1, in the section dedicated to Microsoft, an examination of our conscience that doesn't hurt is not real.

At this point, I must find a systematic way to identify items of potential irresponsibility. These are going to be very close to what the strategist applying the SWOT analysis would call threats and opportunities (and perhaps would add strengths and weaknesses, too). What I look for is also close to what the professional in public relations would list as the relevant issues of the organization at hand. If I were a city or landscape architect, I would look for the hallmarks that make that city or landscape unique, important or bleak, and in need of attention and refurbishing.

Now, what remains to be done is to understand the method for discovering social issues. There's no closed formula with which to scan the corners of the economic system. Porter and Kramer follow the same checklist approach pursued by the Global Reporting Initiative (GRI) – and other proponents of guidelines; scholars, too, in the neighboring domain of intangibles draw up long shopping lists. Porter and Kramer maintain that it is the task of the mid-level, local managers to apply the shared value (their) paradigm, to create a rough list of initiatives that can then be prioritized. The drawing up of a list is an intelligent way to make heuristic knowledge additive. A process to identify issues of social irresponsibility is also a heuristic one for which all sources are good – research and debate within the company, the vocal busybodies outside the company, the press.

The Figure in the Carpet: deriving a framework from the database

I propose four guiding values:

- stewarding the *unknown stakeholder*;
- allowing information *disclosure*;
- developing a culture of *implementation*; and
- exercising *micro-ethics*.

I will call this the USDIME framework.

The *unknown stakeholder* is he who does not share a voice, who doesn't even know he has a stake in the activities of the organization being analyzed. It may be a newborn baby who will breathe what will be left of the air seventy years from now. It may be the reasonable solution to a problem that is proposed by wise people and that local voters turn down, spurred by emotions and demagogy. Stewardship of the unknown stakeholder implies, first, identifying the competitive context surrounding the organization that we are observing. Within this framework, comparisons of performance must be made with competitors and, in the case of government organizations or monopolies, international benchmarks must be provided. Possible government subsidies must be accounted for under this heading.

When we identify economic phenomena in the internal functioning of a company or an institution, particularly intangibles and externalities, then we are listening to the unknown stakeholder. He is at the heart of all research, the silent critic inside us.

An example of stewarding the unknown stakeholder would be Fiat accounting for the government subsidies obtained during the post-World War II decades.

Exercising *disclosure* means to tell and explain to the public the well-known stories relating to the business. Apologies and answers to unasked questions are also welcome. Brevity is a 'sub-value' of disclosure: be brief, do not pad your report.

I propose that disclosure is also about inserting awareness concerning an organization's operations and communicating this, internally and externally, which generates value for the organization itself. This way, research and dissemination of internal information (disclosure) become a key element of CSR. Adding awareness to the list of intangible company values would implement what Marco Ghetti has called corporate 'spiritual capital' (Ghetti *et al.*, 2009).

An example of exercising disclosure is Nike's providing to the public the list of its suppliers and the results of their survey on working conditions at those suppliers' facilities.

The value of *implementation* requires adherence to facts instead of opinion: a culture of implementation vs. politics of announcement. This means developing measures of performance and indicators of intermediate organizational processes. If we have a code of ethics, it is nice that we also have some means of measuring the organizational population's adherence to it. Developing indicators of product quantity and quality is most important in the public and non-profit sectors, where the payer is different from the beneficiary of the service or product. In the public sector, it is most important to understand the nature of the product or service being produced, rather than laboring around the measuring of funds deployed. In times of economic crisis (and in times of economic boom, to avoid busts), it is better to develop summary accounts and benchmarks of actual performance, rather than plans and budgets.

An example of the culture of implementation is BAe Systems' provision of the call log to their ethics hotline.

Living *micro-ethics* does not require heroism: avoid disinformation and do not reveal the faults of others. These are already acts of micro-ethics. I call this ethics 'micro' as opposed to the big ethics, always concerned about whistle-blowing, stem cells, abortion, theft. This ethics is something you live twenty times a day, not once in a lifetime.

An example of the absence of micro-ethics is the persistent organizational divorce in insurance companies between the sales and the claims departments, thus making it very hard for the customer to obtain honest claims processing.

In Chapters 5 to 8, I will illustrate the four values and how they are present in our corporate narratives. I will also present the theory that makes these values interesting in proving whether the organization irresponsible or not irresponsible.

5
The Unknown Stakeholder

Let us recall the formulation of this value as I proposed it at the end of Chapter 4:

> The *unknown stakeholder* is he who does not share a voice, who doesn't even know he has a stake in the activities of the organization being analyzed. It may be a newborn baby who will breathe what will be left of the air seventy years from now. It may be the reasonable solution to a problem that is proposed by wise people and that local voters turn down, spurred by emotions and demagogy. Stewardship of the unknown stakeholder implies, first, identifying the competitive context surrounding the organization that we are observing. Within this framework, comparisons of performance must be made with competitors and, in the case of government organizations or monopolies, international benchmarks must be provided. Possible government subsidies must be accounted for under this heading.
>
> When we identify economic phenomena in the internal functioning of a company or an institution, particularly intangibles and externalities, then we are listening to the unknown stakeholder. He is at the heart of all research, the silent critic inside us.
>
> An example of stewarding the unknown stakeholder would be Fiat accounting for the government subsidies obtained during the post-World War II decades (p. 22).

I start this illustration of the unknown stakeholder guiding value by explaining where the centrality of stakeholders comes from.

Questioning the stakeholder approach

I want to start my treatment of the unknown stakeholder with a reference to the theory of stakeholders that has so permeated CSR – indeed, has given-birth to it.

I will dwell on this at some length, since the stakeholder approach appears to be prevalent and is the preferred way to go about CSR reporting in the public relations industry, which is the leading supplier retained by corporations to run CSR programs and write CSR reports.

The stakeholder approach to CSR action and reporting implies that the relevant stakeholders of the organization be listened to, and this listening be accounted for in the CSR report. So, we read section headings in the reports that list the generic names for the groups of stakeholders: stockholders, employees, customers, suppliers and the rest. These groups are also called the 'publics' of the organization.

I contend that the stakeholder approach might be misused and end up in collusion with sections of the publics involved. It is not enough to run a two-hour focus group with opinion leaders to understand the issues and to certify that the CSR behavior of the organization is OK. It is not enough to get the OK of the in-house trade unions to demonstrate that the organization has fair employment practices: there might be collusion between management and employees on high-salary practices or inefficient labor organization – all things that are against the best interest of consumers and the general public.

The stakeholder approach leads an organization to try to engage with the wrong counterparts; for instance, interviewing young people as representatives of future generations, as a major power utility did. Headquarters representatives of stakeholder organizations are very prestigious to interview, but they may not be very interested or knowledgeable about the specific interviewing organization. They may have to interface dozens of such organizations and not have anything specific to say. I am talking here about an over-rating of stakeholders.

Sometimes, it is easier to convene a generic association in an aseptic setting than listen to an individual stakeholder when he or she is at hand and there is a hot issue to solve: an individual obnoxious customer, a difficult file to process. Besides, interviewing association representatives might very well be an issue of double-counting: first, you interact with an individual stakeholder; then, you ask his association what they think about your organization. You'd be better off asking the individual stakeholder you have at hand and giving an account of that interaction.

Therefore, everything that is not taken into account under the headline of the stakeholder approach I call 'stewardship for the unknown stakeholder'. The theoretical bases of this value reside in the vast literature on non-maximizing, non-efficient, non-effective behavior by the firm, and by the employee especially.

Thus, the first task in drawing up a CSR or sustainability report is to identify the possible unknown stakeholders; that is, those who do have a stake but don't know they do; those who have a stake too small to care about but who are numerous, whose protection would be the government's task; those – the weak – who do not have a press office.

Taxonomy of organizational sectors

Accounting for the unknown stakeholder is one way to identify potential irresponsibilities on the part of the organization. As a first step to identifying the unknown stakeholder, the competitive arena of the business should be provided. We thus derive a taxonomy of the general content of the CSR report by sector of the economy. Government and monopolies should provide indicators of activity; businesses subject to competition should conduct research and disclosure on their activities.

A simple taxonomy according to the competitive environment is:

- government sector (public non-profit sector);
- regulated for-profit private sector (monopoly or subject to moderate competition);
- non-profit associative private sector (not subject to competition: entrepreneurial associations and trade unions);
- non-profit private sector (subject to competition);
- for-profit private sector (subject to competition);
- SMEs (small and medium-sized enterprises).

For an organization belonging to a specific competitive environment, the relevant reporting content would be:

- government sector: indicators of product or service;
- regulated for-profit private sector: indicators of efficiency;
- non-profit associative private sector: indicators of product or service and of efficiency;
- non-profit private sector: indicators of product or service and of efficiency; sources and uses of funds;
- for-profit private sector: data on competition;
- SMEs: additional specific data on financial statements, such as the liquidity of accounts receivable.

In praise of competition

The key driver that distinguishes the different sectors identified is competition – the higher the competition, the higher the likely respect for the customer and the taxpayer. Lower competition inevitably leads to cost inefficiencies and the abuse of customers and citizens.

All organizations – public and private – should provide a benchmark with competition or comparable organizations, be it international or domestic, depending on the level of the reporting organization. Organizations that do not have homologous ones within the country should make comparisons with international or foreign organizations.

Some sectors – banks, for instance – may be subject to competition in theory, but preserve privileges over other sectors. Employee salary is one area where a whole sector might be privileged over other sectors. Accounts of this kind might be provided in the CSR report. The competition that must be reported is the effective competition prevailing in the economy across different sectors, not only within the industry to which the organization belongs.

Much of what I have said so far on the stewardship of the unknown stakeholder may sound excessively trusting of competition; indeed, the notion of the unknown stakeholder is basically used as a synonym for competition. Opposed to such faith in competition, I often hear the phrase 'cut-throat competition' and the 'accelerating' expression: 'increasing cut-throat competition'. We should be starved and dead by now if that were true: cut-throat competition is always feared when we are the losers.

I want to point out that there are instances whereby the absence of competition is merciless. We should think of the absence of competition everywhere there is corruption. We should think of the absence of competition everywhere a service or product could be provided in a regime of multiplicity, also in the government sector, and is not. There is unfair competition in urban traffic when a mass transit vehicle stands in line behind a private car, because the mass transit vehicle bears the cost of congestion generated by private car traffic. There is absence of competition in the labor market when there are government-tenured workers that do not undergo any evaluation of performance. This list could continue. It seems to me that these examples show that the weak in the competitive arena are not always those who define themselves as such. The real cut-throat competition is unrealized competition.

Let us now examine several case studies in capsule form.

Highway system

Three years after its infamous 2005 survey on CSR, *The Economist* updated its position on the subject with a second survey on January 19, 2008. The good news is that, while the first survey was scathing in its judgment, this time space was given to John Ruggie, from the Harvard Kennedy School of Government: 'The theological question – whether CSR exists or not – is irrelevant today. The real question is not whether, but how CSR is done.' Of relevance to how CSR is done is a counterargument from none other than Milton Friedman, in 1970: 'A company's social responsibility is to make a profit.' Friedman's indictment appears terrible, especially when applied within the context of countries that fall miserably short when their governments are charged with monitoring their own companies and bureaus. Milton Friedman had in mind an ideal form of capitalism when he said 'A company's social responsibility is to make a profit.' What is necessary, then, is to specify under what conditions profits are made and what kind of capitalism we are talking about.

A case in point concerns the national highway systems and the individual highway managing corporations of certain countries, the return on equity of which is greater than that of the Medellin cartel on drug dealing. The individual highway managing corporations are licensed monopolies from the Government Unit, ministry or department, for Public Works or Highways. However, Friedman wouldn't call this 'capitalism' but, rather, 'socialism in action,' because the profits of these corporations are not made thanks to the quality of the service offered by the holder of the licensed monopoly. If one is to drive – say, from Milan to Venice – one pays a toll to three different highway companies: the Major (the nationwide highway managing company) plus two smaller local companies.

While the Major, with the use of digital meters installed in 2007, uses speed values to monitor safe driving and fine speeding drivers, nothing of this sort of safety measure is available on the other two highways. Highway signs differ between the Major and the other two routes, and one hesitates to even mention another jewel: the Venice Bypass, which resembles the Naples–Pompeii connection in the 1960s. This bypass falls under the aegis of the Government Agency for Highways, and everybody should be checking it out in order to avoid, perhaps, the waste of another billion or so dollars of asphalt laid for its renewal, instead of suitable signs installed, with the subsequent increase in toll fees because of the extra billions spent. And let's not forget the Brenner Pass Highway that installed a pass-card toll booth system (called the Telepass) in the 1990s in the same lanes as the cash windows, thereby totally negating the effectiveness of the Telepass system itself.

It is clear that the minor highway companies are of lesser importance than the major one, refuting the rule whereby the reason that the smaller companies should exist is to be better than the big ones. If the Government Agency for Highways is not checking the quality of the service being rendered by its licensees, then it is clear that maximizing profits within this framework is terrible. But it's not Milton Friedman's fault: it's confusing model capitalism with ruthless capitalism in action.

I would posit that a more responsible behavior for this is part of CSR. Since the Government Agency for Highways is silent, there is nothing stopping the market and public relations from imposing behavior on these companies, as if state oversight existed. Since most economies do not fall under the Western norm from whence come critics of CSR, this is a good argument for CSR as voluntary competitive behavior attuned to the quality of service and providing information to the public. On a highway, we should not evaluate the drivers but the road, its construction and maintenance; in a prison, not the jailed but the jailers; in the precinct, not the criminals but the cops. What is newsworthy is not the novelty of the contingent data but the analytical method. What is newsworthy is CSR.

Recap: The highway case study invites the careful observation of the behavior of the producer at the expense of the user, consumer, citizen. Often, the producer himself will evaluate his work by detailing the behavior of his clients, but this is not proper. The producer must, above all, evaluate what it is that he is offering and how he does it. Only after this is clear can he talk about how his clients respond. The unknown stakeholder is often a citizen who has been given pseudo-importance. Multiplicity is a good thing.

Gas station owner-operators

CSR in action – as opposed to 'in reports' – was evidenced by a campaign carried out by ERG service stations. In 2007 and 2008, huge posters of the station managers were widely displayed on their premises with the inscription: 'ERG puts a face on it. Steve works here for you.' This is CSR, because the campaign extended accountability by involving its workforce, something clients appreciated and awarded through patronage.

This is an example of widening the sphere of contact between the workforce and the clients in an environment often characterized by the wily hiding of slack work under the guise of privacy and personal security, along the lines of the civil servant in some government bureaux who, when asked for their name for future reference, gave the offending client a haughty once over and kept their mouth eloquently shut.

Publicity garnered from the work itself – courtesy, a name, a friendly face – can be more effective than running around the world slapping logos on the fenders of racing cars.

ERG was a classical family-owned domestic oil company, in the second half of the twentieth century and in the first decade of the twenty-first. It probably wasn't easy for the management to get the station managers to agree to have their pictures on public display. It was probably helpful that the managers were not employees but owners; nonetheless, not all the service stations were identified in this fashion, a sign that there was some dissension. Thus, the campaign was an attempt at communication and internal harmony within the organization, which is an example of the dictum that the best company ambassadors are its employees.

Oil companies were making fantastic profits above and beyond short-term capital. It was acceptable, then, that they were being over-taxed. Oil companies' profits, however, were more an expression of public folly than of greedy capitalist aggression. Despite the high cost of gas, in fact, millions of citizens continued to insist on driving their guzzling SUVs through narrow roads originally built for horse-drawn carts. The car was an imperative – so much so that, during the Winter Olympics of 2006 in Turin, the taxpayers had financed the construction of an underground tunnel in which to lay train tracks in order to recuperate a large swathe of the city, through which the city government decided to build a big thoroughfare. It's this mental hegemony of the car that generated not only super profits for the oil companies, but also the under-use of public transport and alternative vehicles available on the market – after all, hybrid cars were already popular in the United States when barely seen elsewhere.

Recap: The ERG case study, as opposed to that of the highway, is a positive example of giving value to a neglected laborer, a laborer who is often not considered to be one: the small-time owner.

Monopolist air carrier

Writing negatively about Alitalia during its crisis in the mid-2000s would have been a cowardly travesty, since everybody was talking about it at the time. It is a subject, however, that presents five aspects little, and badly, treated: memory, nationalism, consumers, salaries and flagships.

Memory: newspapers have a way of talking about the world as if it is constantly changing. 'Now the game begins,' heralded the *Corriere della Sera* on December 2, 2006, though anybody looking could have said that the company was a drain on its population from the day it bought its first plane. Already, in 1984, you could tell which way the wind was blowing from the way the ground crew couldn't be pinned down to a concrete answer, insolently slouching in their chairs like bored receptionists. 'Their time will come,' people said. Then it was the pilots' strike, and people reported them, were called to testify and nobody knew how the story ended. Then, a thousand stewards called in sick on the same day, showing how big the tumor had grown, both in transport and the health system, with obliging doctors certifying the obvious. Thus, it is clear to folks that the 'game' has been going on for a long time and may still not be over. In fact, Alitalia was merged in the end with its domestic competitor, Airone, in spite of antitrust regulation.

From the contrasting call published by the *Corriere della Sera* in 2007: 'Survey the real entrepreneurial market availability, national and international, to cover the Alitalia risk' and that of a political leader of the center-left, Francesco Rutelli, also mayor of Rome in the 1990s: 'Find Italian shareholders,' the national property prejudice is clear. The political view is understandable – but old news, willfully ignoring statements such as the one by a prominent journalist of economic matters, Massimo Mucchetti, vice-editor of *Corriere della Sera*, who maintained that national property is not a guarantee in and of itself and, furthermore, 'in Europe, governments are not allowed to discriminate in favor of national ownership. Governments have to pose precise problems and ask for precise guarantees not on the nationality of ownership but on what best serves the country's interests.'

Still, the center-left politician was upheld by the Minister for Economic Development, who appreciated the solution of national ownership 'for the national market and employment.' The exact nature of the national market is unclear, whether it is limited to employees of the airline or its vast number of users – a contradiction between national ownership and the good of the economy as a whole, which needs a great deal of service at low cost. Add to this another politician's request for 'a sound employment plan that guarantees the consumer,' even though an employment plan doesn't give a hoot about the consumer. These dissonances already existed thirty years ago, and were soundly denounced in 1990, only to surface again – a conflict between two stakeholders: employees and consumers. A parochial affair concerning ownership that sets aside *ex ante* any benefit to the Italian consumer and Italian businesses, which are an airline's biggest clients.

The calls continued, asking for the removal of those managers who brought the company to this disastrous point despite their enormous salaries. Here, there is short-term memory on two fronts: first, Alitalia's woes are not due to a few years of bad management, or specific managers – some of whom came from the train company and, second, looking at individual salaries instead of the black hole in the government budget. What's several million euros in salaries compared with the billions spent by the government in one year? Besides, Alitalia's last manager got himself a fail-proof contract as befits a manager taking on an impossible mission, the fate of which is already sealed, so why not make a few bucks?

Instead of shooting the bearer of bad news, the politicians would have done well to look back at government spending on Alitalia since 1960, since the days when Gregory Peck and Spencer Tracy landed in Rome to shoot movies about the *dolce vita*. What's really missing is a corporate social report over the years, and nobody knows who should actually write one – perhaps a working group from the House and Senate. No political party is above criticism in this regard; over the years, all have done their share to wrap the company in the Italian flag, pour billions into its management and even blindly support the all-powerful pilots' union for reasons unknown.

A corporate social report on Alitalia would also need to address the lax control of its human capital. Spoiled employees may be the company's worst asset and have probably done more to give the flagship a bad name than anything else.

Recap: In the case of Alitalia, the unknown and ignored stakeholder is the traveler, with emphasis on a key element for said clients: competition. This is why CSR must focus attention on competitive (or comparable) companies and institutions, incorporating also actuation and memory.

Closed-shop recruitment by political parties

It isn't only businesses or institutions that can be subject to competition or the lack thereof, but political institutions, too, can incorporate competition and transparency for the citizen or, quite the opposite, build a collusive cartel against him.

An open letter to an 'Iron Man' politician:

Dear Sir,

I write to you because, during these last few days of the 2008 electoral campaign, I have been carrying on a dialogue with you in my thoughts. You, being an intelligent man, can't be unperturbed by the banality of the campaign posters plastering the city walls or the television babble. In my modest opinion, one of the reasons for the banality of political slogans is the need to make them national – a way to shore up the propaganda being diffused by television. At least, that's what some spin doctor probably told you: vague, short messages like 'Be Safe', or 'Help for Families' or 'Rise Up.' The most evocative is 'Don't ask what kind of party but what kind of country,' rather Kennedy-esque in its vague association with 'Ask not what your country can do for you, ask what you can do for your country,' though it is also deceiving because it does not, as John Kennedy did, call for individual responsibility.

Exasperation with this kind of *erga omnes* communication is due to the fact that one is voting not for people but for parties, since that's the kind of electoral system we have and, what's worse, any talk of reform keeps this central primacy of the party. In effect, parties act as an insulating wall between the people and those they elect. Voting for specific people is hardly being practiced around the world. What is mostly done is that people vote for parties and it's the parties who decide who goes to Parliament.

Voting in small districts would enable a minimum of concreteness, confrontation and responsibility towards the voters. Voting for party lists appears to me to be a true closed shop recruitment carried out by political parties with regard to society as a whole. It makes of you an oligarchy and, while you yourself have contested this accusation by calling yourselves a 'management class,' there is no contradiction here. You are all an oligarchical management class, conducting a personal war of national political consensus against the territories and single citizens, preferring to answer to mute television audiences – uni-directional propaganda disguised in supposedly open debates where not even the most intellectual say anything of merit.

You are not subject to competition, though it is clear that within your parties competition is intense, even if it is back-room competition. The system is not competitive; neither are you as individuals. As a business model, you are the Alitalias of the world, as opposed to the Pan Ams and TWAs, who no longer exist; your only objective is hanging on to your chair, though you could find work anywhere. Service to your clients is the last thing on your mind and this is a cultural fact. You don't care what impact you have, whether or not you've gotten anything done. Politics as tangible effects is foreign to you if not in the most banal fashion, through family connections or monetary gain. You boast of steady hands, but they have never done a day's work; and you float above a constitutionality that even you complained about in 1991, that tries to have the state work like a robot programmed with law while the politicians play 'king of the hill'.

Recap: In this case, the ignored stakeholder is the citizen, who neither has, nor knows how to have, the ability to intervene for change.

Germs of competition

A corollary of competition is the quantification of public activity. It is not often that you read a newspaper editorial like the following:

> A public sector that incorporates 'germs' of competition may be necessary to increase the productivity of the economic system and is a recipe that does not require a great expenditure of public funds.

The first thing that needs to be done to inoculate such germs would be to diffuse corporate social reports in the public sector. The job of a corporate social report is, in fact, to define the (social) product of an institution, and measure its efficiency and its impact (product, in this case, intended in a general sense; it could be a court sentence or an administrative act).

It's paradoxical, but a social report makes more sense for a public institution than a private company. Budget accounts of public institutions serve to certify the legitimacy of their administration but do not evaluate the work of the institution; thus, social reporting could step in to measure the quantity and quality of the work being done. Though it is true that budget reports, estimates and final balances are legally recognized and subject to controls on the part of internal auditors, the Court of Accounts and appointed ministers, they only give an account of the administrative correctness and say nothing about the product of the institution – when this is what competition requires: a comparison between the product and the resources spent. It is only by comparing the social reports of two prisons or health care units that we can see which is working well and which is not.

The use of public funds to undertake this kind of exercise would be limited compared with the benefits, though care would need to be taken not to bristle at the use of outside consultants, since the know-how to apply CSR is lacking in the public sector and would probably entail endless roundtables and seminars in an attempt to figure out where to start. Whether it would take a few germs or a full-blown transfusion is up to the reader to decide...

The value of the unknown stakeholder

Edward Freeman's 'stakeholder approach' method is truly revolutionary and I have, in this section, given examples of how businesses and institutions, from the private to the public to the political, listen to stakeholders, or ignore them. I have also shown that there is a hole in the usual list of stakeholders, which includes clients, employees, owners, suppliers, the community, the state and the environment. The hole has to do with the competitors: businesses and institutions give an account of their work as though they operate in a vacuum, totally ignoring the competition.

The most commonly ignored stakeholder is the consumer – a citizen, yes, but he could also be a clueless employee or workman that needs to be considered – and the key element engendering respect for the stakeholder is competition. In a corporate social report and sustainability report, leaders of the market must be challenged. The names of the competitors should be listed, and faceless averages should be stamped out, because these are always subject to the person writing the report. Performance measures should be included, and benchmarks (against others and oneself, over time). Benchmarks also make sense in the public sector because, here, it becomes a liberating tool for the citizens concerning their government and management classes. As it is now, the citizens are hostage to their governments, which do not compete against other institutions and thus enjoy a monopoly not subject to control.

Questionnaire tool box

To implement the USDIME framework I am going to make each of the four values explicit through a questionnaire that can be applied to any sustainability report in order to check how much irresponsibility is embodied in it. This questionnaire will be a sort of 'decalogue' guiding us in our search for CSR.

Questionnaire 5.1 presents the relevant section for the unknown stakeholder value.

Questionnaire 5.1 The unknown stakeholder

1.1	– The report should frame the organization's operations within its correct competitive context.
	– For the government sector and for monopolies, indicators of product or service must be provided as well as benchmarks, at national or international level.
	– Companies subject to competition should provide some benchmark with their competitors.
1.2	– Does the report make explicit benchmarks with market average or, better, with specific competitors?
1.3	– In the case of monopoly enterprises or central government organizations or local governments, the report should make explicit price comparison (when applicable) with an analogous product or service.
1.4	– When the organization is too big or unique to find a comparable domestic organization, an international comparison of performance must be provided.
1.5	– Comparison must be made on quality of service.
1.6	– Comparison must be made on efficiency and waste (inefficiency, not an environmental notion).

1.7 – Does the report give measures of potential jeopardy to unknown stakeholders – such as, for example, profits or gross margin (earnings before interest, taxes, depreciation and amortization – EBITDA) by country?
1.8 – Does the report show attention to the customer and/or to the employee?

Four lists of questions, like those in Questionnaire 5.1, will be produced, one for each value. The juxtaposition of such partial lists will constitute the questionnaire that I will apply to the CSR or sustainability reports of important global organizations.

In Chapter 6, I proceed to illustrate the second value of the USDIME framework: disclosure.

6
Disclosure

Let us recall the formulation of this value as I proposed it at the end of Chapter 4:

> Exercising *disclosure* means to tell and explain to the public the well-known stories relating to the business. Apologies and answers to unasked questions are also welcome. Brevity is a 'sub-value' of disclosure: be brief, do not pad your report.
>
> I propose that disclosure is also about inserting awareness concerning an organization's operations and communicating this, internally and externally, which generates value for the organization itself. This way, research and dissemination of internal information (disclosure) become a key element of CSR. Adding awareness to the list of intangible company values would implement what Marco Ghetti has called corporate 'spiritual capital (Ghetti *et al.*, 2009).'
>
> An example of exercising disclosure is Nike's providing to the public the list of its suppliers and the results of their survey on working conditions at those suppliers' facilities (p. 20).

Relevance

Hundreds of uncommented key performance indicators (KPIs) won't help disclosure. Certainly, they will be appreciated by the experts. However, it will be nice to point out the few that are critical, explaining why they are critical. So, the key point of disclosure is to point out spontaneously what is relevant and what is not. Candid admission of problems can be revolutionary – and generate attention from the public. The issues dealt with in the CSR report should be those that are on the agenda of top management.

One could provide information that is only apparently an industrial secret: much information is withheld from the public under the guise of industrial secrets. Often, information is also withheld from employees. The CSR report can be an instrument of internal communication. Indeed, employees are severe critics of a CSR report. Not only top management, but also employees look at the CSR report as a necessary nuisance, not a sign of organizational health. The actual watershed doesn't appear to be the confidentiality of information. Rather, it is the organization being aware of it, and knowing and managing that information.

An example of this is provided by Brembo, an international manufacturer of automotive systems, mostly brakes. Brembo has a balanced scorecard of about 60 indicators. Of these, about half are made public in their report (they call it a Statement of Intangibles).

A distinction should also be made between secrets and classified information. Classified information is something that has a positive industrial value. A secret is almost the opposite: information that has a potential negative value for the organization, but a positive value for the public and the community.

It is curious that, when stakeholder engagement is undertaken, it is not easy to find competitors among them. Competitors would know the dirty secrets that ought to be brought to the public, in due time and in due words.

An example is the pricing of electric power in Europe and the inclusion in it of the price of carbon rights for the emission of CO_2. Regulators are correctly including the price of carbon rights in the price of electric power to consumers. This correct micro-economic practice, however, delivers extra profits to the providers of power to the public. In some European countries, there is an open debate as to how such extra profits should be used; in others, there is not. This is an example of a dirty secret that is well-known in the industry and should be brought to the public in CSR reports.

Brevity

'Words, words, words': brevity is another key element of disclosure. The CSR report should list no more than three or four key elements, with a maximum of seven, which is the number of things a person can easily retain by heart. Analysts, after all, are people too.

Brevity embodies the Italo Calvino (1993) value of rapidity: important things are said very quickly. Don Quixote and the windmills take only a couple of lines in the relatively thick Miguel Cervantes epic.

Doubt and vulnerability

Doubt and vulnerability are also good elements of disclosure.

It is very rare that, in corporate documents, organizations acknowledge their limits. It would be very innovative to do so – showing doubts, things that went wrong. It is not necessary to undergo self-criticism, as was done under the Soviet empire. A little active transparency would be a clear hint that the organization knows its problems and is dealing with them, not denying them.

T.S. Eliot expressed very well the importance of what was not said and could have been said at the same time, expressing the relevance of self-restraint: when in the Four Quarters he says something to the effect that our mind is full of memories and regrets of things we could have said and done, and of feelings we could have expressed and he uses the methaphor of steps not taken on some important path. The subjects we did not dare to bring up, T.S. Eliot calls 'the doors we do not dare to open' and the good things we could have discovered and the good results we could have obtained are 'the rose garden' we never discovered, and we keep living in the complexities of our lives, and of our organized world, corporate, public or non-profit whatever it may be.

Let us now examine three case studies in capsule form.

Regional electoral communication

A problem posed by political jurisdictions can be seen in the crowding of the cities, boroughs within cities and *arrondissements*, provinces around the cities, districts, regions and states, not all of which are meaningful or enjoy a clear mission. Thus, political communication in suburban areas, the political representation of which is joined with the city at its center, generates problems in that these suburban areas do not have their own representation. This engenders communication such as: 'We excavated for three years to find 2,000: the Province of Rome gives back to its citizens the Roman Domus,' which the President of the Province circulated with fanfare, despite the fact that there is no shortage of archeological excavations in the country. Or billboards on buses that boast of government progress in employment, career advancement, or the reduction of job-related injuries.

Not that the Province doesn't receive its own black marks: hard as it is to believe, the Province of Rome renovated a building in the center of the city for which it would surely be interesting to know what proportion of the budget was going to the various initiatives planned for the Meeting Building. For now, the only thing being distributed is a heavy, color volume on the various archeological hallmarks in the Latium region, which is nice for the people who live there, certainly, but those citizens would probably find more useful some reporting on the efficiency of various provincial programs, especially the latest figures on personnel costs and the total volume of business. This information, however, is kept in a drawer, and one doesn't even know if such an analysis is possible. After all, what the people want is beauty.

So, you get electoral communication that resembles fortune cookie messages: 'Dream with your feet on the ground.' A democratic candidate was more concrete: 'Enter and leave the City. Easily.' Not bad, but give it a try and you'll soon find yourself at a dead stop on the Orbital Highway around the city, a perennially congested thoroughfare. Telephone the city hotline to get an estimate of the duration of the hold up and a young, energetic operator will happily inform you that this thoroughfare is managed by the Freeway company, dumping the problem back on the hood of your car.

Just an aside, but these ubiquitous call centers are far from satisfactory; however, there has probably been some agreement with a union regarding hiring, and some judge most likely okayed the city hiring these youths, who are thrilled with their luck.

Some slogans are nearly evangelical: 'Transforming garbage into resources'. This is, obviously, a gross exaggeration (not to mention an attempt to hit two issues with one swing). This was already given a try in the 1970s: resolving the energy crisis and unemployment. There's also: 'Free wireless Internet throughout the province' – once again pushing WiMax technology (how that is different from UMTS I still don't know, but that's another problem). The idea is to provide broadband technology to those areas that don't have it and have despaired of ever receiving it. But the pitfall is the free service, showing a desire to expand welfare to things, and even to those who could pay for it without any difficulty – 'The more problems I have delivering a few concrete things, the more I promise!'

Provinces would be interested in getting information on the number of road deaths, since most of these occur on provincial highways; but only if they were to detach themselves from the major cities, since over 80% of the electorate resides there. This is why candidates go to such lengths to attract their attention, though outlandish claims could be modified were there a system like citizen advocates dispersed over the territory, acting as their guardians.

Recap: One element of disclosure is the speed of information and its synthesis. In the case of communication in the Province of Rome, there are positive and negative examples – though it is clear that the freshness and rapidity of some of the campaign promises wilt when under implementation, making it easy to see how little has been done of that which has been promised (it's a problem of honesty).

The European Central Bank

Maybe it's all the negative publicity over the last ten years, but in no place more than a bank does a person feel like a mark, just waiting to be fleeced – and there's good data to prove it. Unicredit Xelion Bank/JPMorgan, in two years of modest profile (70% obligations, 30% shares), lost €2,000; Cassa Lombarda/Aletti Gestielle, in five years of similar investment, shows a return of 1.59% (which they call 8%, omitting a specification that this was obtained over five years); Monte dei Paschi di Siena actually entrusted sales to peppy telephone operators – who are shielded by the fact that they are merely a call center, pushing a well-known comedian to observe that all one has to do is put a call center between a company and its clients and *les jeux sont faits*.

In response to the negative results, salespeople tout the new regulations of the European Central Bank, which will register the needs of the clients and act accordingly, giving them exactly what they want – but, in the forms you get to fill out, there is no place to mention that what you want is not to lose money. Much talk centers on the needs of the clients but, truthfully, there is absolutely no guarantee of neutral advice and there is a strong undertow perceived that they are acting according to dictates: sell this, sell that. It would seem that the European Central Bank attributes consultant status to its salespeople but does not ascertain whether they act like consultants. A consultant has only a partial conflict of interest: doctors, pharmacists, lawyers and engineers are paid regardless of the specific recommendations they come up with for your problems but, if the person selling you shares is paid according to the ones you buy, he is less a consultant than the salesclerk in a fabric shop.

In fact, the European Central Bank is putting its emphasis on the wrong person. Just as in a prison you should be keeping your eye on the personnel, so too in a bank, instead of controlling the clients, it should be controlling the bankers. What it ought to do is publish a CSR report providing bank by bank information on, for example, the formulae behind the salaries of the salespeople, along with a list of the shares portfolio of each bank in comparison with the portfolios of the clients, in order to see whether banks are selling to others what they buy for themselves.

This emphasis on the needs of the client is nothing other than a ploy to force the client to make the first move, something that happens in no other sector. It is up to the seller to offer you a price, whereas in a bank it is you who must come up with your profile, which is just another way of finding out the answer to the question, how much money are you willing to give us? You tell us your profile, how much you want before you get angry, and the rest of the proceeds we will take care of ourselves. While it's true that all is fair between two consenting adults, CSR goes beyond this and reveals the stacked deck. If a person feels vulnerable when dealing with one professional, imagine how much stronger this feeling will be when dealing with international institutions like banks.

Recap: In the case of the European Central Bank, there is a mixture of the absence of genuine attention to clients (unknown stakeholders) with the absence of disclosure – information supplied by banks being controlled by the European Central Bank regarding their internal procedures and salary mechanisms.

ICT pundits

Paris, September 1, 2008, noon sharp, a national public institution, the manager of which sits panting in front of his computer: 'No, that's the old version. What did we call it this time? Where'd I put it?' Finally, the file is found. It's called 'CAP Report pd2.xls.'

Berlin, September 2, 2008, one o'clock, a big private company: same scene. The mystery file is called 'Final_strategic_pole.doc'. It is the 'final' version of a previous document called 'strategic_pole.doc.'

T.S. Eliot said that it's hard to name a cat; he would have found it near impossible to name a file. Even hardened professionals slip up: commercial agreements baptized 'last round.doc' of which no penultimate round exists and there can be no 'very last'; CVs drawn up by young candidates entitled 'curriculum.doc' or at most 'curriculum_Johnny.doc', a coward if he writes his last name.

Without considering the difficulties at the onset, when Wordstar forced us to use no more than eight letters, amputated titles we forgot the meaning of in two minutes flat, Apple and MacIntosh always enabled the use of dozens of letters – Microsoft beginning with Windows95 – and perhaps that's when things started getting sticky. For example, Windows won't back-up or cancel files with long names. Looking at the problem from the standpoint of CSR, it's necessary to reach someone who can influence the situation: Microsoft and Google.

In 2007, Microsoft launched its new Vista system and the new, frivolous Office 2007 compendium: useless transparent icons that disappear when you move them. Getting the consumer to use a variety of symbols, characters and formats at dissonance with the mental mindset in which the document is written is falling into the hands of the ICT giants: formality and little practicality. It is recreating at the level of a product what is happening inside every organization, where the IT people sit in their air-conditioned ivory towers saying 'no' to every request that does not specify the exact nature of the problem – which, if thus specified, would already be resolved. Zero rapport with the final user. Has anybody ever received any feedback from the rather familiar Windows message about communicating problems to Microsoft – Windows' manufacturer?

Here, I turn to Microsoft because what little we have of a global language we owe to it (I've been trying for years to introduce manila folders in Italy, the kind reproduced as a symbol for files in Windows). Microsoft could help users give a name to their files that makes sense, that starts with a key word and not something generic like 'report' or 'letter.' It means taking a moment and thinking in the abstract. As for the version, throw out adjectives like 'last', 'final' or 'definitive' and, instead, insert the date and hour into a file name, along with putting the name of the file at the bottom of the printed page.

Google, too, needs to shape up. The subject of an email, as the name of a file, should not consist of the first words of said mail – 'Here I am!', or 'Part Two' – but should also consist of key words so that, when they are searched for, all the correspondence on a given procedure comes up. In this way, Google could help its clients avoid the pitfall coined by Esso (Exxon) Gas in the 1960s: 'It's useless to put a tiger in the tank if an ass sits behind the wheel'.

Recap: In the case of the products put out by the information giants, criticism leveled at their level of complication is an element of the absence of disclosure.

Questionnaire 6.1 presents the relevant section for the disclosure value.

Questionnaire 6.1 Disclosure

2.1	Brevity: the report identifies the key issues relevant to the organization and the time period the report is written for; the report presents a short list of these issues, which are also easily found in the body of the document.
2.2	The document is easy to read, also from a graphic point of view; contains visuals that are meaningful, also in black and white, not only in full color print.
2.3	The document does not anesthetize itself with the many things done; it is written in the least number of pages; it is understandable so that after two hours of study an expert reader can fill out a first draft of this questionnaire.
2.4	The report recalls the hot questions that were dealt with during the year (the period of time the report covers); it reports, at least, the threats according to the Strengths, Weaknesses, Opportunities and Threats (SWOT) model.
2.5	As an example, the report accounts for working conditions and suppliers in developing countries.
2.6	A second example: the report accounts for casualties in the workplace.
2.7	A third example, relevant in the aftermath of the 2008–09 global financial crisis: the report shows the parameters relevant to the risk situation – quality of accounts receivables, payables and actual terms of payment.
2.8	Doubt and vulnerability: the report admits that not everything was done that was expected to be done, and something could have been done better than it was.

7
Implementation

Let us recall the formulation of this value as I proposed it at the end of Chapter 4:

> The value of *implementation* requires adherence to facts instead of opinion: culture of implementation vs. politics of announcement. This means developing measures of performance and indicators of intermediate organizational processes. If we have a code of ethics, it is nice that we also have some means of measuring the organizational population's adherence to it. Developing indicators of product quantity and quality is most important in the public and non-profit sectors, where the payer is different from the beneficiary of the service or product. In the public sector, it is most important to understand the nature of the product or service being produced, rather than laboring around the measuring of funds deployed. In times of economic crisis (and in times of economic boom, to avoid busts), it is better to develop summary accounts and benchmarks of actual performance, rather than plans and budgets.
>
> An example of the culture of implementation is BAe Systems' provision of the call log to their ethics hotline (p. 18). (We saw this in Chapter 1.)

'Facts, facts, facts': the value of implementation measures the ability to follow suit on plans and declarations. This is what I call a 'culture of implementation vs. politics of announcement'. Especially in certain media, especially in certain countries, announcements of future plans receive a great deal of attention. It is not infrequent for certain governments or large monopolies to publish long-range plans every five or ten years; at every change of top management. Seldom, though, are those plans preceded by an account of what came of their predecessors. It appears to me very difficult to make plans without studying the history of preceding plans, to formulate new intentions without checking the ability of the organization to perform and execute old ones, unless one is satisfied with the sole result that the announcement itself is supposed to provoke.

This is not uncommon in European culture – in world culture, perhaps. In history, there have been many cases of a series of edicts on the same plaguing topic announced every few years but never resulting in a solution; the promulgation of the edict itself being considered satisfactory.

I believe that the credibility of a plan resides in the summary account that precedes it – setting standards, fixing parameters for historical comparison of performance and identifying pitfalls: final accounts instead of budgets; summaries instead of previews and plans; *ex post* checks on what was said; revealed references out of actual money expenditures vs. announcements (Leonard *et al.*, 2007).

In the aftermath of the 2008–09 global financial crisis, there is a need for summary accounts and benchmarks, rather than plans and budgets. In the public sector, stable and disseminated measures of effectiveness of programs are needed as much as the ubiquitous measures of mere expense funds; in the private sector, there is a need for measures of quality of goods and services.

Implementation, therefore, is brought about by a culture that is a complex mix of knowledge, custom and history, while announcement is brought about by politics, which are an articulation of social groups, motivations and goals.

Key performance indicators

One of the reasons that publishing CSR reports has developed at large corporations was the fact that financial statements do not give justice to complexity. Financial statements are the profit and loss account, the balance sheet (made of assets and liabilities) and the cash flow account. So, the CSR report developed the concept of key performance indicators (KPIs), which are what should give substance to the concept of implementation.

In the value of disclosure, I have already said that confronting the reader with a few hundred uncommented KPIs is not very useful. Also, numbers separate from words is a sign of mental divorce in the report writer's mind. So, the use of KPIs should be tempered by the modulation of subjects and issues resulting from the four values of the USDIME framework.

An enthusiasm for technicalities

The value of implementation should also transmit an enthusiasm for the technicalities of work, thus demonstrating the importance of details, which is what matter in implementation. I call this a 'culture of implementation'. Which is not there. Which would be good for society. Which could be brought about by CSR. I have been obsessed with this phrase about the missing 'culture of implementation' and have found in CSR a vehicle to convey this need to the public.

Intangibles and externalities

What is to be measured, then, that is not already quantified in the financial statements? The tautological answer would be everything that is relevant and is not captured by those statements. The backstage of capitalism is full of things: work conditions at the suppliers' sites, casualties on the job, quality of car doors, compliance with intellectual property rights. In the technical jargon of economics, many of these things go under the aegis of externalities and intangibles.

Externalities (external effects) take place outside the ordinary transactions that are the object of accounting registrations. The textbook case is the smoke from the chimney of the pizzeria oven that dirties the drying linen of the adjacent laundry.

Intangibles are things that are difficult to quantify in monetary terms but, nonetheless, are an obvious – and quite often central – part of the production phenomenon. A textbook case is the intellectual capital embodied in the minds and bodies of the employees of an organization.

Memory and time

Memory is a sub-value of implementation. Brute and indistinct memory exists only in computers. People remember and recall what is relevant to them, what is of value, what is related to what is important. So, the CSR report is the place where things are remembered. CSR also profits from things past, both good and bad.

The CSR report is the place where present and relevant things are transformed into the wealth of memory, heritage and legacy. In operational words, this means to recall what has been relevant in the media in the past year and account for it with the benefit of the passage of time.

Memory is fed with time: the report should provide data of the past, not only the present, in order to let the reader understand and form an independent idea on the data provided. The world was not founded last year. Time series are needed.

From strategy to tactics

Statements about sustainability as they are referred in some interviews and surveys appear not very helpful in understanding what is going on and the actual behavior of those who say, for instance, 'leadership will be crucial' (it is of leadership to be crucial), or 'establishing trust' is important, or 'education is top priority'. These are not detailed enough to cut both ways, as any survey question should; that is, it should cost something to answer 'yes' to the question 'will sustainability be embedded in your business?' (KPMG, 2010; Moro, 2010).

In order to take into account the complexity of sustainability, implementation revaluates the long-forgotten companion of strategy: tactics. The difference between strategy and tactics is one of scale and one of time. Tactics is involved with the appreciation of small changes, of details, of those details that might reverse the impact of a measure. Tactics is about the short run, one year, the year that just went by and that we are accounting for in our integrated report and the year that is just begun. Tactics is made of small intervals of possibility. It has been said that often, when overall changes are claimed, this is in order to change nothing and preserve the *status quo*. Well then, we can reverse those cynical statements and change as little as we can and be as concrete as we can (Kakabadse in Kakabadse *et al.*, 2007).

Let us now examine two case studies in capsule form.

Citizen security system

It is unsurprising that politicians rely so heavily on their cowardly insistence on the menace posed by illegal immigration, appealing to the worst in us instead of the best – weekly egotism as opposed to Sunday generosity – giving greatest emphasis on the worst, and the least on the best. One can only hope that they actually put into action far less than they constantly harp on about.

What should cause indignation is the servitude of the managing class, these 'Stalin's barbers' who serve themselves by serving politicians, among which the head of police who in 2007 repeated the same, stale baloney before a Parliamentary commission about the police herding them up and the judiciary letting them go. Since this baloney is exactly the same being bandied about today, it would seem the police are unable to learn from the judiciary. They ought to be arresting those the judiciary keeps imprisoned – quite a number, judging from the overcrowding of prisons. Insisting on useless activities is a waste of state resources; focusing on the arrest of illegal immigrants is financial, as well as managerial, cowardice.

And yet, the American economist William Niskanen (1968) warned about behavior such as that of the head of police in an article in the *American Economic Review*, noting that the top echelons of a bureaucracy will lobby to generate work for themselves: enhancing social demand for the services of their bureaucracies. Like asking the innkeeper whether his wine is any good, the head of police will never say that public order is not under threat. That would be managerial suicide. But the nation-system works better than one might think. In fact, it is not the police that draws up statistics concerning crime but another government agency, the census bureau, the Central Statistics Agency. It was, in fact, data from this agency that 30% of general crime is perpetrated by illegal immigrants. Another example of Stalin's barbers at work: they created a category 'general crime' in order to custom-make a crime rate around a specific group of criminals: a bit like saying that 100% of children were born of pregnant women.

Besides, who's to say that the most prevalent crime in the country is street crime? This kind of crime becomes a national emergency only in the absence of statistics and estimates concerning white-collar crime, such as the arbitrary exclusion of competitors from public works bidding processes. What about administrative crimes, like fraudulent book-keeping? It was de-penalized in the early 2000s. The only thing left is the theft of apples at the market place. Now that's a criminal for you! What's missing is systematic reporting on the judicial system, a class of technical and administrative personnel of professional and ethical quality that can counter politicians and the press with proper analyses and evaluations of public politics.

As for the sovereign population, it was a fine thing to see their own venting made public by rancorous politicians, even legitimizing insulting foreign mothers on the subway. It was a referral to this same 'national emergency' that was made in 2008 by Monique Vaute, then director of Palazzo Grassi in Venice on the occasion of an exhibit entitled, rather less than casually, 'Rome and the Barbarians,' when she said that it was a reactionary way of writing history to insist that the Roman empire was disintegrating thanks to attacks by the Goths, that that civilized population was a victim of barbaric barbarians as opposed to rotting from within. Some politicians in 2008 seemed to be wondering 'Why did we not exterminate all those brutes then, when we had the chance?'

Recap: The case concerning the police exemplifies the value of memory, presenting a correlation to the unknown stakeholder as concerns the independence of the judiciary. The police exhibited a conflict of interest in talking about crime (as we all exhibit when it comes to our own work, for which there is always a need). It is to counter this kind of interested judgment that controls exist for the particularly monopolistic system that is public administration.

We have met the enemy, and he is us

A sustainability report confirms the value of memory, which helps us to understand even things like the financial crisis of September 29, 2008. The first thing that needs to be done is to understand the phenomenon. To this end, was the statement by Nobel laureate Vernon L. Smith in May 2009:

> You end up with an implosion of the markets when banks lend money in the long term to house buyers, and borrow money in the short term from savers without having sufficient capital to cover the fluctuations of savings accounts in the short term. It's worse this time because in 1997 Bill Clinton rendered up to 500,000 dollars' profit from real estate earnings tax free. We all applauded the decision: banks, real estate agents and citizens. We did not help the poor buy homes; we helped ourselves. Better

regulations are now being requested but the problem is precisely the inefficiency of the regulations. The lesson is that taxes should never be lowered on just one kind of investment; taxes on earnings from all capital accounts could have been lowered as long as the capital was reinvested instead of spent. Yes, dear citizens, a home is an expense.

This, then, is the view from the United States.

People around the world and their banks bought shares in the junk described by Smith unaware of the euphoric mood reigning in the United States, similar to the mid-1980s, when even taxi drivers were speculating on the market. The defendant's box is stuffed: in medium-sized countries (say, of 60 million people), there are more than 300,000 bank employees, each of whom is free to work unchecked. Banks got bigger by popular request – so big that they are now too big to fail. Every banker tucks under his arm a copy of the *Financial Times*.

At the very top are National Central Banks (distinct from the European Central Bank): more than 7,000 employees apiece, with oversight officers paid to keep an eye on the banks' gains and the economic soufflé, since 'money breathes,' according to social critic and novelist Alessandro Baricco (2002). The title of his interesting pamphlet is 'Next.' We wouldn't have the things we do unless there were vanity in our desires. This vanity keeps the soufflé full and this is why it is so subject to variations, the so-called economic cycles. Last, but not least, is the market monitoring agency. There is no doubt that all the regulations were respected, and this is the result of having jurists at the helm – no imagination and, therefore, no responsibility. As for the responsibility of the politicians in this mess, not a word.

Savers in some of the Western economies avoid the stock market like a park in the dark, cringing away from government bonds and trusting foreign ones, like demeaning the local fruit seller in favor of somebody we can't understand, and the European Central Bank must now add to the idiotic questionnaire filled out by future savers a warning that, in order to enjoy twice the gains received on government bonds, a saver takes on 200 times the risk. Unless a saver buys government bonds, he is playing Russian roulette – there's always the risk of losing far more than you win. Though it is true that one pays for greater tranquility with less fun and games.

Looking for – and taking on – one's quota of responsibility is transformative and helps us respond to the crisis. This hypothesis is echoed by Smith (2009): 'We have met the enemy, and he is us.'

Recap: During a crisis, it is easy to forget the long-ago causes; thus, CSR is memory, implementation as memory. This case branches off into microethics, which itself requires an examination of one's own conscience on the part of every worker and consumer. If we'd all bought government bonds, none of us would have lost a penny, and there are those among us who did just that, which means that the financial crisis has shown us that they are not stuck-in-the-mud Neanderthals but savvy consumers. And what, then, does that make of those who jumped on the band wagon?

Questionnaire 7.1 presents the relevant section for the Implementation value.

Questionnaire 7.1 Implementation

3.1	The CSR report should identify measures of performance for the issues identified under the value of *disclosure*.
3.2	An example is: if a code of ethics is published by the organization, then there should be some means of measuring the adherence of the organization to it. Publishing a code of ethics is certainly one step, but there must be some means of checking that it is not one more announcement.
3.3	Another example is when the report acknowledges the difficulty of working in delicate contexts from a corruption point of view, and identifies means of tracking the phenomenon.
3.4	The report identifies specific measures of customer service.
3.5	Memory: the report keeps track of data and circumstances of the past because it is not uncommon that what is now perceived as an injustice can be better explained as the consequence of irresponsible past behavior.
3.6	'Denominators' are also an important element of *implementation* and the report should provide supplementary data that help the reader put indicators in perspective and understand for himself the relevance of what is being said. In other words, it is important that each piece of information be put in the correct quantitative perspective; an increment should be related to preceding percentage increments and absolute levels. This is why benchmarks are so important under the value of *unknown stakeholder*.
3.7	Adoption of international standards such as the GRI is important, in any case.
3.8	International standards should be adhered to in a complete form rather than the usual table of conversion at the end of the report, which makes comparisons impossible.
3.9	The report takes responsibility for upstream economic units (such as suppliers).
3.10	The report takes responsibility for downstream economic units (such as customers).
3.11	The report imagines the long-term consequences of the organization's development, such as upstream availability of resources or congestion downstream for its customers; it concretely delineates the meaning of sustainability in its own business.
3.12	The report adopts specific industry standards.

8
Everyman's Decision-Making: Micro-Ethics

Let us recall the formulation of this value as I proposed it at the end of Chapter 4:

> Living *micro-ethics* does not require heroism: avoid disinformation and do not reveal the faults of others. These are already acts of micro-ethics. I call this ethics 'micro' as opposed to the big ethics, always concerned about whistle-blowing, stem cells, abortion, theft. This ethics is something you live twenty times a day, not once in a lifetime. [It is interesting to recall here that the Japanese novelist Murakami Haruki in his *Kafka on the Shore* sustains that responsibility depends on imagination. Lack of imagination leads to a personality that can't take responsibility because it cannot imagine the consequences of actions or non-actions. Murakami also quotes William Yates: 'In dreams begin responsibilities.']
>
> An example of the absence of micro-ethics is the persistent organizational divorce in insurance companies between the sales and the claims departments, thus making it very hard for the customer to obtain honest claims processing.

Ethics cannot be overlooked in a set of values on the social responsibility of organizations. When capital 'e' Ethics are dealt with, I am accustomed to hearing something about abortion or stem cells in private life, or whistle-blowing in organizations – 'to take arms against a sea of troubles', as it were. These are things that have an impact on everyone and are very important; nonetheless, we live a little remote from them, as if ethics were something for specialists, political opinion, legislative discussion. Something you deal with once in a lifetime, perhaps. No, I am not going to talk about those heavy subjects here. I am going to talk about something easier and much more present in everybody's everyday life decisions.

I define here micro-ethics as those specific instances of ethical or unethical behavior on the part of individuals in their daily life within organizations, leading to the overall unethical behavior of the organization: Everyman's decision-making.

It doesn't take a hero to find out, for instance, that the claims department of many insurance companies is often organizationally divorced from the sales department of said companies. This outcome of individuals' behavior makes it very hard for the customer to obtain honest claim processing. So, it can be an effective and responsible practice to tell the truth about your claims management: honesty and candidness can be part of a strategy that is often contrarian and, therefore, successful.

There is an element of micro-ethics in all the instances whereby the decision is taken in the organization to identify and disseminate information about the organization itself. There is an element of micro-ethics in every instance of management that implies compliance with the law, adherence to one's own professional standards, making an effort to bridge the gaps that are always there in an organization, or pursue a new subject that has come to mind.

Micro-ethics, then, avoids disinformation. The CSR report is not an account of donations and philanthropy, cause-related marketing or welfare capitalism. Account should also be given of publicity campaigns that pursue pure image, and often the good disposition of the media towards the advertising customer. Lobbying should also be accounted for under this value.

The organizational model

Micro-ethics – like ethics – is a domain of the individual. Dealing here with organizational behavior, I have to clarify the model I have in mind of the relationship between the individual and organizational responsibility. The relationship that I propose is that organizational responsibility is the outcome of the responsibilities of all the individuals that operate in the organization – each one being responsible for the whole result, if need be. There is no room in the twenty-first century industrial, Western organizational world for the 'I was just executing orders' that was so often heard from Nazis at the Nuremberg trial.

I have in mind a model whereby the product of the organization is not one of rational and purposeful action, whereby a top manager takes all the decisions and everybody else executes them in a mechanical fashion. The product of the organization is the outcome of many, even conflicting, individual contributions for which, however, every member of the organization is responsible, it being his or her own choice to be part of that organization (Allison, 1971).

When I say there is little micro-ethics in a company's CSR report, I do not have in mind a wicked CSR manager governing systematic disinformation, the writing of mere good intentions and avoiding the hot organizational questions. I have in mind a complex interaction of individuals spanning the ranks, each one adding his or her own reluctance to go beyond informational routine, avoiding the challenge of uncertain terrain and the risk of being contradicted by colleagues and bosses. Therefore, a poor CSR report is the outcome of poor individual behavior, not the rational purposeful result of concerted action.

The responsibility that each individual shares in organizational behavior need not necessarily be conscious and acknowledged. Often, the individual's awareness is confined by routine and self-serving excuses. This idea is conveyed by the metaphor of Stalin's barber, who doesn't think he has any responsibility in the dictator's crimes, while trimming his famous moustache, serving him devoutly and perhaps even considering that service a social privilege. We could call this personal social responsibility.

In Chapter 6, on disclosure, we illustrated the example of the inclusion of CO_2 in the price of electric power as an example of a well-known secret in the industry. It is not difficult at this point to see a personal touch of irresponsibility in the behavior of many industry executives who know the secret but do not talk about it – like the fat rabbits in the Richard Adams best-selling novel *Watership Down*.

Another case in point would be the existence of cartels in some European countries well into the 1990s. I am not talking of conscious delinquent behavior. I am talking about unaware, carefree introduction of customer abuse clauses into the public statutes of industry associations and consortia. It is not unlikely that such practices are still in place in many parts of the world.

In the social responsibility report of a large, world-class corporation, one would take things a little further with an eye to organizational behavior and organizational non-ethics embodied in organizational rules and aggregate behavior. Let me give a couple of examples of this.

These statements follow an individualist approach in spite of the diffused opinion that 'the fault is the system's' (Galluccio, 2009). Such approach lays a very heavy burden on the shoulders of each individual (Berta, 2010). However, we cannot deny that organizations, especially the long-established ones and the most successful, do have their own way of doing things; the work of their managers is, in fact, to develop a culture that is conducive to a specific, and effective, way of doing things. And, indeed, predictions can be formulated on the basis of organizational culture (Allison, 1971).

How is it possible, then, to reconcile individual responsibility with the predictive power of the collectivist approach? The collectivist approach has its realm in the positive analysis of organizations; the individualist approach has its realm in the normative domain. If we want to predict what an organization will do, we'd better use a collectivist approach. If we want to account for what does not work within an organization, and therefore if we want to change an organization, if we look for responsibility within an organization, we have to work with a normative, and therefore an individualist, model. In fact, one of the tenets of the change management area of studies is that 'organizations do not change, people change, one at a time' (Hiatt). It is my experience that there are moments within institutions – incremental ones – when micro-decisions are made that lead to reinforce or change that very culture (Schelling, 1978).

Let us now examine some case studies in capsule form.

IBM

International Business Machines, the giant that has thrived in the information and communication technologies (ICT) market over the decades, has a very elaborate incentive scheme for its sales organization. Commissions on sales are paid to entire lines of responsibility. And correctly so. Client account assignments, however, are changed quite often (every year), sometimes within the fiscal year. This generates uncertainty about 'who will be my customer next year' and consequent short-term behavior by the sales force in pursuing customer opportunities and customer service. Accounting for the impact on clients and the use that clients make of what is sold to them would be an honest arena for IBM to open up in their CSR report.

The European Central Bank

The European Central Bank suffers from an analogous strabismus in their customer relations. The European Central Bank and the European national banking systems made much ado in the first decade of the twenty-first century about regulation that would require individual banks to identify each customer's risk profile. This was made with the intent not to sell people financial instruments they would subsequently discover they did not want. I believe too much emphasis was made on so called 'customer needs' (customers basically just want to make money and not lose it), and nothing at all was said about the incentive schemes for sales employees in the banks – which are, at least in part, responsible for what is sold to whom.

More on the media

Another aspect worth mentioning about the media, since it is ubiquitous in our daily lives, is a concept that is often taught on the first day of a communications class and which the populace often must submit to. Television is not the only culprit when it comes to exploiting its clientele. Newspapers, too, though each of us decides freely to read them. Here, the exploitation is more subtle, made up more of calling fabrication truth. In their small way, newspapers do their best to bring out a reader's more negative responses. This can be immediately verified by checking out the latest headlines, such as 'The Recession Nightmare,' 'Utilities Cost More – 50 euros a year', 'Internet Fraud Boom – how identity theft happens,' 'Good-bye to Brothels.'

It would seem to me that all this information is either alarmist or irrelevant. When has there not been the threat of a recession? Have the costs of utilities ever gone down? It would seem the print media is on the look-out for issues that bring out our worries. Instead of providing catharsis – the way Greek tragedies are meant to – newspapers create tragedies without catharsis.

Media focus is on the marginal, while the organized goes without notice. Much is written about identity theft on the part of criminals, but nothing is said about the Monopolist Domestic Credit Card Company – from which one cannot cancel unrecognized debits; the entire card must be cancelled in order to stop payment of a fraudulent entry. Consumers are under the *fatwa* of the European Central Bank, which controls the honesty of (potential) thieves by measuring the naiveté of those from whom they steal. Naturally, talking only about the good things appears totalitarian, but there must be a middle ground between alarms for alarm's sake and putting on rose-colored glasses.

Media focus on what makes the 'best' story, rather than seeking out the root cause of a situation or problem, does not serve us well. Instead of hanging out in police stations to inform us about the latest murder, journalists should be attending the courts so as to give us a sense of how incredibly long it takes to bring criminals to justice. Instead of the media reporting on the estimated level of tax evasion, it would be nice to know how much of that has subsequently been recuperated. If the story is about an immigrant driver who runs over a woman in a car owned by another immigrant who has 500 cars to his name, it is certainly not about the victim or the immigrants. Rather, the core of the story is about the ineptitude of those who work at the automobile register office, which is obviously not monitored and thus never detects the real problems. When we are told about yet another death on the job, why do we never find out how all the trials on similar deaths have concluded?

Recap: The print media is as lazy as we are, and feeds our voyeurism, harking back to public hangings. Responsibility here can be connected not only to a single journalist and the story he writes, but also to individual readers. Timothy Ferriss, in his best-seller *The 4-Hour Workweek*, invites us to stop reading the papers, since you'll find out what's important anyway.

Ethics revealed

You always get a strange reaction when talking about ethics in the business sphere – a mixture of incredulity and cynicism. While lip service is always paid to ethics, any real exhortation in its favor is met with skeptical disdain. These exhortations consist of abstract concepts with no examples, so the disdain is couched in a certain 'been there done that' attitude, or takes the form of self-justification: 'I'd like to see you when the bank manager tells you what to sell by the end of the month and who gives a damn who you sell it to.' Either response is frustrating but, somewhere in the middle, is the practice of ethics that is still a mystery; we can't decide how immoral those folks are that thumb their noses at ethics, or how moral their champions are.

In an attempt to shed some light on the subject, it is helpful to give concrete examples of ethics in action, the voluntary adhesion to correct and proper behavior even if it is not self-serving, either from the purely economic, company point of view or for the individual. There's working harder than just enough not to get fired, paying taxes, paying suppliers quickly, standing in line, not cheating on the books, not selling dud shares to little old ladies. There's not ignoring the needs of the customer, copying brands, and buying phony brands. You can not do many of these things and still stay within the law, which by itself lays bare what hypocrites we are when we clamor for ethics or belittle them.

I propose that we are actually more ethical than the skeptics want to admit. To prove it, I call your attention to sentences issued by the courts many years after the deeds are done and are often in favor of the guilty party. If by acting illegally you gain economically, then it makes sense to do so, since Italian justice appears to be on the side of debtors. At worst, you'll have to pay back what you stole along with interest, but nothing will be said of the increasing value of the damage done over all the years it's taken to come to trial. Time is not a variable in Italian jurisprudence. That justice will be done is mere rhetoric; not only is it far from certain that justice will be done, but where it is done it is often at the expense of the person in the right.

The state itself takes advantage of this situation: a gentleman from Bosnia was awarded €1,000 for having unjustly served five months in an over-crowded prison cell (a television news report on August 4, 2009); that's less than €7 a day. It appears economical for the state to have overcrowded prisons and compensate those unjustly incarcerated with €7 a day instead of building new prisons or taking other corrective measures. It behooves you to act criminally; that the majority does not means that it is acting ethically with no view to self-interest. So, we are more ethical than we say we are; acting like we're not is just trying to look cool.

Recap: Ethics revealed is an attempt to specify in detail the daily moments in which each individual and organization finds itself at the crossroads between ethical and unethical behavior.

Ostrich ethics

Another sidestepping device is the 'sell no arms, buy no tobacco' argument. While I agree that there ought to be a rating of ethics, I mean here to limit myself to the consideration of a sort of ostrich ethics: 'I don't like it but there's nothing I can do about', or a 'not in my name, not in my backyard' attitude. While one would be hard put to decide which companies would appear at the top of an ethical rating, people are quicker to identify those they perceive at the bottom: arms dealers, tobacco companies, gambling outfits. However, not much has been said on the subject by the great moral philosophers and, in the end, who would be the good guys, family TV broad-casters and their serials full of sexual innuendo or the car manufacturers?

Let's take a look at the arms dealers. In the transition from individual (micro) ethics to company (macro) ethics, the idea would appear to be

'Thou shalt not kill. So no arms sales.' But killing is done with far less, and you need more than a weapon in order to do it. You need rage, or motive. Tibullus himself spoke on the subject when he started by deprecating those who made swords only to end up accepting that it is our own darn fault that we have turned weapons made for killing wild animals on each other. And being issued a license to own a gun would appear a good thing when considering some of the lunks seen on the streets with beer bottles in hand. Besides, self-defense is legally guaranteed and going from brute force to the licensing of weaponry appears rather civilizing.

More information ought to be sought before leveling criticism at certain businesses; for example, it would be nice to have a public discussion concerning the Italian aerospace and arms company Finmeccanica, which is reported to receive 30% of all state incentives for businesses. The state has both feet planted squarely in the business of vice but, in so doing, has eroded the profits of organized crime in areas such as gambling – though on other fronts it, too, hides its head, passing laws against prostitution but not escort services, which are actually the cream of the crop. While it's true that there is a dependence of supply on demand, prohibition generally creates more illicit profits (and greater social costs) than less.

When going from micro- to macro-ethics, it is helpful to look for individual irresponsibility. An ethical rating should take account of the core business of a company. Concerning Italian telephone companies charging the highest rates in Europe, what good is a political stand on zero environmental impact when individual clients are being squeezed dry? You could say that telephone rates are the concern of standard business ratings while ethical ratings are measuring something else, but I disagree. An ethical rating ought to be concerned with the response to a problem at the core of a business; otherwise it remains on the periphery of the economy, and of ethics.

Recap: This consideration of isolating as non-ethical an entire organization as simplistic takes us back to the idea of complexity, and judging on a case-by-case basis only.

Conclusion

Putting the accent on the faults of the system has led us to a quantum of personal irresponsibility: speeding on the highway of welfare, we missed the exit of personal social responsibility. This was probably an unintended consequence of the writings of Herbert Marcuse. A philosopher and political theorist at Berkeley, Marcuse was the thinker who fathered the student protest of the 1960s. His key works were *Eros and Civilization* (1955) and *One-Dimensional Man: Studies in the Ideology of Advanced Industrial Society* (1964).

'Ethics: you can't learn it, you just practice it': the do-it-yourself approach often masks a denial of the issues and does not recognize that some ethics are around anyway. You do not need a ghost to visit you at night to become honest with yourself. You can hire a consultant who will tell you a great deal about ethics. The mental disposition of an executive or white-collar, learned employee in a large organization may very well be summarized by the words of T.S. Eliot in 'The Love Song of J. Alfred Prufrock' in which the author creates an atmosphere for the condition of the individual in the organization. His or her mental and emotional states may range from the humility and diligence to undertake projects to the willingness of serving in an almost a-critical, Weberian fashion. Sometimes he may be part of the political game himself or one may very well feel an impulse to seclude oneself while the storms of organizational politicking rage all around him, and hide, like a monk in the middle ages, in some metaphorical hilltop monastery, copying manuscripts and waiting for the barbarians to pass or simply one may feel frustrated and manipulated or, worse still, stupid.

Questionnaire 8.1 presents the relevant section for the micro-ethics value.

Questionnaire 8.1 Micro-ethics

3.1	The report does not look for CSR in the wrong place: philanthropy, welfare capitalism, cause-related marketing.
3.2	When the organization runs pure image campaigns – not subject to full competition – it is not a good sign of CSR.
3.3	In a bad CSR report there is disinformation in what the report says; the report points to other organizations' or people's faults.
3.4	The report accounts for lobbying and institutional relations practices.

The four values in Questionnaire 8.1 are rather loose, but it is not impossible to interpret them with the help of standard sciences such as microeconomics and organizational sociology. Therefore, in Chapter 9 I will briefly talk about the professions of sustainability reporting and the skills needed to do that.

9
Who's Afraid of the Policy Analyst?

CSR is who you are (it is not what you do). To talk about CSR, you need to know what and to be where the company's business is. This has an impact on the studies that you have to do and the general knowledge that is required to carry on this business of CSR.

When confronted with a CSR report from a business or government organization, and the task of criticizing it using the USDIME model, students argue that they do not know enough about the organization itself: you can only criticize the document if you know something about what is outside the document itself. It is not sufficient to read what is in the report if I have to find out what is not in the report that could have been. Is this true?

My hypothesis is that you do not need more information about the specific organization at hand but, rather, that you do need general business analysis and public policy skills to understand and manipulate the USDIME framework. It is therefore interesting to understand which professionals are better equipped for contributing to such a process.

Without doubt, a public relations (PR) professional has an advantage thanks to his sensitivity to the internal dialogue of a company, the press and the vocal stakeholders. The stories in Chapter 1 shed new light on the reflexive function of the PR profession within the corporate environment, according to James E. Grunig's model (1995), which distinguishes between the relational and the reflexive function of PR. This important area of PR is often neglected, and this research is a documentation of it.

Public policy and business analysts, for their part, have their own tools to identify economic phenomena in the internal functioning of a company or of an institution – particularly intangibles and externalities. The policy analyst knows his SWOT analysis, his value chain and competitive context analysis, and is capable of identifying and listening to the unknown stakeholder, which is at the bottom of all research – the silent critic inside us.

The basic tools of the policy analyst include micro-economics, organizational sociology and politics, and statistics. Once you are aware of these domains,

I do not think you need to know more about the reporting institution to be able to criticize its CSR report through the USDIME framework.

Corporate (social) responsibility is a traditional staple of PR. CSR strategizing and reporting in international corporations appears to be a domain of the PR profession. Traditionally, PR professionals have been trained in communication studies. This research now shows, with a variety of examples, how PR professionals could profit if they acquired skills that are taught in government and business management schools. I argue that policy analysts also have a role here. This book is an example of the point of view that the management consultant and policy analyst can provide a fruitful contribution to CSR.

Conversely PR could be taught in business and public policy schools.

Rather than professional fences, I see windows of convergence among disciplines that often make themselves more distinct than they are: intangibles, social capital, policy evaluation. From the disciplines to the professions, I see a great deal of convergence between policy analysis and public relations.

Thus, CSR is an opportunity for PR to free themselves from the fetters of the hidden persuader. It is also an opportunity for policy analysts to have their skills probed. The two professions should be allied in this venture. So, the USDIME framework moves CSR analysis from communication studies to business and policy analysis.

The sorrows of the young CSR executive

I question the concept of the CSR manager used to identify the executive who is 'in charge' of CSR within an institution (private or public) and propose, instead, the use of the lighter concept of CSR 'reportist'. CSR is a responsibility of top management, as is now acquired knowledge; CSR reportists, however, feel too much responsibility. They oscillate between an external excess of responsibility and an internal pessimism – the CSR executive as Stalin's barber (personal responsibility when rubbing shoulders with the powerful) (see also Chapter 8 on micro-ethics.)

The limitations I introduce, however, should not be an excuse. To define the responsibility of the CSR reportist, I develop the analogy of Stalin's barber, who ultimately shares responsibility for the dictator's crimes. A CSR reportist should use all instruments of internal lobbying to put forth the cause of CSR.

Often, CSR executives feel like the black sheep in the corporate herd. Maybe they are right; CSR is not the hottest thing in the corporate hierarchy and the career of the CSR manager does not look as flashy as that of the chief financial officer. However, the CSR manager does have instruments to promote CSR, if he or she assumes internal lobbying as part of the job.

The USDIME framework, CSR standards, and integrated reporting

The USDIME framework does not aim to substitute existing CSR and other standards. I examine here the relationship between the USDIME, the Global Reporting Initiative (GRI), the Committee of European Securities Regulators (CESR) regulations and the possible link to the Japanese-led World Intellectual Capital Initiative (WICI).

The USDIME is something additional to other standards. It should not supplant the other systematic standards. It should contribute to making them more relevant and effective.

The GRI is apparently the most widely accepted CSR reporting standard. I have two points *vis-à-vis* the GRI.

First, the GRI is not applied effectively. All companies' CSR reports I have seen so far have a table of contents of their own, different from the GRI's both in terms of sequence of subjects and in terms of text and graphic image. Between 2003 and 2009, companies learned to publish a cross reference table that maps the GRI indicators over the actual content of their report. This way of showing compliance to the GRI standard is better than nothing, of course, but it frustrates a key element of reporting: comparability, both with the same company reports over time and with other companies' reports.

The GRI standard should be applied in full, including the graphic design suggested in the GRI guidelines. This would make CSR reports much less glamorous, and expensive, but also much more relevant, readable and dependable. This aspect frustrates the standard the most, since the standard is not supposed to push the writing organization out of its comfort zone but, rather, is intended to provide a wide context, across companies and time.

Second, GRI guidelines do not seem to have the 'bite' to get to what is important. Companies write pages and pages of answers to the GRI questionnaire, never getting to a hurting point, to something that reveals data that without the standard would not be provided. This is the task of the USDIME framework: to help the company smoothly to leave the comfort zone of muffled information.

It appears crucial to me that Eccles and Krzus (2010) include the Balanced Scorecard among the CSR reporting standards. This implies, once more, a nature of CSR very much within the core business of the enterprise and CSR reporting as disclosure of corporate critical information.

As we have argued, CSR in the core business leads to integrated reporting, as it demands that CSR be influential in the economic bottom line and in the workings of the corporate activity. It therefore cannot be reported other than where economic activity is basically accounted for. This is true in the private sector; but it is all the more true in the public and private non-profit sectors as, in those sectors, strictly economic and financial reporting is almost meaningless, as will be argued at the end of Chapter 13.

The Committee of European Securities Regulators (CESR) is not a CSR standard, but the CESR is in search of better reporting standards to prevent stock market bubbles and busts. The CESR enjoys the consideration – and embodies the hopes – of European economists, accountants and financial experts but, so far, the CESR statements and documents do not appear to have gone beyond vague do-good exhortations.

WICI is also in search of a standard with the same scope as the CESR. WICI is based on the economic category of intangibles. Intangibles is a serious economic category to which I would grant primacy over CSR. I have argued that CSR can partake of the benefits of intangible management. I have argued that CSR reporting should give account of intangibles and externalities – another serious economic category. It is clear that distinctions (between CSR and intangibles and externalities) must be preserved; otherwise, every-thing gets entangled with everything else in a primordial broth leading us nowhere. However, it is also undeniable that, when we get to organizational operations, a syncretistic approach takes us much closer to reality.

As Antonio Tencati points out in the CSR handbook *Corporate Reporting Frameworks* (2010), there is little room for further reporting frameworks, as he outlines a well-crowded field. However, if reporting standards have to produce a living and growing set of ideas, they must be put to trial *vis-à-vis* experience and criticism (Aras and Crowther, 2008).

Tencati also pointed out that reporting standards – and CSR, in general – are viewed by their students as instruments of strategic management (i.e. geared to answer the question: where are we going to go?), whereas I am putting my accent on the present and past accountability, and the inter-pretation of CSR in public and monopolistic organizations, rather than competitive organizations.

Also, here we must recall Giovanni Moro's criticism of simple definitions and simple rules, and simple declarations of acceptance of sustainability concepts by corporate executives: the phenomenon has an intrinsic com-plexity that is difficult to capture in standard format. That is why the basic idea we are carrying out in this writing is that CSR and CSR reporting is quite close to policy analysis, and issues must be dealt with in some depth. Such depth might lead to excessive work and materials: that is why, in the disclosure value, we put forth the invitation to limit the number of issues to be dealt with. Nothing excludes overall and systematic reporting from still being in order, so that a 360-degree view of the organization is preserved and tomorrow's issues can still be identified.

I wouldn't want to take the issue too far, but I think CSR is an opportu-nity to help us take into account important economic and social theories that, in the decades after World War II, have been formulated but were never actually incorporated into business reporting, given the dominance of legal and accounting (and tax) professions over corporate culture: Herbert Simon's 'satisfycing' (1997); Harvey Leibenstein's X-efficiency (1978); Oskar

Morgenstern's 'Thirteen Critical Points in Economic Theory' (1972). Part of Nobel laureate Herbert Simon's work revolves around the concept of satisfycing in organizational behaviour, whereby employees work towards an acceptable (satisfying) level of performance, but are far from the classical idea of maximization of work effort and economic performance. Different – but also critical of the maximization hypothesis – is the work of Leibenstein on X-efficiency: employees do not necessarily maximize something, they just observe social norm and other pursuits of life. Morgenstern laments the absence of micro-economic theory to deal with that (greater) part of the market that is not governed by the neoclassical tenets of perfect competition.

10
The Proof of the Pudding: Applying the USDIME Framework

Business corporations – much more than government institutions – go to great lengths to show themselves responsible before the public. These efforts are summarized and presented in documents that are very similar to financial statements (which also have the same finality) to the point that they share part of the name: CSR reports or sustainability reports vs. annual reports.

These are documents of length, ranging from 50 to 200 pages, often filled with illustrations inspired to good and beauty, which describe the performance – economic, social and environmental – of the organization *vis-à-vis* the surrounding society: customers, employees, the environment, stockholders.

These reports are the empirical basis for the application of the USDIME framework. The USDIME framework helps to identify places of potential CSIR in the CSR reports, and it also helps to recognize places of responsibility. With the idea that the CSR report should prove the company is not irresponsible – until proven otherwise, I assume the company is anesthetizing itself and the reader with irrelevant accounts of how good it is.

From each value of the USDIME framework (treated in Chapters 5 through 8), we have derived a few questions, general and specific, about information and data to be provided in a CSR report. The juxtaposition of these questions results in a questionnaire. This questionnaire is a guide for a systematic screening or test of a CSR report (when we study one written by somebody else), and a handbook on how to write a CSR report (when we write one ourselves).

Through this procedure, I try to attain what is most essential in corporate behavior: probe the places of potential irresponsibility and check what the organization has to say about them. I propose that this method is more efficient and effective than others proposed and currently in use.

Finding what was expected by the corporation

In order to validate the quality of the USDIME framework, I have screened a sample of CSR reports of large, worldwide corporations, and some more local,

91

domestic companies. In this chapter, I present the information that I found important and in accordance with the USDIME framework, and I highlight the information provided in these CSR reports that makes me think there is some responsibility and awareness in the business of these companies.

British Petroleum (before the Gulf of Mexico)

The 2008 Sustainability Report of British Petroleum (BP) provides an overview on the world oil market, as it shows the market shares of the major oil companies. To do this, it has to mention the names of its competitors. This is not a frequent case; often, corporations seem to operate in a vacuum, alone in the world. This piece of information incarnates the value of the *unknown stakeholder*; that is, it provides the competitive environment in which the company operates.

BP's CSR report is short, just a few dozen pages, and it shows what it thinks are the relevant data in one table, where one of the first indicators is the number of casualties that occurred during the year. This is an important item of *disclosure*.

BP is also concerned about the sustainability of the business, and it provides data on the replacement rate of its oil reserves. This data appears to be a key item in a sustainability report, a very basic way to implement the concept of sustainability (the value of *implementation*). Other oil companies (ENI and Total, as we saw in Chapter 1) see sustainability in their relations with local communities. That is certainly important, but the key point in oil – it seems to me – is that there be oil.

In its CSR report, BP also overtly states that its 2008 profits derive from the dance (ups and downs) of oil prices in that year. This is an instance of *micro-ethics*: people already know that; you say it, and you get good grades. There is no point in looking for a culprit elsewhere, as in the ENI report that deals with this issue only to end up saying the gasoline distribution networks are inefficient.

Toyota

Toyota provides gross margin by region of the world. This is an interesting step forward in the stewardship of stakeholders from the usual data provided of revenues by region. Margin is much more meaningful than mere revenue, since it takes into account prices and it exposes the profitability of the company by regional area.

The Toyota report (2007–08, since their fiscal year does not coincide with the solar year) is also very short and liberally illustrated with tables and visuals that make it easy to follow and fun to read. A sign of *disclosure*.

WalMart

After infinite polemics, WalMart provided data on employee compensation in its CSR report. WalMart is often criticized for its poor employee policy: low salaries, union busting and the rest. In its 2009 report – not called a CSR report – WalMart provided data on the hourly wages of its full-time employees. This is a measure of *disclosure* – though it is partial, since hourly salaries of full-time employees are probably higher than those of part-time employees.

It would be nice, however, if other organizations followed WalMart's example and provided such data because of the potential moral hazard [conflict of interest] between employees and customers as far as factor remuneration is concerned. This is an important item of stewardship of the *unknown stakeholder*, since factor remuneration (i.e. employee salaries, in certain industries [sic, not 'companies']) might be higher than in others. Often the issue at hand appears to be the opposite to that of the WalMart case: we see employees in entire sectors or industries of the economy being better remunerated than others. I think it is an item of CSR that these data become public and are considered part of the domain of CSR.

It is a consequence of what has been argued by *The Economist* – in their industry-famous 2005 critical survey on CSR – that this provision of information (once considered company confidential) doesn't have anything to do with CSR but is simply a correct managerial practice and use of the media. I like to see something more than just straightforward management in such communication events. After the media wave has washed away, a residue is left on the shore that was not there before. A new habit is started. A discontinuity has taken place that characterizes innovation. Innovation is often the daughter of ill deeds or diversity: also, the Nike disclosure of supplier information (see Chapter 1) stemmed from polemic and pressure from the public and journalistic accounts. The CSR report is the summary of what the press said – a question of memory, in order to not forget what was said and to build on it.

ING Group

In the aftermath of the 2008–09 financial crisis, it is logical to look for information about the ownership of Lehman securities in the sustainability reports of financial institutions. So, I found out that Ing Group, the Dutch giant, couldn't bring itself to utter the word 'Lehman' in its 2008–09 CSR report. Compared with that, the less worldly Italian-based institutions Montepaschi and Unicredit fared better, both providing some data on their involvement with the bankrupt institution.

Unicredit

Unicredit may not be one of the leading financial institutions in the world but I think their CSR behavior is relevant here just the same, because we do not all buy our goods and services only from world-class corporations. Even the most cosmopolitan of us lives life with domestic supplying companies and local shops. It will not be difficult for the reader to relate less well-known names and brands to the ones he or she uses every day. The ultimate meter of CSR, after all, is the individual.

The reason I mention Unicredit here is, however, unique, I think, in the landscape of CSR and CSR reporting. In its 2008 CSR report (published in 2009), Unicredit reported a procedure that manages disputes between its own employees. This is of no small import: everybody knows that the corporate – indeed, all of the organizational world – is full of infighting and politicking. It's human. But overtly recognizing this and trying to work on it is a very nice piece of doubt and vulnerability: good elements of *disclosure*.

I think of this as an instance of *disclosure* and *micro-ethics*. Micro-ethics: there are fights among employees all over the place, micro-behavior, individual responsibility on the job – how much of that is generated by individuals not pausing and thinking about themselves a little bit? *Disclosure*: let's acknowledge that. Let's not hide our heads in the sand. Everybody talks about it.

Also, the data provided by Unicredit were quite interesting in their detail – the number of formalized files open during the year, the closed cases and their outcomes, thus providing an example of the value of *implementation*.

As far as the ubiquitous business of the Lehman bankruptcy, Unicredit gave the total number of clients that held Lehman securities in their portfolio. They did not provide the amount of these securities. Montepaschi, another financial institution, gave a less transparent number: the percentage of its customers that held Lehman securities.

Intesa San Paolo

Intesa San Paolo is another bank that is not a world class operator in the financial landscape but, nonetheless, is a strong European player. In their 2008–09 CSR report, Intesa Sanpaolo gave a measure of customer satisfaction *vis-à-vis* market average and, basically, came out saying: we were below industry average but we checked and our direct competitors were below us. This is quoted here as an example of absent *micro-ethics* in action. Mentioning competition only generically, without data and in a negative way, was an obvious case of petty one-upmanship. Micro-ethics is also avoiding such base speech.

From an industry point of view, the statement in the Intesa Sanpaolo report is quite interesting: the big players' performance is below average. This implies that smaller banks are consistently better than big banks. This is good fodder for central banks' and market supervisors' reports.

Finding what was expected by the values

How did the USDIME framework fare *vis-à-vis* each CSR report value? Was it really helpful to identify key areas of irresponsibility? Albeit difficult to state scientifically what was expected and what has been found (this is not physics), in studying the reports there have been quite a few instances where I felt that I was reading something that I had envisioned should be there, content that I would have put it in had I been writing that report. Insights: moments of 'Aha!'

Unknown stakeholder

According to the unknown stakeholder value, the CSR report must present the competitive context where the company operates and the rules it is supposed to obey. Specific benchmarks with the competition must be provided and, where this is not possible (as in the case of government institutions that are unique in one country), an international comparison would be in order.

Companies never do this in their reporting; be they CSR reports or financial statements, they seem to operate in a vacuum, a world with no competition. Competitors are never in the array of stakeholders.

BP did break this code of silence and provided the global framework for the oil market: nothing fancy, information that is available in specialized websites. It is important, however, that the point be made: we are not alone.

Regarding Toyota, I had noted on the pages of all reports that give revenues by region of the world that the margin should be provided, instead of the revenue. That would have been a more telling measure of respect for the consumer; so I was pleased to see the Toyota report give this more relevant information.

It is regrettable that, under the unknown stakeholder value, no company gives explicit and detailed (distribution) data of the time they take to pay account payables to their suppliers. In particular, big companies should do that, since they have high market leverage (i.e. power). It's one more element of fair competition. Large organizations have SMEs and individuals working for them, and they set the standards for the overall market.

Disclosure

While it was logical to search for the 'Lehman' reference in the text of the reports of financial institutions, in my opinion it was not logical that some institutions didn't even name it.

Unicredit struck me with their data on internal fighting among employees. To this date, I am incredulous of what I read; I doubt I understood it.

Implementation

The value of implementation is more about creativity to figure out indicators and ways to capture what cannot be captured with standard instruments. Imagination is needed to identify responsibilities.

I'd like to mention here the BAe Systems independent study to ascertain the fairness of BAe prices to the British government, and the McDonald's special study to determine the economic impact of its restaurants on local communities. Also, the number of calls to the BAe ethics hot-line was a simple and telling indicator of the significance of the hot-line service itself, once the comparison is made with the number of BAe employees and the volume of its business worldwide.

On the irresponsibility side, we find all the financial institutions examined in our study so far. They all talk about the necessity of controlling the underlying risk of securities, but a measure of such risks is never to be found.

Measures and indicators are key-words in the value of implementation.

Micro-ethics

Ethics is always a touchy subject to mention. You get a lot of skeptical reactions to it. However, when I came across the statement 'Our performance was below industry average, but we checked and our direct competitors were lower than us', I was sure that I was hitting an ethics matter. As Potter Stewart, Associate Justice of the Supreme Court of the United States, wrote in his concurring opinion in the obscenity case *Jacobellis v. Ohio*, 378 U.S. 184 (1964): 'I shall not today attempt further to define the kinds of material I understand to be embraced within that shorthand description [hard-core pornography]; and perhaps I could never succeed in intelligibly doing so. But I know it when I see it, and the motion picture involved in this case is not that.'

The general feeling is that CSR reports are better when they are specific, with fewer words and more data – easy to read and to capture in their essence.

Towards an open source community of CSR rating

The USDIME framework can be used to grade a CSR report. Each item of the questionnaire can be answered with a score ranging from 1 to 5; 1 is bad, 5 is very good, 3 is satisfactory. Each value can then be scored by averaging the scores of each question, and an overall score can be obtained for the report. Once you do this for several reports, a ranking can be obtained.

Numbers alone do not mean a thing. They help, however, to reason and probe one's own evaluations. I ran the procedure (see Table 10.1) and a few questions sprang up immediately: why did I assign a score of 5 to BP's reserve replacement data and a score of only 4 to Unicredit's internal personnel procedure? Unicredit's procedure was very creative; however, BP data are more in the core business of the firm. Oil reserves data strictly belong in the core business of the oil company whereas personnel data – though more creative and innovative *per se* – do not belong in the core business of the company.

Table 10.1   The USDIME framework applied

	Sector	Corporation	US	D	I	ME	AVG
1	Energy	British Petroleum	3.5	4.0	2.5	3.0	3.2500
2	Auto	Toyota	3.0	3.0	2.3	2.0	2.5833
3	Retail	WalMart	3.0	3.0	2.0	2.0	2.5000
4	Auto	Fiat	2.0	2.5	1.8	1.5	1.9500
5	Energy	Snam Rete Gas	1.0	2.0	1.0	3.0	1.7500
6	Energy	ENI	1.3	2.3	1.3	2.0	1.7083
7	TLC	Telecom Italia	2.0	1.8	1.0	2.0	1.6875
8	Bank	Montepaschi	1.5	2.0	1.5	1.0	1.5000
9	Bank	Unicredit	1.5	2.3	1.0	1.0	1.4583
10	Bank	ING	1.5	1.3	1.0	1.0	1.2083

Also it was good to notice that the low ranking of the banks did not come out of their negative economic results in 2008 but from their reticence to speak about the underlying risk of their business, which was a cause – not a consequence – of the international financial crisis.

One final observation: responsibility is the same for everybody. There is no *a priori* ranking between industries: a banker is as responsible as a journalist or a car-maker or an oil wildcatter.

All evaluations imply a degree of opinion, of personal feeling and priorities. No question about it. The good thing about the USDIME framework is that it defines a procedure, explicable and therefore falsifiable. In one word: scientific.

You may certainly dissent from these evaluations. The good thing is that these evaluations come from an open system. Each agreement that is reached over such valuations can be made cumulative into the system.

Existing CSR rating systems are proprietary themselves – as most corporate information pretends to be – and this is hampering the development of valuation and the transparency of markets. The USDIME framework can be the base for an open source community of CSR rating. It is open to contribution for a learning experience for everybody, not least for investors.

Conclusion

In conclusion, companies appear to make an effort to tell their own story with some honesty. A great deal of work and resources are spent in order to collect the necessary information, put it into communicable form, publish and disseminate it.

There is still a great deal of room for improvement, however. I propose the USDIME framework as a means for leveraging corporate reporting resources. It is detrimental to the organization to have reports drafted that are perfunctory, both financial and non-financial statements.

The 'weak' theory of CSR that I have proposed here carries an element of effrontery with it, a *chutzpah* that is not to be found in other frameworks of CSR: strategic management, cause-related marketing, strategic philanthropy, and shared value with the non-profit sector. CSR as defined operationally by the USDIME framework is different from these. CSR is who you are, it's not what you do.

USDIME Framework Course Work

Tables 10.2 and 10.3 present the applications of the 'decalogues' developed in the previous chapters.

Table 10.2 USDIME framework course work: Telecom Italia and Vodafone

Company	Telecom Italia	Vodafone
Document examined	**Sustainability report 2008**	**Social responsibility report, 2007–08**
DISCLOSURE		
Identification of 'emergencies': offers a brief, easily identifiable and located list of the company's hot issues.	On p. 21, the table is clear but its contents are rather general.	In ch. 1 (Who We Are, Where We Operate), in particular.
	Noteworthy is the indication of a section in which each item is given greater detail.	Page 23 prioritizes activities under thematic headings.
		Less clear than the Telecom report, but located fairly easily just the same.
Easy to read graphic lay-out, easy to read tables also in black and white.	Easily found and downloaded off the internet, but hard to read the very small print.	Easily found and downloaded off the internet; well-spaced text is easy to read.
	Considering the length of the report, there seem to be fewer tables and diagrams with respect to Vodafone.	Numerous tables and diagrams. Clear also in black and white.
	At times, the black and white printout renders the information inaccessible.	

(continued)

Table 10.2 Continued

Company	Telecom Italia	Vodafone
Document examined	Sustainability report 2008	Social responsibility report, 2007–08
Does not 'anesthetize' with too much information.		Number of pages fairly contained (90) and easy to read. It is easy to find what one is looking for.
Accessible length and content so that, in two hours of attentive study, the reader is able to fill out this questionnaire.	Number of pages acceptable (106), but the amount of text is a bit excessive. In two hours one can get an idea, but it is difficult to later fill out the USDIME framework with explicit references to the text. While legitimate (the reason is obvious), it is distracting to be constantly referred to the criteria, standards and institutional norms with which the company has complied (footnotes may be preferable). The overall tone is sometimes excessively self-congratulatory.	Two hours are sufficient. Never boring.
Confronts issues encountered during the year.	Does not seem to.	Does not seem to.
Writes up risks according to the SWOT analysis.		
Gives examples of hot issues: details working conditions of employees and suppliers in developing countries.	N/A	Not found but ought to be, because Vodafone is present in 25 countries (among which, for example, Ghana and India). However, this report relates to Vodafone Italy so could, as in the Telecom case, be not applicable.
Another example of a hot issue: job related deaths in Italy, 2008–09.	Page 84, under the 'Accidents' heading when considering their increasing seriousness as compared with the previous year.	Not found (perhaps there weren't any?) but accidents (on the decline) are dealt with on pp. 67–8.

Another general example for 2008–09: considers the implications of the financial crisis by evaluating, for example, risk parameters (debt, credit).

Doubt, vulnerability: contains admissions of not having done what was supposed to be done, or of having actions be insufficient.

Of the two non-professional deaths, the cause is given; cause is not given for the professional death.

There is a table on accidents.

No reference to the financial crisis.

On p. 16, 'Economic value of product', devaluations and debts connected with the management of non-financial credits are mentioned.

Sometimes deduced from the tables, but not explicitly declared.

Seems unlikely that there is nothing to say here.

There is also a table.

Not found, perhaps because the budget refers to 2007–08 (1 April 2007–31 March 2008). The 2008–09 budget is not yet available.

On p. 24, mention is made of an 'uptake in inflation'.

Not classified.

An interesting section is the 'Opinion of the Commission of Experts' (p. 6), which contains a list of members, the conclusions concerning each variable of the AA10000SS, and a table with the main observations and suggestions for every variable. It is a good idea to put parts of these evaluations, both positive and less positive, in the text itself, 'signed' by the evaluator.

Valid in terms of disclosure also is the reference to the termination of a branch of the company in favor of Comdata Center SpA, which had generated some noise (pp. 11, 63) and other similar initiatives that involved employees.

(*continued*)

Table 10.2 Continued

Company	Telecom Italia	Vodafone
Document examined	**Sustainability report 2008**	**Social responsibility report, 2007–08**
		On p. 75 the report mentions 'Churn', the subscriber tax on clients as at March 31 2008 (23%).
		Laudable.
Grade for Disclosure	***1.8***	***2.8***
IMPLEMENTATION		
Adopts performance indicators; offers measures of performance in relation to the 'emergencies' in Disclosure.	Yes (KPI); about 200 on p. 10. On p. 37 the report talks about 'the definition of over 193 performance indicators that allow for monitoring and improved services supplied to internal clients and suppliers.'	Yes (KPI). The procedures are briefly described on p. 49 and the possibility of adding new ones is also foreseen (p. 71). For example, these are clearly present in the section concerning the environment and environmental sustainability; less so in the section concerning suppliers.
Is there a code of ethics (a good thing) and is its application measured?	There is a code, mentioned on p. 8; it can be consulted via the Internet (though, as at the time of writing, the site is not interactive).	A Code of Ethics exists and is part of the 'Organizational Model'. The two documents are easily accessed on the company website (also in English).
Are indicators identified to measure its implementation?	No measures to implement the indicators are listed.	Numerous self-discipline codes have been adopted along with the Code of Ethics, the Organizational Model and the Sarbanes–Oxley Act (p. 18).

Mention of work undertaken in delicate circumstances *vis-à-vis* corruption and indication of specific measures.	Reference is made to anti-corruption practices (p. 7, for example, where the annual Corporate Governance report is found). There do not seem to be specific, more precise measures in place. The section entitled 'Financial communications' is interesting (pp. 87–8).	There is reference to a Controlling Agency (p. 15) and it is also stated that, as at the time of writing, 'there have not emerged any particularly critical aspects related to the actuation of the organizational model nor any reports regarding violations of same or the Code of Ethics.' It then goes on to talk about the activities of the controlling agency. 'Integrity in relations with suppliers,' a section on p. 71. The 'Speak Up' program to allow suppliers to report corruption or non-ethical behavior in contrast with the guidelines contained in the code of ethics and the business principles of the company.
Considerations of the clients (consumers and users). Does a code of service for clients exist (when it ought to)? Does the report measure its implementation?	Service cards exist (p. 8); here, too, the reader is directed to access the various company websites (though not directly, cfr. 2.2).	Reference is made to a Client Card for landline telephones and one for mobile phones. The report states that the company 'monitored the difficult and complicated enactment of Bersani's law and contributed to its evolution, also by means of participating via the ASSTEL association in related Parliamentary hearings.'

(continued)

104

Table 10.2 Continued

Company	Telecom Italia	Vodafone
Document examined	Sustainability report 2008	Social responsibility report, 2007–08
MEMORY		
Keeps track of things that happened a long time ago that may still have an impact currently or in the future.	Not relevant.	It could be better. From a 'historical' point of view, the section on the evolution of the telecommunications market (pp. 24–5) is interesting.
DENOMINATORS		
Compares numbers in such a way that the reader is able to come to a conclusion regarding their relevance.	Yes, but could be better. In view of the hefty text there are too few tables and diagrams as compared to °VODAFONE, often examining three-year data.	There are numerous tables and they are very clear, though often they, too, are examining three-year data.
Adopts international standards.	The Principles of the Global Compact, GRI, ISO 9000 and ISO 14000 certification for systems to manage quality and environment. Principles of the International Labour Organization Convention on the rights of workers; Social Accountability 8000 standards (SA8000) finalized to favor respect for human rights and working conditions on the part of companies and their suppliers; OHSAS 18001.	GRI (2006) G3, AA1000 (also, for example, standards inspired from international standards on human rights, p. 71). Also p. 21, 'Guidelines for CR'.

Correctly implements the standards adopted (GRI and others)	GRI (declared conformity A+) and also others from 2.7 (an entire section dedicated to the company's position with regards to indices, p. 14).	GRI (2006) G3 with declared conformity B+.
Takes responsibility for upstream activities (payment of suppliers, for example).	Selection, evaluation and controls are foreseen also for suppliers (some data is provided concerning controls). Each company supplier is requested to declare intent, both for itself and for eventual authorized sub-contractors, collaborators and employees, to observe the ethical-behavioral principles contained in the Code of Ethics and Company Behavior Code. The reader is directed to the company website for further details. A vendor rating indicator exists (p. 38) to evaluate the overall performance of the main suppliers, as do performance indicators that allow for the monitoring and management of the services supplied to suppliers (cfr. 2.1).	Emphasis on the quality of chosen suppliers and mentions the possibility of enriching the evaluation parameters for the qualification of suppliers along the lines of indicators regarding Health and Security, as well as adhesion on the part of suppliers to CR principles by way of questions posted directly to suppliers and to their personnel. Insertion of an ethical code for acquisitions. Suppliers must adhere to this code of ethics or a standard equivalent, the contents of which conforms to international human rights standards, in order to do business with Vodafone. However, no mention is made of on-the-job accidents by suppliers. Mention is made of the insertion of parameters concerned with CO_2 emissions in work carried out by suppliers, but no precise data is provided regarding waste recycling and disposal. Mention is made of controls but less data is supplied than by Telecom.

(continued)

Table 10.2 Continued

Company	Telecom Italia	Vodafone
Document examined	Sustainability report 2008	Social responsibility report, 2007–08
	A second survey of satisfaction has been undertaken (early 2007) concerning Purchasing and Telecom Italia as a whole on the part of the company's main suppliers.	A Risk Matrix is introduced to evaluate risks to suppliers, including an analysis of risk associated with CR performance.
	The first e-community of the company's main suppliers has also been activated regarding work behavior, with the aim of improving communication to and between suppliers, mainly along thematics concerning company and environmental sustainability.	
Takes responsibility for downstream activities (clients).	Obvious mention is made of electromagnetism (conformity with norms declared and reference to scientific studies), but it is reasonable to doubt that this is all there is.	Here, too, mention is made of electromagnetism (declaring conformity with norms and reference to scientific studies), but it is reasonable to doubt that this is all there is. (A real sour note is the affirmation on p. 28 of an 'excessive worry on the part of the population about the effects of electromagnetic emissions'.
	There are initiatives for customer satisfaction.	
	A report by consumer associations is cited to note 'conciliation procedures' undertaken to resolve controversies with clients (p. 35).	As for Telecom: campaigns on the responsible use of mobile phones aimed at children and youngsters and their parents (p. 58).
	The company pledges to reduce the territorial and socio-cultural digital divide.	

	Mention is made of the protection of minors with 'Alice Total Security' and 'Alice Magic Desktop'; the former to exercise parental control, and the latter to guide young users in computer applications and allow for control on the part of parents.	Parental control systems, Family Filters inhibiting the transmission of questionable content.
	Activities and communication undertaken to fight pedophile pornography.	Nothing on the digital divide. Much more could be done.
	An Abuse Desk monitoring chat lines, forums and blogs offered by service suppliers.	
	I give the initiative a 3 but more could be done.	
Considers the long-term consequences of company development (for example, the availability of suppliers/environment upstream, client congestion/environment downstream).	Not mentioned.	Not mentioned.
Adopts specific industrial standards.	Explicitly mentions DLNA standards, UPnP Forum and OPEN IPTV Forum with regards to technological innovation (p. 66), but I imagine others are also adopted.	Yes (for example, on p. 33, where Health and Product Security is mentioned, and on p. 38 where CO_2 emissions are mentioned).
Grade for Implementation	2.3	2.4

(continued)

Table 10.2 Continued

Company	Telecom Italia	Vodafone
Document examined	**Sustainability report 2008**	**Social responsibility report, 2007–08**
MICRO-ETHICS		
Stays on the subject: does not present philanthropy, welfare capitalism or market-related causes as social responsibility and sustainability in business.	It gives information on these subjects, but distinguishes basic business from initiatives for the community, investments in the community or free markets according to London Benchmarking Group guidelines. It advertises self; the tone is a little triumphant.	It advertises itself, but perhaps a bit less loudly.
Company engages in socially damaging actions.	Not found.	Not found.
Company engages in disinformation: denying what's in plain view, calling tardiness a time change, makes affirmations that appear contradictory, accuses others of wrongdoing.	Not found (though nothing final has been decided concerning possible electromagnetic effects. Report includes a detailed bibliography on the subject but, not having read it, I can't make any judgment about it).	Doesn't appear so, but the report could have been more prudent as far as possible effects of electromagnetism. As for Telecom, references to scientific studies on the subject laudable.
Lobbying. What relationship does the company have with those agencies meant to regulate this sector or with legislators? Gives an account of company lobbying activities. Here, too, *excusatio non petitae* are interesting.	Not found, but possible? It cites a reduction in litigations as a result of effort, but only on p. 42 and only concerning the access network in the competition section concerning external stakeholders. I'll give them a 3 to be on the safe side.	Seems to be well-inserted in the Italian and European legislative context (pp. 26–9). Some reticence concerning litigation (no numbers) but they are, at least, mentioned.
Grade for Micro-ethics	*3.0*	*3.5*

UNKNOWN STAKEHOLDER		
Taxonomy of responsibility: locates the company in a competitive context; public sector and monopolies (also international indicators and comparisons); competitive sector (comparisons with competitors).	Refers in a general way to the competition on p. 100 in the 'Internal control system' section, where it mentions the recent integration of the Code of Ethics with a reinforcement of the concepts of correct and fair competition. There is an entire chapter dedicated to the competition in terms of external stakeholders, in which it talks about associative and collaborative activity on the national and international level, but it is all very general. On p. 42, however, there is a more detailed account of the access network.	On p. 53, there is mention of heavy competition among the main operators on the business market 'which has resulted in a significant pressure on prices.' On p. 11 there is a diagram indicating market shares of the main mobile telephone operators.
Gives benchmarks to the market average; better: with specific competitors.	Not found.	Apart from the diagram mentioned above, nothing.
In the case of a monopoly enterprise or a state or local government administration, as pertains to its clients, does it make a comparison on the prices requested by analogous services?	Not found.	Not found.
Also, on the international level, given the vast and important nature of the company in the national or local Italian panorama.	Not found.	Not found.

(continued)

Table 10.2 Continued

Company	Telecom Italia	Vodafone
Document examined	**Sustainability report 2008**	**Social responsibility report, 2007–08**
Comparisons of the quality of service.	Not found.	Not found.
Comparisons of efficiency/waste.	Not found.	Not found.
Provides measures for behavior in relation to the unknown stakeholder: for example, provides profits by country.	Not found.	Not found.
Demonstrates attention to clients, employees.	Yes. There is much use throughout the text of the words client/clients/clientele.	Yes. There is much use throughout the text of the words client/clients/clientele.
	There is a chapter dedicated to the client as an external stakeholder.	One section is entitled 'Attention on the client' (pp. 50–4), mostly in terms of greater information on such issues as the digital divide, the relationship between minors, and the responsible use of mobile phone technology and the transmission of data.
	Customer satisfaction is mentioned, distinguishing between 'cold' and 'hot' monitoring – table on monitoring 2008.	
	The same occurs for employees, with investigations concerning the company climate (questionnaires, 'group photos') and attention given to the health and security of employees (pp. 82–3), along with training and professional growth programs (pp. 77–80) and welfare and well-being activities (described on pp. 75–7).	Greater clarity and transparency in terms of the materials of communication (better legibility of legal notes with fewer acronyms).
	Some feedback should have been included.	The Consumer Delight Index (CDI) is interesting (too bad no examples are given).

Attention for employees also declared (there's a section entitled 'Attention on human resources'), especially in terms of health and security, training, and the analysis of the company climate through initiatives such as the Vodafone People Survey with subsequent definitions of specific actions made for improvement. There, too, lack of data.

1.2

2.5

Grade for the Unknown Stakeholder

TOTAL AVERAGE GRADE   *2.1*

Table 10.3 USDIME framework course work: ENI

Company	ENI
Document examined	**ENI 2008**

DISCLOSURE

Rapidity: identifies 'emergencies'; offers a list of hot issues that are easily identified and located in the document.	Identifies the company emergencies, but not enough synthesis (pp. 16–19).
Easy to read graphic lay-out, contains tables that are easy to read also in black and white.	Both in terms of the graphics of the tables and the text, the use of black and white renders immediate comprehension of the data difficult.
Does not 'anesthetize' with too much information. Accessible length and content so that, in two hours of attentive study, the reader is able to fill out this questionnaire.	Heavy anesthetizing with information of everything that's been done. Two hours' study are not enough to fill in the questionnaire.
Confronts issues encountered during the year; writes up risks according to the SWOT analysis.	Yes, considers recent issues such as the financial crisis (p. 10), the role of alternative energy (p. 13) the fight against climate change (p. 16). Nonetheless, the report appears to lack synthesis.
Gives examples of hot issues: details working conditions of employees and suppliers in developing countries.	Yes, ample space given to the analysis of the frequency of on-the-job accidents (p. 34).
Another example of a hot issue: job related deaths in Italy 2008–09.	Yes, notes that in 2008 there were 17 deaths, of which 5 were of employees and 12 contracted workers (p. 34).
Another general example for 2008–09: considers the implications of the financial crisis by evaluating, for example, risk parameters (debt, credit).	Yes, guidelines for the identification, measure, management and monitoring of economic and financial risks facing the company and its subsidiaries have been defined by the Board. A diagram illustrates (pp. 31–2).
Doubt, vulnerability: contains admissions of not having done what was supposed to be done or of having actions be insufficient.	Fairly self-congratulatory; no mention of things that aren't working but only that the company aims to improve and strengthen various sectors (p. 23 and more).
Grade for Disclosure	*3.0*

IMPLEMENTATION

Adopts performance indicators; offers measures of performance in relation to the 'emergencies' in Disclosure.	Only in terms of the fight against climate change and emergency efficiency is a performance indicator provided regarding the energy of electric plants, and an index of energy-refinement (p. 49).

(*continued*)

Table 10.3 Continued

Company	ENI
Document examined	ENI 2008

Is there a code of ethics (a good thing) and is its application measured? Are indicators identified to measure its implementation?	There is a code of ethics and the role of the guarantor for the code of ethics is given to a Control Agency. There is no indication of the implementation of the code itself (p. 29).
Mention of work undertaken in delicate circumstances *vis-à-vis* corruption and indication of specific measures.	ENI only mentions that it chooses its suppliers and monitors them continuously with regard to those aspects concerning human rights and the politics of anti corruption (pp. 78–9), but does not identify specific measures.
Considerations of the clients (consumers and users). Does a code of service for clients exist (when it ought to)? Does the report measure its implementation?	There is no code of service. The report does state that dialogue with consumers occurs through meetings with Consumer Associations or the public sector agencies (p. 74).
MEMORY Keeps track of things that happened a long time ago that may still have an impact currently or in the future.	There is no reference to things that happened in the past that could have an impact on the current situation.
DENOMINATORS Compares numbers in such a way that the reader is able to come to a conclusion regarding their relevance.	Lots of numbers are provided in diagrams and tables. Sometimes the reader is able to come to some conclusion regarding the subject being considered (e.g. Fatality index on p. 36), but in other cases this isn't possible because there are no denominators (emission of GHG from flaring, p. 16).
Adopts international standards.	Adopts GRI and IPIECA.
Correctly implements the standards adopted (GRI and others).	There is a table illustrating the correct use of the above-mentioned parameters.
Separates the implementation of standards from the presentation of emergencies.	Yes, usually it presents emergencies (such as research on renewable energy resources, p. 25) and then details what is being done to implement standards to resolve them (collaboration with MIT Boston, p. 25).
Takes responsibility for upstream activities (payment of suppliers, for example).	Yes; for example, it notes initiatives undertaken to reduce gas flaring in Algeria, Republic of Congo, Libya and Tunisia for investments of €1.26 billion in 2009–12 (p. 48).

(*continued*)

114

Table 10.3 Continued

Company	ENI
Document examined	**ENI 2008**
Takes responsibility for downstream activities (clients).	Yes, client satisfaction is indicated on an annual basis using a customer satisfaction index. In order to meet client needs, services besides gas offered at gas stations have been increased (p. 76).
Considers the long-term consequences of company development (for example, the availability of suppliers/environment upstream, client congestion/ environment downstream).	ENI often emphasizes its dedication to fighting environmental pollution by reducing gas flaring both in Italy and in its supplier countries.
Adopts specific industrial standards.	Yes
Grade for Implementation	***3.8***
MICRO-ETHICS	
Stays on the subject: does not present philanthropy, welfare capitalism or market-related causes as social responsibility and sustainability in business.	Yes; for example, emphasizes company activities related to the promotion and safeguarding of human rights (p. 18) and the support of diversity (p. 44).
Company engages in socially damaging actions.	Company engages in strong image work, but I don't believe any socially dangerous message is being conveyed.
Company engages in disinformation: denying what's in plain view, calling tardiness a time change, makes affirmations that appear contradictory, accuses others of wrongdoing.	It states that the decrease in the cost of crude does not correspond to a decrease in the cost of gas because of, among other reasons, taxes and the low diffusion of self-service stations (p. 75).
Lobbying. What relationship does the company have with those agencies meant to regulate this sector or with legislators: Gives an account of company lobbying activities. Here, too, *excusatio non petitae* are interesting.	In a table on p. 33, there is a list of court cases regarding the environment and procedures tied to antitrust and other regulations. Nonetheless there is insufficient information concerning the cases themselves.
Grade for Micro-ethics	***1.5***
UNKNOWN STAKEHOLDER	
Taxonomy of responsibility: locates the company in a competitive context; public sector and monopolies (also international indicators and comparisons); competitive sector (comparisons with competitors).	No reference to competition.

(continued)

Table 10.3   Continued

Company	ENI
Document examined	**ENI 2008**
Gives benchmarks to the market average; better: with specific competitors.	No.
In the case of a monopoly enterprise or a state or local government administration, as pertains to its clients, does it make a comparison on the prices requested by analogous services?	No.
Also, on the international level, given the vast and important nature of the company in the national or local Italian panorama.	No.
Comparisons of the quality of service.	No.
Comparisons of efficiency/waste.	Talks often about efficiency referring only to itself.
	There are no comparisons.
Lobbying. What relationship does the company have with those agencies meant to regulate this sector or with legislators? Gives an account of company lobbying activities. Here, too, *excusatio non petitae* are interesting.	In a table on p. 33, there is a list of court cases regarding the environment and procedures tied to antitrust and other regulations.
	Nonetheless there is insufficient information concerning the cases themselves.
Provides measures for behavior in relation to the unknown stakeholder: for example, provides profits by country.	Does not appear to provide information regarding profits.
Demonstrates attention to clients, employees.	ENI puts a great deal of attention on people (p. 26).
	Initiatives are planned, aimed at increasing the organizational welfare of its employees through, for example, the ENI Nursery School.
Grade for the Unknown Stakeholder	*0.7*
TOTAL AVERAGE GRADE	*2.0*

Part II

From CSR to Politics:
The Competitive Divide

Not only international companies, subject to international competition, are prone to irresponsibility; but more so are monopolies, regulated industries, government bodies and other non-profit institutions, and finally politics itself. In this second part, consequences are thus drawn from the findings of Part I and extensions are made to all other economic sectors.

If CSR is in the core of the business for companies that are subject to competition, then CSR is even more important for companies that are not subject to competition, and it is extended to the private non-profit sector, to the public non-profit sector (public administration) and to the practice of the public arena *par excellence*: politics.

In Part II, the fluid boundaries between the private and the public sectors are examined. CSR seems to belong only in the private sector. And it is implicit that we know exactly what that sector is. It is clear who is listed at the stock exchange and who is not, but we did not need the financial crisis of September 15, 2008 (Lehman's bankruptcy) and the consequent bail out of many private institutions by the public sector to find out that the boundaries between the private and the public sectors are rather thin and that there is a great deal of grey.

Following a bottom-up methodology, we have seen it in the examples of the four values of the USDIME framework in Part I, where not all the cases were from the private sector in the restricted acceptance of the word. We will make it explicit in Part II. The end result is that CSR is for all sectors – each sector having its own peculiarities. We will examine each sector in turn, from the monopolistic sector of utilities and financial institutions to the private non-profit sector, to the public non-profit sector (i.e. government or public administration), to the political arena and the political systems. This will be dealt with in Chapters 11 through 14. All these chapters will be followed by case studies to exemplify what we mean by accountability and accountability studies.

Finally, Chapters 15 and 16 will deal with the opportunities that accountability opens up for society and the values that it helps us discover. A perspective will thus be derived on the future, and what can be done to bring about accountability and social responsibility.

11
The Neighborhood Bullies

In this chapter, companies subject to regulation and living in less competitive environments are analyzed. They represent the standard complex of a modern economy: utilities, banks, large service providers (transport). The conclusion is that the less competitive an environment, the less responsibility is generated.

A case study is presented whereby the USDIME framework is applied to a set of European banks from whom results are relatively scarce.

In this chapter, we will review companies subject to regulation and less competition. Companies have been chosen as an almost complete sample from the utilities and regulated industries sector, ranging from the telephone company to a water supply company, from railways to power production and supply.

We have included the financial services sector here, banks and insurance companies. These are subject to competition. However, in some countries of the Western and non-Western world these institutions are rarely subject to lay-offs or worker compensation programs, a situation that does not apply to the manufacturing and construction sectors. Also, these institutions are subject to regulation and specific government bodies are in charge of overseeing them. Central banks, for instance, often perform a role of oversight *vis-à-vis* these institutions. So, we have included them here, in the vast realm of the regulated economy.

The reality that we are about to describe is hardly hellish – sunny earnings and beautiful people who work little; small entrepreneurs who struggle to pay salaries at the end of each month and small entrepreneurs who struggle to help other small entrepreneurs. Nonetheless, the metaphor chosen of a descent into hell doesn't seem peculiar, even though we're dealing with the economy and work.

The descent into work begins with the circle of monopolies. Contrary to Dante's Hell, however, they won't first encounter the lesser of evils and then the worst of them. Instead, the criteria necessary to understand the theme we are dealing with will lead us – after an initial, grueling journey – straight into the heart of issues that are, let's admit it, splitting hairs.

Thanks to monopolies, each day we have electricity, water, gas, public transport and a series of other things that we are barely aware of; this could, hopefully, help us keep to the spirit of work presented herewith with greater interest and conviction.

Our journey begins with the monopolies sector – not because it is less polluted with lies and embellishments, but because the issues that are connected with this sector appear to be the most comprehensible, even to those readers who may not be versed in these things.

Whether what comes first is contempt towards the electorate which uses services or towards consumers and clients, whether it is companies or politics that have instigated the national tone, is a matter of opinion. For the love of concreteness, we will start with the big – particularly, the very big – companies over which the state could and should keep watch.

The consumer and the telephone monopolist

It happens that a passer-by or a bus driver wags a finger in disapproval, or shakes his head in disgust at a driver who has stopped an inch beyond the stop sign, but this gesture of condemnation is even more understandable when the driver is behind the wheel of a sports car – black, with a 3,200 cc engine, 200 horsepower. The undisciplined driver cannot complain if people feel provoked – he's done everything in his power to attract attention. It would behoove said driver more than anybody else to toe the line. Applying the law of Caesar's wife, it is best for those who cannot avoid the eyes of the public to behave honestly and to demonstrate it. As Shakespeare would have it: 'Caesar's wife must be honest and must show that she is honest.'

This is certainly debatable, but it is the most effective way to explain the anger that sometimes makes us rail against an injustice when it is nothing more than a simple management limitation on the part of a monopoly. At the dawn of the twenty-first century, telephone monopoly companies covered cities with advertisements of aggressive, buxom women ready to do whatever was necessary to have you make a telephone call. The public face and private affairs of such companies' top executives generated resentment when they perpetuated the old monopoly model of bullying clients. At that time, it was not unheard of that the telephone lines of a small company – a micro-client of the giant telephone company – were cut for three months because of an unpaid bill, and only after labored investigation and hours spent listening to the muzak version of Judy Garland's 'Somewhere over the Rainbow' was one able to discover that it was all because of a presumably unpaid last installment payment for the lease on the office network switchboard.

When dealing with a monopoly, one interacts only by telephone through a call center, where you never talk to the same person and the right hand doesn't know that the left even exists. For one thing, many call centers don't keep copies and do not have access to pertinent documents. In theory, you could send a fax to them, but it would have been hopeless: as soon as you tried to get the fax line an electronic voice would come on with a farcical 'Dear client, all the lines are busy' and there you'd be, at the mercy of Ms Garland.

Monopolies all over the world were introducing doing everything by telephone – cost-cutting, it was called – but making administrative services available over the telephone should also have been an element of quality and not only an opportunity of firing suddenly superfluous personnel.

The long-term industrial vision should be based on the understanding that, if you give your clients trustworthiness and sovereignty, you reap tomorrow greater sales and a leg-up on your competitors. But here's the hitch. There is no competition. In order to deal with the new telephone service companies, with their catchy names, you still had to make it through the Caudine Forks of the main supplier and nothing could be done unless you took the issue up with it. The ancient historian Livy says that the Samnites, after winning a battle, had the Romans perform the unnecessarily humiliating task of passing under a yoke: likewise in spite of liberalization, you still had to go through the monopolist's yoke.

Customers could turn to consumer organizations, but that was jumping from the frying pan into the fire because organizations to protect the consumer sprouted out of labor unions of the monopoly workers themselves and clearly operated within a conflict of interest. They considered it logical to defend, at one and the same time, both the worker and the consumer against the capitalists; they did not, however, understand – or refused to – that while, figuratively and emotionally, a consumer was bullied by capitalists, in everyday life he was equally tormented by the employees of the monopolies themselves – a state of affairs for which the owners were responsible, but so were their employees.

It was time to overcome the outdated Marxist idea that distinguished responsibilities of owners and employees one from the other. When dealing with operations each is responsible for what is done. One could no longer, at the start of the twenty-first century, explain industrial development through passive logic or its pretence, such as the mere 'taking orders' behind which the Nuremberg defendants hid. This point should be emphasized: in complex organizations, responsibility is shared by all. The idea that it is the owner's responsibility and everybody else passively obeys his orders like the cogs of a wheel was a sociological hypothesis from the early 1900s, one that was extremely important for the science of organizational behavior but not articulated to the point that it could explain the world – not even the one in which it was conceived. What is meant here is that employees are equally responsible for company behavior both as a whole and individually, and this is the key point of the hypothesis proposed herein.

Clearly, each individual is not responsible for the whole thing. However, everyone shares a responsibility according to his or her own role. We will keep coming back to this idea. Literature of organizational behavior implies such a consequence on personal responsibility: for instance, Graham Allison's models of organizational behavior and of personal political position power imply such a responsibility by individuals in the organization (1971). Such an implication could also be a consequence of Allison's rational model, which depicts an organization where all actions are the consequence of a rational choice under perfect information and perfect consensus by every employee, a Weberian bureaucracy. In fact, in the twenty-first century, in a relatively well-functioning democracy and in a labor market that allows for some leeway of the individual employee, adherence to an institution implies sharing in the responsibilities of that institution's actions: Weber does not apply any longer. Weber is dead.

The mother of all proof concerning the obtuseness of monopolies was the simple fact that they wielded boundless power over their customers. They could hook up your telephones one day and unhook them the next, and forever after.

The irresponsibility of the freeway company

There's half a death too many in the freeway company's accounts for 2005. The digital billboards along the roads kept a tally:

2 deaths out of 5 due to distracted drivers
1 death out of 5 due to drivers asleep at the wheel
1 death out of 2 caused by speeding.

If we bring the last datum up to 5, we get: '2.5 deaths out of 5 caused by speeding'.

Summing up the data in the three propositions: 2 + 1 + 2.5, we get 5.5. Therefore: '5.5 deaths out of 5 are caused by all listed factors'. There is a half a death too many. Certainly, there could be more than one cause for the same accident but, if a company is going to be this categorical, it is important for the numbers to make sense to the audience, especially to those nitpickers who actually add them up.

After the introduction of a driver's license penalty point system, numbers abound with regards to the freeways. The license penalty point system works as follows: your driving license is initially endowed with 20 points. Each ticket you get, a few points are subtracted, proportionately to the infraction. When you run out of points, your driving license is withdrawn and you have to go through a very long procedure before you can sit at the wheel of a car again. Numbers are at home on the freeways, without overdoing it. In fact, numbers are a friend of corporate responsibility; let's appreciate them.

Arithmetic is far more efficient than a smarmy 'Drive carefully' – a sunny, superficial phrase that had no intention of having a real impact. An attempt was made to give it some weight with admonitions such as: 'Avoid committing a crime: drive carefully' but, after the first blunt exhortation, the concept was muted with the rest of the phrase. The freeway company management correctly considered it a gesture of responsibility to supply data that it pretended it knew nothing about just days before: corporate responsibility, in fact, is taking care of issues that go beyond the strictly legal, like the innkeeper who attempts to convince a drunkard to stop drinking as he pours him more wine.

Along these lines, the corporate reporting of the freeway company could develop rapidly, with data available concerning service and quality: total number of hours per means of transportation spent on the freeways; total number of hours wasted in traffic jams; and the ratio between these two measures represents an index of the efficiency and fluidity of traffic along the freeways. Aware that it was operating in an imperfect market, with its sole competitor the railways, the freeway company instigated a benchmark using international counterparts: the Basel–Frankfurt freeway is compared to the Koln–Paris freeway. A virtual market made up of numbers and comparisons thus takes shape.

Thanks to this enlightened way of measuring its performance, not only do the specialists of asphalt and white lines begin to reason, but the reporting of freeway corporate responsibility gives economic relevance to transportation services. This is not an insignificant cultural event because, up until that time, had some hapless traveler called a newspaper to report some misadventure on the road, a gentle voice would have explained that 24 km of traffic jam was hardly an economic disaster – it was newsworthy, just like the dog owner who bites the dog.

And the traffic information radio station acted *vis-à-vis* the freeway company like a reveler at a bar. It informed listeners that the 4 km jam between Exit 13 and Exit 14 was 'due to heavy traffic', but failed to let them know that the cause was the bottleneck represented by a two-lane tunnel on an otherwise three-lane freeway. Heavy traffic played a part, but it was merely the outcome; a lie, therefore, but effective because not many of us were outraged. We are always ready to justify any political or managerial snafu while considering as a natural phenomenon things caused by the precise incompetence of fellow working citizens, while normal working people – like the radio station employees – can be irresponsible all the same.

There's also an element of the Stockholm Syndrome in those zealots who, at every stage of work, amplify the irresponsibility already present in the hardly socially responsible instructions given by company heads. As irresponsible as their heads, the average worker does his damndest to distance himself from any kind of responsibility as much as possible. In fact, the radio station broadcaster, candidly responding to complaints concerning the lacunae in the information provided, said: 'This is the information we receive from the freeway company.' Every single day obvious things were repeated, such as 'traffic slow-down on the Freeway A4 between Exit 15 and Exit 16', but never would they say: 'Send a cop because it's not possible that it's always the fault of those drivers who love driving in "heavy traffic"'.

These institutions (the radio station and the freeway company) were held by the state holding company. There were many such holdings throughout different countries. Some of them dated back to the aftermath of the 1929 Great Depression, their ancestor and model being the Tennessee Valley Authority in the United States.

Emergencies are hardly wise counselors. Should a snowstorm upset the agendas and appointments of half a country's population, in the freeway bedlam responsibility escalates to the political level, allowing some to profit from the situation by passing new legislation and making investments in gravel and asphalt.

Responsibility and its acknowledgement do not emerge on the spur of the moment, but are the result of an examination of the conscience during a daily routine. This is the only way responsibility is revealed – office by office, desk by desk: thoughts, words, reports and omissions.

Another example is that during 2006 it was hypothesized that Abertis, a Spanish freeway company, would buy the private Italian Autostrade. Good heavens! The changes at the helm and the delocalization of the decision-making centers were feared, but these have nothing to do with the service provided to consumers, or the responsibility of those who are part of the institution. The fact that this acquisition was born and died in the arc of a few months helps us to focus on the fact being emphasized here: besides high-flown politics and power play, it is important to pay attention to the operational reality and the implementation of intent, to the various phenomena that involve large numbers of employees.

The irresponsibility of banks

Around the year 2006, a strange feeling was experienced by the clients of a bank as they waited their turn. There was something different about the place: spacious, elegant, a wealth of goods – marble, flat screen computers. One was struck by the fact that all the banks looked like this. In other businesses you had the higher and the lower ranges represented, while all banks looked the same. They were luxurious, and there was good reason to be suspicious, as confirmed by the story told by my financial consultant when I went to see him to check the status of my savings.

His bank had recently changed hands. The company emblem of a Dutch group had been substituted with that of an Italian bank. The Dutch were weak in Italy, while they maintained a discreet position in Poland. The Dutch and the Italians then held a mini-Yalta Conference, like in 1945

Roosevelt, Churchill and Stalin had done to divide Europe into areas of influence. So, the Dutch 'ceded' Italy to its current owner, obtaining in exchange a reinforcement of their network in Poland. This consultant basically told a story of how his owners had plotted to damage their clients and the principle of competition in force in the European Union. Nonetheless, there was not a trace of this affair in the numerous bank reports published on corporate responsibility.

To be emphasized is precisely the moment when proposals, declarations and laws are concretely analyzed. We are dealing here with issues that are so pervasive that it is enough to flip through any newspaper of that period and find that there isn't a day that this kind of affair wasn't in the news. On May 28, 2007, professor of statistics and prominent pollster Renato Mannheimer warned the banks: 'After the mergers, think about your clients.' The next day, in a free paper distributed nationwide, the headline on the front page read: 'The Antitrust to the government: "Banks not transparent".'

All hope of being competitive price-wise lost, the banking sector could have quickly rehabilitated itself with two initiatives that bow to transparency. The first was the disclosure of data pertaining to the risks being faced by savers. After the important failure of Cirio and the non-existent reimbursement of the bonds that had been sold to savers by primary banks, banks began to publish statistics on the risk levels that each saver underwrote when buying bank shares. Banks could have published some good books and the Italian Banking Association could have offered a Clear Pact program. In both cases, this meant tables on the client risk profiles registered in the banks' databases. In fact, banks undertook the diligent data entry of the paper forms that clients filled out in order to avoid the alterability of those documents through computer database certification. Next to those first tables, other tables were published with the risk profiles of the stocks held by said savers by the risk level accepted and, finally, a third series of tables on the risk profiles that same said savers declared in interviews once outside the bank. This quibble of tables served to explicate – with the help of an able public relations man – whether there was a delta, a difference between the free (but not always static) intentions of savers and the reality of their financial acquisitions. The tables served to demonstrate how ignorant the saver actually was, whether goods were being palmed off on him that he didn't want and if, when face-to-face with a bank employee, he signed papers he didn't read or understand – the essential and salient points of which were not illustrated.

It was often heard that there was a national predilection for real estate, investing in property rather than stocks. From this, one can believe that this preference comes from some genetic strain in the population, but it may also be the result of the whiff of something rotten caught by the otherwise ignorant citizens. As one director at McKinsey once said, 'Nobody is so stupid that he doesn't understand that you think he's stupid.' What they were trying to prove with the publication of the data was that little old ladies were not being sold risky stocks unawares; that, actually, those who were buying risky products coveted the lavish revenue such products promised – a little like Scrooge McDuck when drawn with dollar signs in his eyes.

Money was reimbursed (only 1.1%, it would seem) but that was not the kind of responsibility being looked for. Along with the loss, disappointing was the 'to sever, to smother' – along the lines of Count Attilio's motto, a famous quote in Alessandro Manzoni's 1842 novel *The Betrothed*, whereby the nobleman is trying to keep under control his crooked nephew's attempt to seduce a young woman on the eve of her wedding – that hushing up of things without providing a plausible explanation. The tables only filled in an information gap, the total absence of serious newspaper articles that explicitly explained what was sold to whom.

The second initiative in the name of transparency that the banking system could have instigated in those years had to do with the reporting on stocks. This, too, stank a little bit – the benchmark; that is, the comparison between the various products available to the saver. When a person bought shares, for example, in an investment fund, the bank demonstrated how it achieved results that were higher than the benchmark – the benchmark at the time consisting of a sum of indexes. But a real fund had a manager who worked morning, noon and night to optimize performance with respect to reality; this was not the case for the index. So, the banks could have started to use real objects as benchmarks; for example, the funds of other banks, which the saver could use for an alternative comparison. However, if a comparison is going to be made, you cannot compare a *cappuccino* made with milk from Rome with a Brazilian *moka*. You have to compare *cappuccinos* made in different cafés.

Faced with this innovation, the diligent employees of the private banking system shuddered in dread and exclaimed: 'This is only done by certain magazines; our clients should buy those themselves and should not be asking us to do this for them.' They did not carry out their mission as consultants to their clients, and it never occurred to them to provide as complete a service as possible. So, once again, good customer relations and the instigation of transparency was in the hands of the individual agents. They themselves could have photocopied the financial magazines, since they read them every day, and given them to their customers as a personal touch – but they didn't and, in not doing so, allowed sand to sift into the competitive mechanism. They could have oiled it, but they ruined it instead.

The power company report

In 2004, the power company sustainability report struck the reader for its segregation of numbers from words – 90 pages of words against 12 with numbers. It was for the good, naturally; the result of a human communications effort to meet the reader halfway. In fact, in a chapter entitled 'How the power company communicates' the manner in which the company presented itself had been considered ethically. It was the first time that an effort of this sort had been made, by which a not insignificant theoretical principle was defined: communication has to be done with responsibility, and this responsibility must not be an artifice of communication. In that chapter, the report presented the company's advertising campaigns and its global visibility index in print and on television, which turned out to be triple the average (the box on page 81, however, did not better-define this average). In order to make the data concerning visibility more significant, it would have been useful to compare it with the money spent by the power company on advertising in order to obtain a kind of Relative Citation Index, putting the quantity of publicity obtained in relation to the amount of money spent for advertising in magazines and on television. In fact, one could have asked if the high visibility in the media wasn't perhaps simply the result of the large amounts of money spent by the power company on advertising.

The power company report was honest – as it had been in 2002, when it revealed that certain executives were under investigation. It didn't so much avoid issues as skim over them, as had been the case regarding the position taken by the president of the Antitrust on the scarce competitiveness of the national energy sector. The president of the Antitrust defined as incredible the cost of the electricity and gas bills that the consumers are forced to pay the power companies – far higher than is paid by consumers in other countries on the continent.

In subsequent editions, the report could have focused its attention on one of several specific variables: developing a reflexive and educational function of public relations by elaborating on pertinent areas in that context; providing a comparison between the cost per kilowatt-hour at a European level and the cost of work per unit of product – a mythical index that was prevalent in financial magazines during the 1970s and which suddenly disappeared precisely when the opportunity arrived to use it to provide an important parameter for measuring corporate responsibility.

The idea of focusing attention on a particular aspect in each annual report could have become a general trend in the analysis of corporate responsibility and its disclosure. One particular theme developed subsequently was the analysis of the average amount of time spent on hold when phoning a call center, as there should have been for the telephone monopolist. There was much hoopla when this variable dropped to three minutes, or sixty rings.

A CSR report can also reveal its dynamic by articulating various subjects between editions, as well as in annual variations of data. But, when it had to confront the hole in the ozone layer, the report lost ground. It assured its readers that the power company would play its part, but this did not coincide with the views of the Executive Director: 'Reaching the target of 6.5% less of emissions by 2012 will cost us at least €5 billion, that is 0.3–0.4% of the GDP – a Herculean effort, while for others it's a walk in the park. Thanks to the efficiency of our electric production, for us, the cost necessary to bring down a ton of CO_2 is higher than for our partners ... our competitiveness will suffer, energy prices will increase.'

In the same publication, those views were supported by the Environmental Protection League. Too bad that neither knew anything about the carbon rights mechanism, created specifically to equalize the costs of the Kyoto standards among different countries. The carbon rights mechanism is so attractive because the damage to the ozone layer from the emission of a tonne of CO_2 is the same regardless of the country from which it comes. In fact, CO_2, once expelled from a factory, an electric plant or an automobile, settles in the atmosphere according to rules that have nothing to do with the place of emission. Since this is a law of physics, the goal of reducing CO_2 emissions is to be pursued whether the operations are easy or not. In order to follow a criteria of economic efficiency, the program had to begin in those countries where it was more economically viable to contain or reduce these kinds of emissions, but the Kyoto agreement (1997) allowed those countries where the cost of reducing CO_2 would have been greater to buy emission permits from the better-off countries. Environmentalists and industrialists worked in synergy to exploit the situation. The former wanted to see CO_2 reduced by others, while the latter aimed for the state to pay for the enterprise rather than the companies.

The unbearable communication of the water company

Yet another public sector utility – water. No objection to the water company ads prevalent from April 2006 to May 2007 on city buses and sign posts: 'Water is your wealth. Don't waste it.' And the picture they chose was quite effective – a diamond choker laying at the bottom of a sink, about to go down the drain. The ads represented a heroic enterprise because they were trying to change the public perception of the value of water solely through the persuasive capacity of a publicity campaign at a time when people were numb to sky-high prices and used to paying €1.5 for a liter of gas. This kind of courage went against all faith in the economy and materialism; it was a poster campaign against the price system.

Nonetheless, the public relations folks, the lobbyists, who work out company strategy by suggesting advertisements and actions, could have carried the project out through to the end and inserted into the work plans a means with which to measure the efficiency of the ads. This time, it could be done. All you had to do was run a series of regressions into the consumer model that the think-tanks of municipalized companies had been making available for some time. The think-tanks of the municipalized companies were represented by the Confederation of the public service sector of local entities – from time immemorial, in the hands of the Left.

There was, therefore, room to introduce analytical instruments to support government decisions, especially with regard to the in-house local services, which had been recently discovered by the Northern Right. The in-house were share companies owned by the public sector, especially local entities. Through their introduction, local entities avoided opening to competition the analytical services being discussed here. This mechanism was appreciated by the parties of the right as well, since the ethic of competition was only in the collective imagination by this point.

It was clear that no individual communications consultant could question his client and so did as he was bidden, but the public relations association could have gone to the policy-makers and producers and said, in effect: 'Water is precious and ought to be paid for more than symbolically. We realize that, from the political point of view, providing water at a fair price is hard-going, but getting hard truths accepted is our job and we can help you. We can get the issue to the forefront, sponsor conventions with people from other places who can talk about how sustainable production works. We've already got a slogan: "Responsibility and water – what future?"'

Obviously the water companies would have to do their part. They had to be a bit more transparent and accountable – in terms of their nominations, their results – and then decide what to do with the additional profits that water bills worthy of the name would bring. Projects needed to be developed to put those resources to use, and these needed to be publicized. They needed to set benchmarks against other countries and demonstrate that they were not less efficient. They had to open themselves up to competition, justify their salaries, which were suspected of being at a banker's level with regards to those paid by companies subject to competition. A national program could be instigated to monitor water consumption per family. As it is, water bills are paid in tandem with condominium expenses and they are so low that it's not worth checking the meters.

If all these things were done, and the price of water actually represented the availability of this resource over the long term, a suggestion might be to insert this price into the current bills – experimentally, as additional information rather than money to be paid, in order to make people aware of its real value. In other words, there's a whole new industry to be created, and they're still campaigning for voluntary rationing.

Reforming paternalism in the media

Any time some VIP left his ivory tower of caterers and guided tours, the way the legendary prince Siddhartha Gautama (later to become the Buddha) left his princely palace, he discovered the suffering of everyday life in the beautiful country (Hesse, 1951). This is what was accounted for in a front page article: 'My train trip was an odyssey – dirty cars and thousands of difficulties. Second class was an adventure.' A few decades later, another article had been published along the lines of Italo Calvino – *If on a Winter's Night a Traveler* – reporting about arriving at midnight at Main Station in Rome and not a taxi to be found. But the real news was the publication of a critical piece about the railways company – though be aware that it was a piece signed by someone outside the paper.

Should a VIP get hacked off and write first-hand, the ad salesman could easily explain to the press agent for the railway monopoly company that the director of the newspaper couldn't say no because 'the person charged into the office like a bull', but all the while assuring that the editorial stance of the paper had not changed and they didn't have to worry. Business would go on as usual: automobile accidents would continue to be caused by fog and never by the absence of police patrols or a non-existent freeway company. And if some radar malfunctioned, questions were asked about the predictability of the accident, but the absence of systematic reporting on the part of journalists was never questioned. This was the key to the impossibility of the development of information, and it was justified by hiding behind a generic 'My dear lady, this is what the people want,' which was false because, as American economist John Kenneth Galbraith taught us, people want – or better, passively accept – what you give them: dependence effect. Galbraith developed the concept of the dependence effect in his book *The Affluent Society* (1958).

And we still remember the fanfare with which the appointment of a newspaper readers' guarantor was announced in the 1980s, who never began work and was only ever a self-referential guarantor of that which was read and never of the readers – and, as such, was superseded by the idiotic national movement for privacy. In fact, having given said guarantor a limited and distorted function from the beginning – as a guarantor only of those mentioned in the press and not of the quality for the readers – when a state authority was formed to carry out the former function, it was not considered necessary to have an internal vestal; in other words, a guardian with pure intent like the virgin priestesses of ancient Rome.

One could have read Antonio Gramsci (2008) to map out the change: 'If you want to know something concrete, you have to walk into a government office – a police station, a prefecture. There, in the office of the officer-in-charge, or the waiting room of the prefect, you will find the state in the flesh, having ceased being an idea and become a man; an employee, if you wish, but a reality that can be observed, experienced, and studied.'

Thus, you didn't have to go far. It was enough to change the focus of attention: the policeman, not the criminal, in a police station; the stretcher-bearer, not the wounded, in the first-aid station; in parliament, not the chattering of politicians but the sloth of their assistants. If the focus were changed, the contents would be different and one could have read a different railways company responsibility report, one that would supply disaggregated data on quantity and quality of service and would not simply have kept repeating: 'We have 16,000 km of railway' – just as it had been doing for the last thirty years.

The railways company

In 2007, the railways company laid out their usual plan for the future in 2011, while the simoniacal press unfurled indulgent pages. But nobody thought to make note of the promises made in the early 1980s, or the hockey sticks (rosy plans) of administrators since the reform – formulations of plans that were never reported. John Maynard Keynes is apropos here, with his well-known 'In the long run, we are all dead.' Perhaps the company turned Keynes's logic upside-down and considered it useless to give an account of the implementation of their long-term plans, in the hopes that those who could remember would already be dead. The railways company heads considered the world to have begun when they were at its helm: the 2007 diagrams start with 2006 data. On the contrary, Keynes wanted to say that promises for the far future, as rosy and brilliant as they may be, have no pull on human beings, who are by nature myopic and oriented in the present. One function of the responsibility report is to give account of things people have forgotten by their human nature.

Another way to take into account the short-term view of people is to consider the costs of transitions. Perhaps this is the reason why the residents of the valley through which the Lyon–Zagreb high-velocity train is to pass have decided that five to ten years of inconvenience due to the work undertaken aren't worth the well-being of their children and the nation. Work plans should have paid greater attention to the timelines, considering the inevitable inconveniences regarding liveableness and mobility in the course of construction. It would have been more effective to have asked for work plans from collaborators and companies, rather than throwing concerns and good sense to the wind and blindly pursing the future at the expense of the present. They should have suspended activities and asked for reports concerning work, and serious plans would have emerged.

Responsibility lies in the long term, and the long term is in the sustainability report. Corporate responsibility is an instrument to widen reporting, as there is no plan without a report. The credibility of future plans resides in the accountability of past plans.

The name of the euro: the National Central Bank

A corporate responsibility report bespeaks the institution that has drafted it, and its impact on reality. One can talk about an 'emblematic' case in this sense when a regulating institution, such as the Central Bank, is involved. The position of the central banking institute with regard to issues that are particularly critical and pertinent is well-illustrated by two imaginary papers that could have been elaborated by the same study center.

First, no foreign groups are represented in bank property. This is not an apodictic affirmation, merely to protect the *status quo*. The first paper demonstrates the negative effects of this eventuality. Governed by folks who do not wash their laundry in the Arno river, decisions are made on the other side of the Alps and there is a decline in the managerial capacities to be found in Rome and Milan, with salaries migrating towards the Thames and Main rivers. Non-indigenous politics deprive high technology sectors, such as the food processing industry, of bank credit, with a decline in the industrial system. There are no savings to be had in the costs paid by the bank's national customers. There's no closure of the spread between active and passive taxes, which Carlo Callieri complained in the 1990s were double the norm. The profits of these new banks are provided to foreigners because Italians are not allowed to buy foreign bank shares.

Much damage and no benefits. As should be the case, the politics of the regulating institution aim to defend society at large, rather than the producers of a service. The plans of the transportation sector, on the contrary, are often completely different – aimed for those transporting, not those being transported. Bank dependents don't get a leg up from those workers who face competition (barmen and street peddlers, shopkeepers and freelancers), but the dependents of the study center itself float over them all. In effect, this position paper is totally in favor of the Italian consumer, with sacrifices from the dependents of the banking system, anxious about comparisons with different management systems.

The center not only deals with socio-economics but also with psycho-economics, as demonstrated by the second issue, which deals with the high cost of living generated by the changeover from the lira to the euro. 'Cash effects of currency changeover' had already been transmitted in 1998 to the Treasury, where it remained at length – ignored (today it has finally been published). To summarize the article briefly, it examines the consequences of the psychological perceptions regarding money at the moment in which the relationship between the denomination and the reality it represents changed. Since the euro is expressed in far smaller numbers than the lira, one is invited to use caution with regard to the symbolic value of the numbers themselves. The Kabbalah and the Book of Numbers both evoke the magic of numbers and their power, which cannot be diminished with a simple ban; one feels that they can be vindicated with a cost of living that is frightening. The paper, updated for the occasion, demonstrates how the government itself, in order to impress the masses, purposefully communicated some values in lire: '9,000 billion in public works initiated.' Finally, it revives the proposal to adopt pricing in both euro and lira until further instructed.

Beyond its denomination, we have assimilated the value of numbers from the time we were on our mother's milk, and a long time will have to pass before we are able to perceive it differently. Money weighs as much as the number it is associated with. Money is all in the number; in truth, numbers are all that we have, so we can join in the same epilogue as in Umberto Eco's *The Name of the Rose*: money is just numbers, and all we own are the numbers.

Conclusion

In this chapter, we have uncovered the social responsibility of monopolies and companies subject to limited competition. Among the latter we have included banks, which do not seem to be aware of the competition both for reasons of the existing veiled collusion and because of the focus of attention on their own dimensions, on governance, on European integration – but, in any case, not on the care of their customers or cost containment.

Natural monopolies – electricity, water, gas, transportation, and so on – were subject to periods of liberalization and privatization from 1990 onwards. These operations can create the illusion of there no longer being any reason to speak of monopolies, but we maintain that, in terms of the social responsibility of the dependents working in these organizations (accounting for work done is the task we have set here), these dependents still have to be considered dependents of monopolies, because these companies provide monopolistic services in any case, in the sense that an individual consumer has no choice with regard to the supplier of said service. The use or suspension of a service was the fruit of collective action, not the act of a single individual. This is the reason for which the industries in which these specific companies work were regulated and made subject to government control (the efficiency and effectiveness of which we have already considered).

Generally, the employees of the companies dealt with in this chapter enjoy work contracts that are advantageous with respect to those dependents in competitive sectors, working in those industries that are subject to international competition. Those employees also enjoy real power with respect to the managers, who prefer to dedicate themselves to projects of technological development and massive investment expenditure rather than trying to improve the motivation and productivity of their personnel. The former are more interesting and manageable; the latter boring and difficult. In the end, however, things come to a head. Take, for instance, the national postal service: when it undertakes a large technological project, its competitive advantage cannot consist in the sole trump card that the postal service has with respect to the banks, represented by the diffuseness of its branches. Such diffusion of the postal service branch offices is, in fact, nothing but the territorial expression of its large quantity of personnel. Thus, tossed out the back door of ease of management, the necessity to manage personnel slips back in through the window of competitive advantage.

After having examined the responsibility demonstrated in the work of dependents in the monopoly sector, we maintain we have shown that this responsibility can be greatly improved.

Case study: applying the USDIME to a sample of European banks
Case study authored by Paolo D'Anselmi, Simone Morganti, Margherita Cappelletto, and Alessio Richichi

What exactly do we mean when we say 'irresponsibility'? Starting with this chapter, we will provide cases of applications and attempts to overcome irresponsibility. Simple accounts that would, however, deliver a lot of transparency to organizations and would very much benefit their constituencies.

Following is a case where a set of banks is evaluated, based on their social responsibility statements (Table 11.1). While doing so, where appropriate, I express what kind of information it would be necessary to have and what

Table 11.1   Applying the USDIME framework to a set of European banks

Company	ING Group	Intesa Sanpaolo
DISCLOSURE		
Identification of "emergencies": offers a brief, easily identifiable and located list of the company's hot issues.	Does not identify.	Does not identify.
Easy to read graphic lay-out, easy to read tables also in black and white.	Very few tables, lots of text, legible in black and white.	Few tables.
Accessible length and content so that in two hours of attentive study the reader is able to fill out this questionnaire.	Not much synthesis since it is mostly text.	Not much synthesis since it is almost only text.
Doubt, vulnerability: contains admissions of not having done what was supposed to be done or of having actions be insufficient.	Everything appears to have been done well; no mention of Lehman.	Mentions Lehman without numerical references; reduces by more than 51% from one year to the next its range of stocks without indicating awareness of vulnerability.
Confronts issues encountered during the year, for example sensitive issues such as the financial crisis by evaluating risk parameters (debts, credits and effective payment terms).	Covered in above-mentioned section.	Covered in above-mentioned section
Grade for Disclosure	*1.0*	*1.4*

kind of phenomena would be desirable to control, thus providing a constructive idea of accountability.

The good thing about the USDIME framework is that it creates a story and is (it should be) readable also by those who do not have a view on the primary sources (i.e. the original corporate responsibility reports). The readers of the evaluation, to some extent, can evaluate the evaluation in their turn. They need not put any faith in the reviewer. Not only do they not need to apply faith to this domain, but also they are enabled to build, criticize or go forward on the research that they are presented with. Other evaluation rating systems are a dead end: readers have no instruments and insufficient information to move forward. The USDIME might be sampling, sketchy – it is however fertile and additive.

Montepaschi	UBI Bank	Unicredit
Does not identify but does have a table in which there is an attempt to synthesize.	Does not identify.	Does not identify.
One table giving synthesis.	Lots of crowded tables, hard to read in black and white.	Few tables, lots of text.
Presents an attempt at synthesis.	Schematic but no attempt to rationalize the whole.	Not very schematic.
Mentions Lehman with numerical references.	Mention is made of the crisis but nothing specific about the bank is said. Vulnerability is implicit in the 'Objectives for improvement' section but these have not been quantified.	Writes about internal controversies and related damage payments; presents data on Lehman clients in absolute terms.
Covered in above-mentioned section	Covered in above-mentioned section	Covered in above-mentioned section minus the internal controversies which are not current.
2.6	*1.4*	*2.0*

(continued)

136

Table 11.1   Continued

Company	ING Group	Intesa Sanpaolo
IMPLEMENTATION		
Adopts international standards (GRI and others) and uses them correctly; contains performance indicators in relation to the 'emergencies' in Disclosure, for example data on underlying risk.	No data.	Includes a table on patrimony indicators with no explanations.
Is there a code of ethics and are indicators identified to measure its implementation?	No.	No numbers.
Mention of work undertaken in risky circumstances *vis-à-vis* corruption and indication of specific measures.	Absent.	Absent.
Considerations of the clients; does a code of service exist; does the report measure its implementation; denominators: offers comparisons such that the reader can get an idea about general relevance?	No data.	No data.
Takes responsibility for upstream (payment of suppliers) and downstream (clients) activities; considers long-term consequences of its development (sustainability of returns in the medium and long-term).	Scarce.	Scarce.
Grade for Implementation	*1.0*	*1.4*
MICRO-ETHICS		
Does not present philanthropy, welfare capitalism or market-related causes as social responsibility and sustainability in business.	Emphasis on donations.	Emphasis on donations.
Report does not hide important issues or muddy them, or blame others.	Appears reticent.	Muddies information concerning customer satisfaction vs. the market.

Montepaschi	UBI Bank	Unicredit
No data; good GRI: an attempt has been made to organize the second half of the report along GRI.	Indicators are present throughout the text but not in relation to emergencies, which are lacking. Only one table on GRI conversions.	Neither data nor explanations.
No numbers.	There is a code of ethics but no indicators.	Presents numbers concerning internal controversies.
Absent.	Mention of non-involvement in controversial sectors (arms).	Absent.
Data only on itself and not over time; not detailed; qualitative.	Consideration of client (there is one paragraph dedicated to this subject) but no data.	Data only on itself, not over time, not in detail, qualitative.
Scarce.	Says a supplier roster exists but it is only cited.	Nothing on payment times to suppliers.
1.6	*1.7*	*1.8*
Emphasis on donations.	Emphasis on donations.	Emphasis on donations.
It doesn't say much.	It doesn't say much.	It doesn't say much.

(*continued*)

138

Table 11.1 Continued

Company	ING Group	Intesa Sanpaolo
Company undertakes (and report notifies of) campaigns purely for image.	Information absent.	Information absent.
The level of disclosure demonstrates the absence of company collusion.	The little disclosure demonstrates company collusion.	The level of disclosure is greater than the ING Group (retribution of women employees).
Report is explicit about the company relationship with regulating agencies and legislators (lobbying).	Hardly.	Hardly.
Grade for Micro-ethics	*1.2*	*1.6*
UNKNOWN STAKEHOLDER Taxonomy of responsibility: locates the company in a competitive context (competitive stakeholders), for example, by presenting market quotas.	Does not do this operation.	Provides market shares.
Stakeholder clients: compares prices with market average or specific competitors.	Does not do this operation.	Does not do this operation.
International stakeholder clients: compares analogous services also at the international level, provides profits by country, which is a measure of the relationship with non-organized stakeholders.	Ignores the international dimension.	Ignores the quantification of the international dimension.
Comparisons of the quality of service.	Does not develop this point.	The reduction in options is an implicit element of client care.
Comparisons of efficiency; comparisons of remuneration and hourly wages.	No information on this subject.	Data on compensation of women employees
Grade for the Unknown stakeholder	*1.0*	*1.8*
TOTAL AVERAGE GRADE	*1.1*	*1.6*

Montepaschi	UBI Bank	Unicredit
Information absent.	Information absent.	Information absent.
Level falls between ING Group and Intesa.	Little disclosure on retribution of women employees, better on clients.	Level of disclosure superior to ING Group (retribution of women employees).
Hardly.	Hardly.	Hardly.
1.6	*1.6*	*1.8*
Does not do this operation.	Some examples of competitors.	Does not do this operation.
Does not do this operation.	Does not do this operation.	A few examples of competitors.
Ignores the quantification of the international dimension.	Ignores the quantification of the international dimension.	Ignores the quantification of the international dimension.
Does not develop this point.	Provides complaints.	Provides complaints.
Scarce.	Very scarce.	Specific data on the retribution of women employees.
1.2	*1.8*	*1.8*
1.8	*1.6*	*1.9*

12
The Profits of Non-Profit

I would like here to consider responsibility in the realm of non-profit organizations – not only charities, but also those organizations that exist to make money for those they represent, such as business and worker unions. Let's first state, once and for all, that non-profit is not no-profit.

The mistaken assumption that these organizations make no profit is, in a sense, a lapse of an associative kind: I am dedicated to non-profit work; therefore, I eschew making a profit. That there must be an ideal sort of profit is understood by all; less understood is that there must also be real profit, in the purely economic sense. The organization must earn money – this means orphanages, hospitals and churches.

Economists have a saying, 'There's no such thing as a free lunch,' which seems to have come from the practice of certain restaurants to offer a free lunch with paid drinks, or to the third party in a group (buy two get three). Obviously, unless the restaurant is to go bankrupt, the third man's lunch is being paid by the first two. At the end of the day, money is important, even for the altruistic: to achieve good, there must somewhere be a surplus of resources that is then devoted to the recipients.

The main difference between non-profit organizations and for profit ones is that, in the case of for profit organizations, the person paying is the one receiving the organization's benefits while, in the case of non-profit organizations, the person paying is not the one receiving the benefit. This is, for instance, the case of government. Government is a non-profit organization the largest of non-profit-making organizations.

A no-profit organization simply cannot exist – however noble its intent – because it cannot work. It cannot deliver on its noble intent. Doing good is making a profit.

This sticking point bears significant consequences because it shows that – as far as money consequences to the public and money for the general fund are concerned – there is no difference between services that government renders with its own personnel and public contracts can be outsourced to private firms who make money, by controlling the prices through competition. A case in point is reflected in privately-run prisons, or government-guaranteed services to the public which it does not itself provide. Quite the opposite are some government buy-outs of failing companies for purely nationalistic reasons, guaranteed to make no profit at all.

Philanthropy does not mean responsibility

The June 29, 2006 cover of *The Economist* had a photograph of Bill Gates with the title: 'Billanthropy.' *The Economist* has no change of heart concerning CSR. The good deeds of Bill Gates? Microsoft. By this, *The Economist* meant that donations made by Gates were not relevant to CSR and confirmed the magazine's position articulated in the 2005 survey, that there are business people who think money is dirty and can be cleaned only by aiming for CSR. *The Economist* did not change its mind because it is correct. Philanthropy is spending money in such a way that it is not connected at all to company business, which is a far cry from CSR. Non-CSR expenditure includes spending to create a consensus concerning the company, thus spelling the tautology that everything that is useful for the corporation is CSR: many things may be useful, but not everything is CSR.

I do not intend here to demonstrate that *The Economist* is incorrect from a micro-economic point of view. However, if the champion of capitalism feels the need to take on CSR, that means that the issue is global, so it is worthwhile taking up the challenge and parrying the thrust. I now propose an approach to CSR that accepts the criticisms and delineates a point of view that is compatible with the position of *The Economist*. To summarize:

1 CSR by for-profit companies is defined within the context of competition among companies whereby this competition also includes transparently accounting for the impact of a company's activities through information to the public. CSR is research and disclosure; this is basically the message of the USDIME process framework proposed in the previous chapters of this book.
2 The theoretical difficulties concerning CSR and philanthropy are only relative to for-profit companies, those to which *The Economist* is referring. For the non-profit, public and private sectors, it is far easier to make a case for CSR.
3 CSR is not connected to philanthropy or patronage.

It appears that non-profit organizations engage in CSR that also includes philanthropy in order to obtain theoretical support for their own financing by for-profit companies. Comprehensible, but hardly defensible. Another route was taken by *The Economist* (2006): it maintained that charity is harder to do well than business. It also stated that charities behave as if they were unaccountable, and noted that, in America, a large part of the money given to non-profit organizations comes from their users or government. CSR is necessary also for non-profit organizations in order to justify their funding; engaging in accountability demonstrates the usefulness of non-profit organizations. If non-profit organizations followed accountability through CSR, they would demonstrate their being more successful than government agencies in a variety of tasks.

The Jesuits' accountability

CSR reports are an excellent tool for non-profit organizations, both public and private, because the variables cannot be summarized with simple accounting. In a non-profit organization, if you didn't measure it, you didn't do it. A good example is the Jesuit Refugee Service (JRS), a refugee assistance agency run by the Jesuits, a non-profit holding in existence for nearly 500 years. The JRS is a global network in support of people who have been forced to leave their countries of origin. It also lobbies for legislation concerning political asylum and human rights.

Among the documents produced by the JRS, the annual report best relates the social outcomes of its work, containing organizational charts detailing the various activities undertaken: food kitchens, health services, legal representation, employment assistance, schools and lodgings. The report considers each activity in detail, providing charts to quantify the benefits. A website provides this same report in part, adding some statistics regarding the various services. Accounting for the success of an activity such as an Italian school for beginners in transition is not easy, and finding a way to do this denotes institutional know-how – the simple constant in attendance would appear to indicate success.

However, not everything can (or should) be quantified. If an abstract indication of why one does what one does is valid for a for-profit company, it is doubly so for a non-profit organization because it is intrinsically tied to personal social responsibility, since most often the people who work in non-profit organizations do so because of a personal moral guide, a personal ideal. It is legitimate, therefore, to write in a CSR report that the organization assists the weak of the world because that is the way taught by Christ. It is the formulation of a mission and it helps to articulate it.

In another instance, emphasizing such a mission of assisting the weak of the world for the simple fact that that is the way taught by Christ would have helped the Roman Catholic Church in taking care of its ailing Pope John Paul II for purely compassionate reasons, instead of trying to keep him alive like a secretary of the communist party in the former Soviet Union. Imitating Christ is the mission of the institution of which the Pope is the spiritual guide, and accepting one's own suffering is, for the Pope, an expression of that mission.

The American Cancer Society: no need for indicators

With some technological savvy, one can access the corporate report of the American Cancer Society (ACS) online, searching for different sections, of which there are a great number. Founded in 1913, the American Cancer Society not only funds scientific research, but also underwrites education, information, prevention, lobbying and assistance to cancer patients and their families – including the logistics for those patients who must be hospitalized far from home. The entire operation earns US$800 million.

The percentage of funds going to scientists is 15% of the total, with similar percentages accounting for the other services, adding up to 71% of the total budget. Only 7% goes to administration, while 22% represents fund raising. Consider: in order to take home the equivalent of €800 million, you need to spend €150 million to organize events and campaigns. In other words, to earn you have to spend. The American Cancer Society is in 10th place in terms of earnings among American non-profit organizations (McKinsey Quarterly, 2002), and published on its site are its company tax returns.

Let's take a look at scientific research, a popular subject these days in which there is much talk about both scientific and technological progress and decline. Published on the ACS site are lists of projects that have been financed; examining them is a pleasure because they are divided either by the geographical provenance of the researchers being financed, or by scientific area of specialization. A million dollars out of US$200 go overseas – not a great deal, but consider: it confirms that pragmatism, and not just philanthropy, spurs giving money to those who can give nothing in return, beyond the myopic reciprocity prescribed by diplomacy: the disheartening *quid pro quo*.

In detail, the table listing the money ending up in California runs to 206 pages. You can click on the list and every line in the table can call up a couple of pages concerning the team receiving the funds, the denomination of the monies and the scientific abstract of the project. The numbers are not immense – US$100,000 on average, marginal funds that are enough, however, to finance multi-year projects. What's interesting about the names of the projects is their minute specificity.

Consider: the *ex ante* evaluation of whom to finance is carried out with a peer review made up of colleagues whose first and last names can be consulted. Also foreseen is the involvement of the stakeholders, those who are not scientists but are dedicated to the American Cancer Society and have a vote on the funding to be provided. The more malicious among us might wonder whether they do not perhaps represent the more wealthy donors, given in this way a manner in which to verify the use of their donations.

In the *ex post* evaluation, the ACS shows some pride when noting that, in the last sixty years, it has financed 38 Nobel prize winners at the beginning of their careers, long before they received the recognition. Lacking, however, is data that would allow some comparison among institutions; instead, one gets a reel dedicated to research milestones. The capacity for selection and the specificity of the detail is laudable, but missing are indicators and numbers. Final consideration: is our rather European insistence on numbers our only guarantee of a transparent, agreed-upon process? Our obsession with numbers in CSR reports is evidence of a lack of clean procedures with the checks and balances so dear to our forefathers.

Professor Jeffrey Sachs' recipe for international aid

Aid to developing countries is a vast area for private non-profit organizations and *The End of Poverty*, written by Jeffrey D. Sachs (2005), supplies technical advice that can be useful to a potential donor stakeholder, often skeptical about the benefits of such aid. Chapter 16 of the book starts like this:

> Everything up to this point is fine and good, except for one matter: it ignores the human factor. Take the case of Africa. Africa needs around $30 billion per year in aid in order to escape poverty. But if we actually gave that aid, where would it go? Right down the drain if the past is any guide. Sad to say. Africa's education levels are so low that even programs that work elsewhere would fail in Africa. Africa is corrupt and riddled with authoritarianism. It lacks modern values and the institutions of a free market economy needed to achieve success. In fact, Africa's morals are so broken down that is no surprise AIDS has run out of control. And here is the bleakest truth: suppose that our aid saved Africa's children. What then? There would be a population explosion, and a lot more hungry adults. We would have solved nothing.

This paragraph, which seems entirely plausible is, instead, a trap, since the professor goes on to say:

> If your head is nodding yes, please read this chapter with special care. The paragraph above repeats conventional rich-world wisdom about Africa, and to a lesser extent, other poor regions. While common, these assertions are incorrect.

And the professor goes on to explain, one by one, what's wrong about those assertions. The book cover abounds with portentous statements: 'The End of Poverty – Economic Possibilities for Our Time', and in chapter 16, entitled 'Myths and Magic Bullets,' the professor begins by taking by the horns those people who are already thinking: 'Sure, we're all for clinical economics without macro solutions; we like technical advances like energy-efficient cooking devices in the Savannah or cures for the HIV-positive in Nigeria, but what about the sociopolitical situation in Africa?'

Professor Sachs refutes each time-worn assumption. Concerning corruption, for example, he says 'as a country's income rises, governance improves ... slower growth is caused, in my opinion, mainly by Africa's adverse geography and deficient infrastructure.' As for the absence of modern values and problems like 'the resignation to poverty, low priority for education, apathy and diffidence outside the family,' he notes that in 1870 it was written about Japan that: 'Wealthy we do not think it [Japan] will ever become ... the love of indolence and pleasure of the people themselves forbid it.' He also notes that Max Weber, in the early twentieth century, explained the low incomes in Ireland and southern Europe by attributing them to Catholicism's static values with respect to the entrepreneurial values of Protestantism; nonetheless, by the end of the twentieth century Catholic Italy had a higher income than Protestant Great Britain.

One can object that the examples he uses required a far greater time span to come about than the mere twenty years he posits to reach his objective; the message appears to be this: donate money and something good will come out of it. Some insist that, were the problem simply one of collecting enough money, it would have been solved long ago; but Sachs reconciles a person with the act of giving – and if something gets wasted, so be it. It's something that happens in every kind of development. Following a dream is good for the heart and, if it weren't impossible, it wouldn't be a dream.

The Vatican's accountability: the Devil's tail

One of the preferred misnomers of social (ir)responsibility is free services. A green card is free, as are a colonoscopy or CAT scan under the Italian national health service. The huge concerts 'sponsored' by telephone companies and banks are free, as are symposiums 'offered' by the city in newly-built venues, to which the average taxpayer has no idea how much he has contributed. Bus tickets are cheap, and so are Buddhist retreats and theater galleries. So many things appear free that one goes back once more to the illusion there really is such a thing as a free lunch, but the truth is that you're paying for every one of them, particularly with your time. By standing in line.

Lines are an example of cut-throat and inefficient competition, a useless excess, and nobody is spared. Both the wealthy tourist and the humble immigrant stand in lines, though the line is usually longest for the poor. The poor lose more time standing in line than others, although for the poor more than others time is money, as work by the poor is more likely to be paid by the hour. Standing in line is like a tax on the poor – and on women, who are more likely than men to be riding the bus.

There are circumstances in which standing in line is a valuable way to spend your time – to vote, for example, or to view the body of a dead Pope. These are moments of collective togetherness.

Some headway has been made to improve this phenomenon. The installation of numbered tickets in the post office has taken the chaos out of unruly lines, but not decreased the time spent waiting.

Token payments for health services are, in fact, token, for they in no way cover the costs of these services and one still pays for them with one's time. There's worse: how about disincentives for eliminating lines? Like buyers of ferry or theater tickets who acquire ahead of time only to be penalized with a pre-sales tax – a true insult to the science of economics. Obviously, buying in advance tangibly benefits those offering the service but there are also intangible benefits, such as precious information: if a theater manager knows ahead of time how many people have bought tickets, he can far better organize repeat performances or cut them short. Those who buy in advance ought to be rewarded with lower prices, not dissuaded with extra charges.

Volumes have been written on theories concerning lines (queuing theory), but in vain. All attempts to rationalize the situation have been perceived by the humanities portion of the population as scientific assault – spiritual engineering. There is a sort of social connection forged in lines: one joins a crucible line in India before a bank window as a tourist, convinced that being immersed in that fetid human-generated heat will be an 'experience' to write home about. Theoretically, one could go back to the medieval rite of payment in kind, in this case using one's time as capital: you could sweep the streets or clean the sidewalks, for example, earning 10 points; 30 would get you into a symposium free of charge.

Of all lines, the worst is that to be found for tourists waiting to visit the Sistine Chapel in the Vatican City. Starting at the entrance on Viale Vaticano, the line winds to the right along Viale dei Bastioni di Michelangelo, spills into Piazza Risorgimento, hangs a left along Via di Porta Angelica, stretching all the way to the Bernini Colonnade. One wonders what tourists think of the 'made in Italy' slogan during the time they have to contemplate the issue. It is not possible that there is no way, via the Internet, to institute a manner in which to reserve entrance to the Sistine Chapel. In Switzerland, they even stamp your skis so that you don't have to wait in line at the ski lift. One might say that a bit of penitence does no harm but, if that's the case, then the crowds of tourists might well take the pilgrimage to heart and join in singing some Exodus psalm from the Promised Land.

Accounting for the industrialists' association

The corporate social reports of many industrialists' associations, as reported by the press, contain broad categories in vague descriptions: 'new and improved', 'high priority', 'efficiency', 'focus on youth', 'innovative technologies'. A detailed reading, however, in the light of the research, disclosure and diffusion of information that are meant to characterize a CSR report, uncovers some missing content that it would be good to know – such as the amount of money spent for lobbying government, or the fact that the industrial complex receives more money from the government for research and development than it invests of its own. The industrialists always come out ahead, even when justifying the use of government funds for research that would not otherwise have been undertaken because it is innovative – that means risky, with returns that may or may not be seen somewhere in the future. It would be good to know what the association does do that the individual entrepreneur is incapable of doing of his or her own: some issues of corruption or organized crime would be key areas for collective action and a key justification for the very existence of the association itself.

Case study: a comparative analysis of research institutions
Case study authored by Andrea Lapiccirella, Fabrizio Tuzi, Paolo D'Anselmi and Simone Morganti

The following institutions are examined: the Max-Planck-Gesellschaft – MPG (Germany), the Centre National pour la Recherche Scientifique – CNRS (France), the Consejo Superior de Investigación Científica – CSIC (Spain), and the Consiglio Nazionale delle Ricerche – CNR (Italy).

The following case study, and the cases in Chapters 13 and 14, have a different cut. They belong to a subset of the USDIME framework: implementation. They are meant to show in detail what can be done to make organizations that are not subject to competition more accountable than they are today. They are shown to clarify the proposed concept of organizational CSR in the non-profit sector, in government and in the political arena.

Cases shown here imply no aspiration to originality of methodology. This section provides a benchmark analysis of European research institutions deemed to be of equivalent status. The idea is to show some of the basic variables and comparisons that can be made in order to evaluate the productivity and the effectiveness of institutions.

Table 12.1 compares the financial and human resources available to the institutions in the two-year period 2001–02. Table 12.2 analyses the structure of the scientific network and its development in the two-year period 2001–02. Table 12.3 compares the scientific output of the various research institutions in terms of their journal citation reports (JCR) publications. Table 12.4 compares the market funding capacity of these institutions over the period 1999–2002. Table 12.5 shows the results of a survey on the publications of European generalist research institutions.

Table 12.1   Financial and human resources available to research institutions, 2001–02

	CNR		CNRS		CSIC		Max-Planck	
	2001	2002	2001	2002	2001	2002	2001	2002
Budget (€/million)	793,000	814,000	2,457	2,533	404,000	562,000	1,261	1,253
Personnel	8,082	8,015	23,094	25,231	7,678	8,738	11,612	12,049
Researchers	3,693	3,610	11,643	11,643	2,259	2,713	3,116	3,509
Budget per member of personnel (€)	98,119	101,560	106,391	100,392	52,618	64,317	108,595	103,992
Budget per researcher (€)	214,672	225,485	211,028	217,556	178,840	207,151	404,685	357,082

Sources: DAST; CNR editorial group elaboration.

Table 12.2   Structure of the scientific network and its development, 2001–02

	CNR		CNRS		CSIC		Max-Planck	
	2001	2002	2001	2002	2001	2002	2001	2002
Number of institutes	108	107	1.640	1.256	108	123	80	80
Budget per institute (€/million)	7.343	7.607	1.498	2.017	3.741	4.569	15.763	15.663
Researchers per institute	34	34	7	9	21	22	39	44
Personnel per institute	75	75	14	20	71	71	145	151

Sources: DAST; CNR editorial group elaboration.

Table 12.3   Scientific output of the various research institutions (journal citation report publications), 2001–02

	CNR		CNRS		CSIC		Max-Planck	
	2001	2002	2001	2002	2001	2002	2001	2002
Publications JCR	4,941	4,916	16,492	16,229	4,362	5,140	7,554	7,699
Publications per member of personnel	0.610	0.610	0.710	0.630	0.570	0.590	0.650	0.640
Publications per researcher	1.340	1.360	1.420	1.390	1.930	1.890	2.420	2.190
Budget per publication (€)	160,494	165,582	148,981	156,079	92,618	109,338	166,931	162,748

Sources: DAST; CNR editorial group elaboration.

Table 12.4   Market funding capacity of research institutions, 1999–2002 (%)

	CNR	CNRS	CSIC	Max-Planck
1999	26	8	30	4
2000	35	11	33	5
2001	31	14	32	2
2002	26	12	40	6

Source: DAST; CNR editorial group elaboration.

Table 12.5   Survey of publications of European generalist* research entities, 1996–99

Institutions/university	CNRS	CNR	CSIC	University of London
No. of publications	23,784	18,833	16,133	85,182
No. of citations	130,105	66,626	50,681	550,278
Field norm citation score	1.190	0.850	0.840	1.290
Field of activity:				
Agriculture		5	1/3	1/3
Basic sciences	1/3	1/3	1/3	1/3/4
Biological sciences	5	1/3	1/3	1/3/4
Biomedical sciences	4		3/5	1/3/4
Clinical sciences			5	1/2/3/4
Earth and environmental sciences	1/3/4	1/3	1/3	1/3
Engineering	1/3	1/3	1/3	1
Chemistry	1	1/3	1/2/3	1/3/4
Physics and astronomy	1/2	2	1/3	
Mathematics and statistics				1/3/4
Computer science	5	1/3	5	1/3

Key to performance by field of activity:
1 most actively publishing institution in field by country;
2 at least 25% of total publication output across the 11 broad field is within the marked field;
3 highest number of citations in field by country;
4 impact above world average (≥ 1.20);
5 highest impact score in country by field but below 1.20.
*The term 'generalist agency' means a research institution which carries out its work in many different scientific fields.
Source: Science and Technology Indicators (2003).

Staff comparison between the Max-Planck-Gesellschaft, CNRS and CNR

This section provides a comparative analysis of personnel in three of the four institutions examined. A comparison of the breakdown of staff reveals the differing staffing structure of the three establishments, by:

- different legislation regarding the recruitment of fixed-term and indefinite-term personnel; and
- different number of layers in the organizational pyramid.

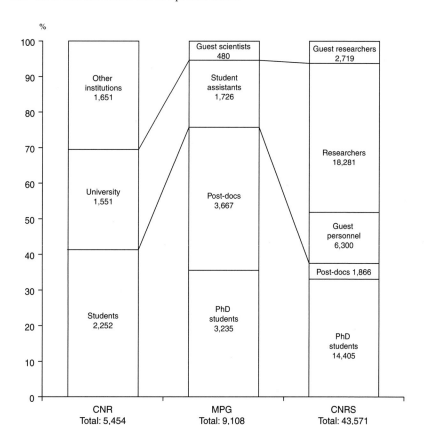

Figure 12.1   Direct external co-workers at CNR, MPG and CNRS: head count
Sources: DAST; CNR editorial group elaboration.

I present an analysis of the external staff involved by institution (Figure 12.1) and a reclassification of the professional profiles, in order to make a preliminary comparison (Table 12.6, section(*b*)).

The first point to be analyzed, then, is the breakdown of the direct external co-workers of the three research institutions (Table 12.6). Max-Planck has a large number of personnel on fixed-term contracts; the personnel we are referring to as 'external co-workers' are mainly young researchers or guest researchers. Max-Planck employs a total of 9,108 external co-workers, equivalent to 4,489 researcher-years. CNRS employs, in turn, a total number of 43,571 external co-workers. Unlike MPG, the external co-workers with CNRS are not only research personnel, but also technical and administrative staff.

The second point is the reclassification of the professional profiles. Table 12.6, section(*a*) shows the different staff posts in each instance: researchers,

Table 12.6 Research staff typology, by institution

Type of contract	CNR		MPG		CNRS	
	No. of persons	%	No. of persons	%	No. of persons	%
(a) Ordinary staffing plan						
Researchers	4,284	53	3,883	32	11,648	46
Technicians	2,632	33	5,644	47	7,569	30
Administrative	1,099	14	2,522	21	6,014	24
Total ordinary staffing plan	**8,015**	**100**	**12,049**	**100**	**25,231**	**100**
(b) Enlarged staffing plan: personnel + leverage						
1 Researchers	4,284	39	3,883	32	11,648	25
2 Guests and young scientists (person-years)	3,088	28	4,489	27	18,636	40
Total researcher personnel (1+2)	7,372	66	8,372	51	30,284	64
Technicians	2,632	24	5,644	34	9,324	20
Administrative	1,099	10	2,522	15	7,409	16
Total personnel + leverage	**11,103**	**100**	**16,538**	**100**	**47,017**	**100**

Table 12.7 Mean expected citation rate (MECR)

Institutions	Countries	MECR	No. of publications (Science citation index)
1 INSERM	France	6.090	3.848
2 Max Planck Society	Germany	5.970	4.369
3 Oxford University (+ Radcliffe Hospital)	UK	5.50	2.734
4 Cambridge University (+ Addenbrokes Hospital)	UK	4.990	2.816
5 Leiden University	Holland	4.980	1.441
6 Karolinska Institute Stockholm	Sweden	4.880	2.150
7 Amsterdam University	Holland	4.750	1.287
8 Utrecht University	Holland	4.670	1.575
9 Heidelberg University	Germany	4.560	1.528
10 CNRS	France	4.400	11.022
11 London University (all colleges, institutes and hospitals)	UK	4.200	10.613
12 Helsinki University	Finland	4.160	1.502

Table 12.7   Continued

Institutions	Countries	MECR	No. of publications (Science citation index)
13 CSIC	Spain	4.120	1,974
14 Milan University (San Raffaele Hospital)	Italy	4.110	1,721
15 CNR	Italy	4.080	2,767
16 Leuven Catholic University	Belgium	4.060	1,044
17 Uppsala University	Sweden	4.040	1,581
18 Munich University	Germany	4.030	1,866
19 Copenhagen University	Denmark	3.900	2,019
20 Rome University (La Sapienza + Umberto I Policlinico)	Italy	3.760	1,632

Note: Mean impact factor and compared total publication output of the most active European research institutions in 1992. Ranked by mean expected citation rate (MECR).
Source: Second European Report on Science and Technology Indicators (OECD, 1997).

technicians and administrative staff. This calculation has been made in terms of two situations:

• the so-called 'ordinary staffing plan' – the staff directly employed by each research institution; and
• what we call the 'enlarged staffing plan' – which also takes into account the human resources that gravitate as external co-workers around the entity.

A comparative analysis of these cases reveals differences between all the tables. But, in all cases, there are also similar proportions – most of the human resources are researchers, while the administrative staff are always proportionally fewer.

Finally, Table 12.7 shows a comparison of the effectiveness of different institutions, as measured by accepted and published international standards. This is only shown here as an example of metrics available at an international level that can be used to evaluate and account for the work of each institution.

13
The Autarky of Public Administration

From international corporations (analyzed in Chapter 1) to monopolies (dealt with in Chapter 12) was a difficult step, since the names are no longer familiar. International companies are easy to talk about: everybody knows them, everybody thinks they know them, a great deal is said about them. Monopolies were more difficult to deal with: the names are no longer familiar; they are often local companies; everybody tends to think they have their own predicament which is different from that of others. Nobody is interested in Lilco (the Long Island Lighting Company, in New York), and speaking of Electricité de France (EDF) might be regarded as an exquisitely European matter, even though Lilco and EDF are very similar to any large power company, like tens – if not hundreds, perhaps – of other power companies around the world. The non-profit world can be somewhat similar to international corporations as there are world class non-profit organizations but, when we come to public administration or government bureaucracies, when we come to politics and political systems, everybody is on his own. It is the war of all against all – notwithstanding the well-known and primary impact of government on development (Perkins in Perkins *et al.*, 2006; Draghi, 2010; Tabellini, 2010).

Thus, individual bodies of millions of employees live in the ultimate autarky; that is, doing everything unsupervised – no benchmarking, no comparison is made, no cross-country learning is available. Marginal attempts are made in the technical fields, like information technology, where – once again – international corporations, driven by the need to sell their products, play the non-indifferent role of inseminating diverse government and public bodies with the same ideas.

Public administration appears to be tied too much to the history of the country and its legal system. How many times have we heard the theme: 'They have Roman Law and we have Common Law so we cannot compare', or vice versa? Public administration is bound by language. To many people, it is heresy to have their official government documents translated into English, as they do in Sweden and The Netherlands. Comparative public

153

administration is the realm of lawyers and constitutionalists with their bird's-eye-view approach.

All of this ignores the simple fact that – paraphrasing German poet Gertrude Stein (who wrote 'a rose is a rose is a rose,' meaning things are what they are and we can't fiddle with them for our own little purposes) – a jail is a jail is a jail: many government services are identical all over the world. Reality is the same everywhere and human beings are the same. There are universal rights recognized and, in spite of this universality in 'demand', no universality in answers to those rights is pursued. Thus, it is not difficult to understand and adhere to the libertarian concept that the peoples of different countries are held hostage by their governments.

Complaint about government is a basic staple of anti-politics: we shall deal with this in Chapter 15. Suffice it here to report one more professional point of view on the deficiencies of bureaucracies. 'Bureaucratic practices rely heavily on symbols and language of the moral boundaries between insiders and outsiders, a ready means of expressing prejudice and justifying neglect. Thus, societies with proud traditions of generous hospitality may paradoxically produce at the official level some of the most calculated indifference one can find anywhere' (Herzfeld, 1992).

Nonetheless, all this having been said, we are going to embark now on a short trip across some examples of CSR in government.

Turning back the brain drain

More difficult to handle than the concept of brain drain is the concept of 'brain come back.' When it comes to the attempt to turn back the brain drain and lure talented scholars and scientists back to their home countries, various projects are underway – tax breaks, among other things, for those that come back home to work. The underlying idea, rather racist and autarkic, is implicitly that a given country can better benefit from those people it has personally educated rather than from any man or woman of good hope and will. Were the true intent of attracting scientists greater economic advantages and national pride, or the possibility of giving students better and more immediate training directly in national companies; were the true aim a wider support of the sciences in general, then young graduates from all over the world would be equally welcome.

The ethnic focus of efforts to get nationals home from foreign institutes backfires right from the start because one of the things scientists appreciate most about research organizations abroad is their international atmosphere. Since a scientific system is a cohort of public and private research institutions, and companies that use their results and financial institutions (such as banks, using both), opening this system is the first step in enabling it to engender the other properties of a vital system: competition, multiplicity, an abundance of ideas; that 'chaos and cacophony of unfettered speech which is the strength of our liberty,' as noted by a famous Philadelphia Court ruling of 1996. In Philadelphia on June 12, 1996, a panel of federal judges blocked part of the Communications Decency Act of 1996 (CDA), saying it would infringe upon the rights of adults to free speech. The CDA was the attempt by the United States Congress to regulate pornographic material on the Internet. On June 26, 1997, the Supreme Court upheld the Philadelphia court's decision. The Communications Decency Act of 1996 (CDA) was the first notable attempt by the United States Congress to regulate pornographic material on the Internet.

The decision of the three judge panel in *Reno v. American Civil Liberties Union*, issued June 11, 1996, grants the most complete First Amendment protection to the Internet imaginable. The three judges – Dolores K. Sloviter, Ronald L. Buckwalter and Stewart Dalzell – did their jobs to the fullest.

> Just as the strength of the Internet is chaos, so the strength of our liberty depends upon the chaos and cacophony of the unfettered speech the First Amendment protects. (Judge Dalzell, CDA panel)

The Supreme Court upheld the Philadelphia court's decision, stating that the indecency provisions were an unconstitutional abridgement of the First Amendment right to free speech because they did not permit parents to decide for themselves what material was acceptable for their children, extended to non-commercial speech, and did not define 'patently offensive,' a term with no prior legal meaning.

What can be done? Set one objective at a time; for example, build a system that is attractive to everybody. An attractive system means that it will be competitive and open to all, which would mean eliminating the requirement for citizenship to compete for state, university and research job positions; betting that offering, for instance, job stability will outweigh the low entry salaries. One could consider abrogating the administrative status of higher education degrees, thus decongesting the universities and giving more value to subsequent degrees, awarding the dedication of those who study and teach and opening the job market to those most capable. One could provide tax breaks to those private companies that request work from public research agencies and universities, thus enabling a greater financing and finalization of research, giving decisions about the work to those who are actually carrying it out.

The accounts of the courts

The centrality of justice in the economic system is certified by the fact that judges are invited to speak at economic symposia, and this is newsworthy. For one light that shines, however, there are also big swathes of shadow.

International statistics and comparisons are made on objects easy to count: the number of rulings by judge, and the number of new lawsuits by judge. Thus, one of the conclusions from a congested judicial system could be that the people are too litigious. It's the people who seek a judge's ruling too much. What is the role of a minister of justice, if not that of telling the citizens the truth about the uselessness of their going to the judges? And, to do this, he would need statistics that are more difficult to calculate.

That the system is congested does not, in fact, appear from the statistics of input and output, because those data show a system that is in equilibrium: so many rulings per year (output), the same number of new lawsuits per year (input). There is no congestion. Congestion comes into play when you do the numbers on the length of the trials. Congestion comes into play when you do the numbers about the final outcome of trials: what really happened when the final ruling was implemented. Was the final ruling implemented at all? Here, no statistics are available. We are in *terra incognita*. No international comparison is available.

It is not uncommon in the circle of political value to witness an inversion of roles on the part of ministers: the minister should be the expression of the citizens' demand for justice and act as the citizens' advocate *vis-à-vis* the judges, who here represent the supply of the service. The minister should act as the employer of the judges, not the advocate of the judges. It so happens that ministers represent the supply of government services, while they are appointed to represent demand for government services.

Another hard item to monitor would be the qualitative performance of judges. Evaluating the quality of the rulings is useful and necessary, since evaluating the work force is a central element in career development and the overall health of any organization; merit must be the guiding factor and not, as so often is the case, seniority. In justice, too, an evaluation on the basis of performance would appear to improve the quality of the system as a whole.

The judicial system, with its trials and appeals, is already a sort of peer review, with each judge's sentence being reviewed by other judges; however, it needs to be better articulated. One could create a report card for a judge trying a case for the first time based on the confirmation of his sentence in subsequent trials. If, on an appeal, the original sentence is modified, then his grade is not good; if it is confirmed, then it's positive. But if the third and final appeal overturns a previous one and confirms the original sentence, then his grade is good again. Each judge could be evaluated according to running statistics concerning sentences that are confirmed or modified, and the plentiful transfers seen in this sector practically guarantee unbiased appraisals. Judges could boast about their percentage of confirmed sentences the same way a baseball player boasts about his batting average. All you'd need is a Microsoft Access database, and a group of brilliant and willing analysts.

Shylock industrial policy

An unanticipated nod to social reporting of productive and judicial activities can be seen in the movie *The Merchant of Venice*, in which Shylock gives a lesson in industrial policy. This story has been around for 400 years courtesy of Shakespeare, but thanks to Al Pacino, Jeremy Irons and Joseph Fiennes – a winning team if there ever was one – it has been given new prominence.

Antonio despises the Jewish merchant, Shylock, but for reasons of the heart he needs money and so he goes to him for a loan. Counting on his ships at sea, Antonio, out of spite, agrees to an absurd deal. If he does not pay back the loan on time, Shylock can have a pound of his living flesh. As one could expect, all of Antonio's ships go down at sea and Shylock, before the Doge's court, demands his payment, his slice of Antonio. There is much gnashing and gashing of teeth in Antonio's defense, but the Doge cannot but uphold the law, horrendous as it is and as unjust as it appears. Why is the Doge so implacable?

Shylock:

If you deny it, let the danger light/
Upon your charter and your city's freedom ...
If you deny me, fie upon your law!/
There is no force in the decrees of Venice.

Doge:

Upon my power/
I may dismiss this court.

Portia, acting as a legal representative:

Of a strange nature is the suit you follow;/
Yet in such rule that the Venetian law/
Cannot impugn you as you do proceed.

Bassanio (Antonio's friend) to the Doge:

And I beseech you,/
Wrest once the law to your authority./
To do a great right do a little wrong./
And curb this cruel devil of his will.

But Portia replies:

It must not be; there is no power in Venice/
Can alter a decree established:/
Will be recorded for a precedent,/

And many an error, by the same example,/
Will rush into the state; it cannot be.

In just a few lines, the Bard has dramatized a key point concerning industrial policy: the quality of justice. Courts must work effectively, otherwise
economic development plunges. The Doge is inflexible because he dreads
the economic consequences of uncertain law.

This could be an advocacy role for the Minister of Industry. The Minister
of Industry, representing the interests of the producers, could go to the
Minister of Justice and ask him for an account of the trials overseen by the
judges hearing civil cases. He could thus evaluate the performance of various judges in terms of sentences upheld and those overturned on appeal.
Thus, as a privileged stakeholder, he would be invited to the inauguration
of each judicial year, where he could show up with a copy of Shakespeare
in his hands.

Dirigistic milk pricing

'Don't cry for me Argentina.' When the price of milk reaches inexplicably
high levels and the government calls all the parties in the sector together –
pharmaceutical industrialists, distributors, pharmacists, supermarkets and
consumers – and talks tough until everybody agrees to give up a certain
portion of their earnings, you do get a flavor of an Evita kind of action to
protect babies and their mothers. In particular, the pharmaceutical companies agreed to spend less on advertising and save consumers money in terms
of prices.

A hypothetical case history of this event could subsequently be published in
the social report of the Ministry of Health detailing the hypothetical actions
undertaken by the government in response to a market failure which required
such strong and Peronist correction from the top. After receiving angry pro-
tests from consumer associations, the government activated and involved
those institutions that control the market – the Antitrust in the lead.

On the supply side, it was found that there are no milk producers willing
to market a 'no logo' brand that would cost less. Partly, it is because the
country has a low birth rate and thus accounts for a small market portion in
an otherwise lucrative business. So not, as some would have had it, a cartel
of villains like the insurance companies.

On the side of misleading advertising, it was found that mothers were not
being coerced into buying something they didn't need. Milk was sold both
in pharmacies and in supermarkets, and there was no pricing blackmail
where a seller might risk losing his supplies.

On the demand side, it was ascertained that the information provided to
those who had the power to influence milk consumption – pediatricians –
was correct and mothers were free to evaluate the price/quality relationship

themselves. In truth, however, that opportunity didn't exist because all milk was the same. There were no differences in price between brands. What did exist was a certain rigidity of demand. Mothers bought the most expensive brands because they were convinced they were the best – a kind of conspicuous consumption *à la* Thorstein Veblen, except complaining about it upon leaving the store. Veblen, an American economist, developed an economic theory based on the story of a woman appreciating and buying a piece of cloth for the very fact that it was expensive.

If this market failure ended up an occasion for politicians to kiss babies on television, well, so be it. Even politicians deserve a Kodak moment. In the end, the producers themselves decided that negotiating with the government was preferable to submitting to an unannounced government inspector, and this socially newsworthy event confirmed once again how difficult it is to create a market that operates properly, and how preferable it is for the producers to frame the marketplace as the Wild West and propound that social justice can only be had through command and control and not, as some would have it, that it is the market that engenders justice.

Far from being coarse, the market is actually a delicate and complex thing itself. This is why so many institutions and people work with it. In its own way, the market, too, is a baby, though its mother is unknown.

Micro health services

There is a small department within one of the local health units that works particularly with HIV. Its mission is to serve people by providing them with medical and psychological assistance, particularly aimed at those at risk of contracting HIV/AIDS. Along with the routine assistance of patients, the department also tests for HIV and provides counseling in an attempt to modify dangerous behavior. Between 1992 and 2003, 2,278 people visited the department, autochthonous citizens and foreigners, the majority of whom were sex workers.

The qualitative efficiency of the work being done can be summarized by saying that a large number of people modified their behavior. The quantitative demonstration of this was the subject of scientific papers written by professionals within the department. In the space of the 11 years under observation, the prevalence of HIV-positive people dropped by 32%. In only 15 cases was there a shift from HIV negative to HIV positive, the last of which occurred in February 2000, confirming the positive impact of the department. Among transsexuals, there was a decrease in the number of HIV-positive people, from 57% in 1992 to 12% in 2003, while the use of condoms increased from 43% to 79%, even among those who declared they had a steady partner.

The department is part of one local health unit, to which it supplies detailed information about its activities, particularly the number and type of visits effected. The Italian national health service reimburses certain things: €13.63 for a specialized visit, €2.58 for a blood test. A consultation with a psychologist, usually €19.37, is free for HIV patients. The report does not compare the data with anything else, and only in the case of a diminished number of patients treated from one year to the next would the station request an analysis. In fact, the only numbers provided consist of the earnings and the small annual procurement budget, which in 2003 amounted to €4,815.

What would be useful, however, would be to calculate the entire cost of the department, which is probably around €200,000 to €300,000 per annum including salaries, benefits and rent; it would be useful both for those working within the sector, who sometimes think the government doesn't spend enough on them, and for the patients who are paying €2.50 for services that, at full cost, exceed hundreds of euros (perhaps even complaining about it when they leave the department and head off to buy themselves a pack of cigarettes costing €4).

In the absence of trends, it is neither possible to see what threat might be lurking nor to hear whether there are alarm bells going off, but there are: the risk of contracting HIV has grown for those people not considered at risk by public opinion and who, therefore, do not perceive themselves as being at risk. Numbers are insufficient to calculate this phenomenon because it is hard to identify the basis upon which the number of positive cases was calculated. Those who undertook to test themselves for HIV are already a self-selected group and do not represent the population as a whole. Counter-intuitively, the testing process – including an informative talk, secrecy and sealed envelopes – can impede the spread of the test and restrict the audience undertaking it, thus limiting the generation of statistics capable of evaluating the incidence of the phenomenon in order to understand whether it is increasing or decreasing. Taking away the shroud of secrecy might end up favoring a wider application of the test and, therefore, greater control over the phenomenon.

Public sector accounts

The social report of the public sector comprises certain specificities that the Global Reporting Initiative itself considers in the Public Sector Supplement to its general guidelines. The primary consideration appears to be that the economic bottom line of a public sector institution ought to be in more rigorous detail than that of a private company. This apparent paradox is due to the specific goals being taken on by accounts produced by public institutions: certify the legitimacy of the administration rather than explain its activities. In this way, the corporate social report considers the quantity and quality of the work undertaken by the institution – which is, in essence, the economic bottom line.

Public institutions provide budget expense estimates and final statements that are strictly controlled on the part of internal comptrollers, and yet all they provide is an account of the correct administration of receipts and expenses. They do not go into the product of the institution. For this reason, the first task of a public social report is to define the (social) product of the institution and attempt an evaluation of the institution's efficiency and impact in producing it. The final impact would be the outcome of institutional activities.

Examining the origin of the receipts of a public institution, it is clear that much is either obtained from the government or received in the form of taxes or local tariffs. On the contrary to a company that operates on the free market, therefore, registering the receipts of a public institution is only a partial indication of a favorable public attitude towards the institution's product. These receipts are not had from the free choice of the public; they accrue from a combination of factors that have little to do with any perceived value of the institution's social impact, such as political opportunism or bureaucratic inertia.

A social report must explain what outcomes are had by supplying the institutions with funds to operate. Thus, the social report of a public sector institution becomes a central component of the overall political value resulting over time from an election. Only a social report provides the quantity and quality of public production. It is an instrument to ensure the transparency of the main activities of public sector institutions. The economic bottom line thus assumes a broader meaning than its use in the private sector and could, therefore, be called the 'institutional bottom line.'

At the end of Chapter 9, I argued that CSR in the core business leads to integrated reporting. I would only add here that the 'institutional bottom line' is the public sector deployment of integrated reporting.

Case study: reverse engineering in the police force accounts
Case study authored by Paolo D'Anselmi, Romina Giannini, Simone Morganti, Riccardo Coratella and Lorena Mazzenca

This case, too, is shown to exemplify what I mean by accountability. I zoom in on the implementation value and its specific value of benchmarking, comparing different situations and different institutions, including different situations over time.

Competition among police forces is not new to most countries, be it at the national level or the local, state and federal level. Let's see what can be done in this setting, and then we'll debrief what we find. These are examples of implementation whereby the efficiency is in details. The basic idea is to mix physical resources with monies and activities – mix and relate these variables.

Police forces keep strict records of what they do. Conveniently, these are made public in their aggregate form (except where we have militia). An overview includes a synthesis of three force resources – three national police forces; reverse engineering of organizational structures (cost accounting/ management control); zooming in on and benchmarking emergency number calls/nationwide benchmark; and a cross-facility benchmark: the example of correctional police.

Synthesis of three force resources: three national police forces

We start with a simple benchmark of three forces. Two of them have very similar tasks, the third overlaps a little. These forces do not produce reports that make explicit the resources with which they are endowed, or the use they make of those resources. However, they do produce operational reports whereby they report the numbers of personnel they have and the operational activities they perform. The work, then, is to collate different public sources. The work done here is, therefore, one of reverse engineering.

From the government budget, we derive the total cost of these three police forces (A, B and C), and we also derive the total cost of salaries of personnel. From the operational reports, we have the total number of personnel in the forces. So, we find out the three forces total a 2006 budget of €15.4 billion with a total 286,000 people on the payroll. Making the ratio between the two variables, we obtain the varying cost per person (Figure 13.1).

A good anecdote about these data is that they were shown to the relevant government-level official. He said he was given different numbers (and evidently no methodology behind them) until he quit asking.

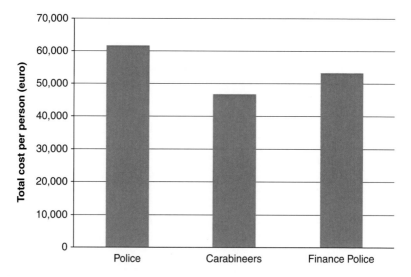

Figure 13.1 Varying cost per person, by police force

Reverse engineering of organizational structures

The main source of data for police force A is their operational report, a very thorough document whereby a wealth of data is provided about police operations. No mention is made in this document of money or funds, the cost of different operations, or of different police activities. Reconstructing such a link between resources and activities is exactly the task we have given ourselves.

Data about the organizational structure of police force A is publicly available, as is their personnel. The organizational structures are presented in Table 13.1. The main areas of activity are also defined by the police themselves in their operational reports.

On the basis of these data we have hypothesized the personnel resources absorbed by each activity and derived Table 13.1. We assigned people from the organizational structures to operational activities. This is what we called 'reverse engineering' of the police force. This is done only to exemplify what would be nice were it done by the police forces themselves and – perhaps – communicated – at least in part – to the public. We approximate the cost of activities by the cost of personnel since, in the macro data on the budget, we saw that personnel are a very high percentage of the total.

In Table 13.1, only the last column is actual and publicly available from sources for police corps A. The rest of the table is an educated guess. Once the resources spent on individual activities are identified, one might want to decide whether the result is in line with government priorities. Ask questions such as: Is it right that we spent X% of our total resources on crowd control and Y% on law enforcement against organized crime? That is the kind of question that would make the organization responsible to the public about its own activities.

Zooming in on and benchmarking emergency calls

Operational reports, however, do provide a wealth of data that at least elicits even more detailed questions. And we can conduct reverse engineering. We can push the reverse engineering further and reconstruct the process ensuing from an emergency call and figure out the total cost of such an important service and operations of that kind.

Table 13.2 shows how the number of personnel involved in first total of the first column of Table 13.1 was derived. Once more, the translation of the data in the first column was given in the police force A report; the number of personnel involved was hypothesized.

The total number of personnel involved in this activity is not important *per se*, it's just interesting to know. Calculations of this kind make us realize that the 'health' of a nation is a relative measure, a product of unknowable reality and of the society's organizational effort to police it. Had we given this activity more resources, we would certainly have had different results concerning the crime rate and the overall situation.

Table 13.1 Personnel distribution on activities

Organizational structures	Operating activities						Specialist activities	Total
	Emergency call centres	Crime prevention	Organized crime	Immigration	Drugs	Public order		
Headquarters	437	326	169	382	166	265	100	1,845
Schools						4,247		4,247
Precincts	15,989	10,709	13,574	13,273	12,803			66,348
Traffic/railroad police							13,660	13,660
Special forces							16,424	16,424
Anti-Mafia			6,287					6,287
Total	16,426	11,035	20,030	13,655	12,969	4,512	30,184	108,811

Source: Elaboration from'Forze dell'ordine. Dar conto del lavoro pubblico'.

Table 13.2   Cost analysis of emergency call service 'dial 113'

1 Activity detail	2 Activity measure	3 Personnel unit involved	4 Full cost/year (€ million)
Answered calls	6,779,614	276	17
Actions after call	2,483,322	12,010	740
Acceptance complaints	519,298	4,140	255
Total		16,426	1,012

Source: 'Forze dell'ordine. Dar conto del lavoro pubblico'.

Enter police force B. Using the fact that a parallel national police force is also active in the country, we can run another pseudo-experiment. A more detailed problem of implementation emerges when we look at the data for the emergency call service of police force B. In 2004, the total number of calls is 6,168,301. This number, however, cannot be used to make a useful comparison with the same number regarding police force A, which was 6.7 million. In fact, police force B only reports 275,000 on-site filed field patrols. This number compares with 2.5 million reported by police force A.

It is clear there are different policies for data collection and/or different policies for intervention in the field. These data make for very interesting work to be done in the brand new police coordination effort undertaken to build a national interface for police coordination. These examples are meant to exemplify the possibility of formalizing and quantifying the decision-making processing of a police force. At the time of writing, these processes are either totally implicit in the decision-making, or are not made explicit, and least of all communicated, to the public. The basic idea is, once more, if you do not measure it, it's as if you did not do it.

Cross-facility benchmark: the example of correctional police

Another example of benchmarking is across homologous organizational structures of the same police force. Correctional police, for instance, operate at different correctional facilities. One way to look at their productivity is to work on the personnel to inmate ratio. This is both a measure of quality and of supervision, when one hypothesizes that a higher ratio allows for more care. It is also a measure of cost, since more personnel are involved. It is, therefore, interesting to analyze the personnel to inmate ratio at different correctional facilities. Figure 13.2 shows the ratio in the facilities located in different districts across the country. We observe very different ratios, which would warrant further investigation of why this is so.

We observe the same variance, albeit with very different absolute values, before and after an amnesty was granted because of jail overcrowding (Figures 13.3 and 13.4). The same is true for specific large correctional facilities. In conclusion, different structures of police force generate a multiplicity of institutions, which is, counter-intuitively, a fertile situation. Competition among police forces is not new to most countries, be it at national level or the local, state and federal levels. This appears to be wrong but, counter-intuitively, this, too, is a fertile situation. It is an opportunity.

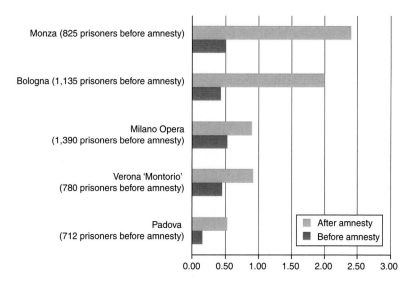

Figure 13.2   Officers/prisoners ratio before and after amnesty

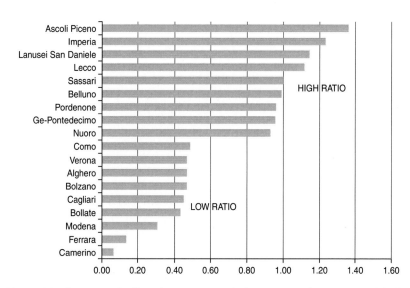

Figure 13.3   Correctional officers/prisoners ratio before amnesty, by correctional facility

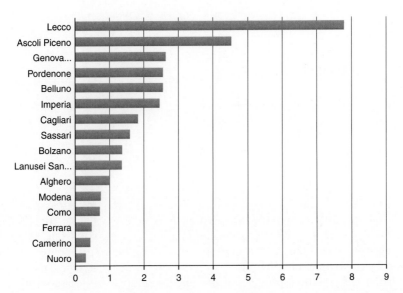

Figure 13.4 Correctional officers/prisoners ratio after amnesty, by correctional facility

14
Irrelevant Politics

The skeptical title of this chapter does not aim to be anti-political – that is, that all politics is just a power play, politics are bad and just coffee-shop talk. The title 'Irrelevant Politics' aims to be realistic: it has to be considered that politics and its specific embodiment in time and space – the specific polity at hand – may have different degrees and capabilities of affecting the reality it wants to govern.

Indeed, it can be said that politics is important in and of itself, even when it might be irrelevant with respect to the social and economic reality. That is exactly the reason why it is crucial that the political sector (i.e. political institutions) is not left out of the circle of accountability: they are the most exposed to public opinion, and they often govern and set the standard for accountability in other sectors.

Political institutions, such as elected or non-elected bodies, parliaments, executive branches, ministers and secretaries, are a conspicuous example that people follow in all areas of work. Moreover, everybody looks at their own political system as being one of a kind. Therefore, we will look only at two very general issues in the hope of dispelling this sense of uniqueness: the budgeting system and the electoral system. Everybody all over the world has a budget, democracies as well as dictatorships – even Mother Theresa's sisters, who live hand to mouth. Electoral systems are less disseminated than budgeting systems, as they are confined to the democratic countries of the world. Still, this is not an insignificant fraction of the world, without factoring in a wide grey area. I believe well over half the members of humankind today live in relatively democratic countries.

Let's start, however, with a discussion of the accountability of supra-national bodies and the attempts of countries and people to join in federations and other supra-national bodies.

Supra-national bodies

It is standard procedure in CSR to concern itself with future generations. It is, therefore, necessary to listen to what young professionals have to say.

A common refrain is the need to 'create a European public sphere, to create a framework by which a populace may be formed that is also European and not tied only to a nation-state, as is the case today.' A public sphere means a polity, a space for pan-European consensus and dissent. Freedom is participation.

Why ought we be interested in creating a European public sphere? Because the lack of such means ignorance about European legislative and executive processes and, thus, no incentive for the new European managing classes to promote coherence and efficiency in their policies. This results in two negative outcomes: scarce accountability, and little efficiency in carrying out decisions made regarding third parties (i.e. the rest of the world).

Scarce accountability means, for example, that nobody knows who the European deputies are, let alone what they are doing for the populace. Little efficiency in the implementation of European policies means, for instance, that, quantitatively, the European contribution to Overseas Development Aid (ODA) is higher than that of the United States, and lower in terms of efficiency. The United States spends 0.19% of their gross domestic product on development aid, while EU countries spent 0.50% – a sum meaning little, considering the small portion the EU actually manages.

In response to doubts about European citizens caring that much about the situation, the young professionals insist that it is in their interest to control the legislative activities of the populace and to promote executive actions that protect their interests. Seen thirty years later, it appears that things haven't so much evolved as become more concrete. The world did not begin yesterday and somebody has already thought about these things. Much about this has already been said. This European framework could materialize in a simple European license plate, or a unifying electoral law for the election of European deputies, perhaps even a single European language (English?) in which to write public documents – CSR reports – for instance, on the part of the public sector.

Primary elections

Electoral systems are of import with regard to the accountability of the political system and its individual members. There is no golden rule, however, and everybody is unsatisfied with their own system. Take Great Britain, for instance. In the year 2010, they were discussing some sort of mitigation of their single-member district system. The structure of this system is the following: each electoral district elects only one member of Parliament. That member is elected on a simple majority basis: the candidate that obtains the greatest number of votes, relatively speaking in comparison with other candidates, is elected ('first-past-the-post'). This system generates local accountability of the elected member of Parliament, as it makes it easy for the citizens to know who their elected member is and, therefore, it is less complicated for them to figure out what he or she stands for, and what he or she is doing in Parliament.

The single-member district system also favors alliances within the district, as it is sufficient to gain the relative majority of votes to be elected. This system, however, does not guarantee consistency at the national level, as elected members – very strong in their districts – may have no cohesion across districts. It may therefore become difficult for Parliament to make decisions at the national level, which is – after all – what elected members are meant to be doing. For this reason, in Great Britain they were unsatisfied with their single-member district system and were considering introducing some sort of proportional rule that mitigates the dispersive local effect and generates a premium for candidates of the same political orientation.

At the other end of the spectrum are systems based on large multi-member districts. Here, candidates of the same political orientation are organized in lists, and members are elected on the basis of the total votes obtained by those lists. Accountability becomes very blurred.

Single or multi-member though the districts may be, a corollary to these systems is the system that is used to decide who the candidates are in each district. It seems a riddle, but it is quite an important step in the electoral process and in the accountability consequences of it.

There are two basic ways to decide who the candidates are: centralized decision-making by some secretariat of political parties and primary elections. In centralized decision-making, the nomination of candidates is usually the responsibility of the political party organizations themselves and does not involve the general public. A primary election is an election in which voters select candidates for a subsequent general election.

The way candidates are selected is a key step in generating loyalty by the candidates and future members of Parliament. It is clear that, under a centralized decision-making system, the elected members will, first, have to be grateful to the party hierarchy and then to their people and their constituencies, since their re-election will depend on the party hierarchy in the first place and only subsequently on the voters. And it is fair to assume that re-election is the first objective of anybody who is elected.

For the sake of accountability, then, the way candidates are selected for the general election becomes more important than the electoral system itself since, in principle, one could run primary elections also within a system of proportional general elections. The basic idea I want to convey here is that primary elections are key in order to generate accountability of elected members of Parliament to their constituencies.

Budgetary shortcuts

We all know that politicians rarely supply a comprehensible, detailed accounting of the work they do and results they obtain, but politics isn't just a question of results; it is also delineated by decision-making processes. So, an accounting of one's work does not consist solely of numbers, but also of a correct process of collective decision-making – something the British call 'due process'. As an example of due process in the private sector, consider the importance of the relationship between a corporation and its stakeholders.

In the public sector, the most important decision-making process concerns the government budget. Traditionally, this yearly ritual would begin with the value of expense increases and then proceed with budget cuts in certain areas. Which areas to cut are decided on the basis of least resistance. In an attempt to rationalize this practice, a government could institute a spending review (as was done in Britain in 2006) whereby each ministry is presented with its budget of the preceding year (baseline) and asked to choose and justify any increases within 2% of the given baseline budget.

Both methods, however, appear to be rather feudal: the individual spending institutions (the ministries, the departments) are seen as a private hunting reserve of their chief (minister or secretary), and there is no evaluation of their achievements, or of their priorities and effectiveness. There is no basis on which to create a (social responsibility) report of government that could delineate the quantity and quality of the work being done by each institution. With no verification or dialectic, with no attempt to quantify, even arbitrarily, the terms of a debate, everything becomes *politique politicienne* and politicking.

It is true that the many civil service sectors account for over a million employees (a two-digit percentage of the working population), making a detailed analysis of the work of each ministry an almost heroic task. Perhaps a starting point would be to apply a reasonable benchmark for personnel in any given area of the public sector: an X number of police or judges per inhabitant; a certain number of teachers per pupil. The difficulty would lie then in the details, in analyzing whether the Coast Guard really needs those extra ships they asked for; whether more teachers in a school will produce something extra in social terms, or what exactly is the social result of a school. The risk is that arbitrary measures are instituted, but doing nothing is worse still.

The basic idea I want to convey here is that an attempt must be made at evaluating the government departments' jobs. The task of accountability is to expose the purposes of government action and attempt to make explicit the expected results. This might be a difficult task, even conceptually; it might be problematic to do so. The tone of the debate would, in any case, be enhanced.

The value of politics

Once an electoral storm is over, the temptation is great to just go back to work as usual – but conclusions must be drawn; debriefings must be held to establish whether the electoral campaign was successful, or what ought to be done when general political disaffection appears to be growing among the electorate.

During an electoral campaign, there is much excess and resulting disgust – as a result of which people begin to believe they want nothing to do with politics; the risk of becoming anti-political is there and, yet, there are reasons to put up with the electoral exercise. Politics – a collection of people and rituals – ought to be appreciated, because it keeps some people out of trouble. It is a good thing to have a non-violent electoral process, a good thing to have a well-paid Parliament. It is useful because it holds off the hoards, the armed bands that would otherwise operate unseen. Politicians are an energetic, charismatic bunch with a mission – at least, they had one in their youth – and they put forth a great deal of effort to bring it to fruition. Without this system we call 'politics' (a system designed to give them social status), these people would express their potential in ways that would be more costly to society as a whole.

Another way to consider national politics is to compare it with a condominium meeting. When we are part of a collective ourselves, we behave just as badly as our politicians, as any condominium member will attest, pointing to the lousy maintenance of one's building. Politics is a glass that should be looked through from the bottom. In mathematical and economical terms, one needs to calculate the 'shadow value' of politics, the cost society would pay if politics did not exist. It would be like living in Afghanistan.

Case study: if you do not measure it, you did not do it
Case study authored by Paolo D'Anselmi, Simone Morganti, Margherita Cappelletto, and Alessio Richichi

How European Union Structural Funds Policy is defined in Lisbon and frustrated in Eboli

Here is a further case about the difficulty of implementing general strategic goals, formulated at the political level and frustrated at the implementation stage. Cases shown here imply no aspiration to originality of methodology; they are only intended to show, in practice, what can be done to make organizations that are not subject to competition more accountable than they are today. They are shown to clarify the proposed concept of organizational CSR in government and in the political arena. The case studied here is an example of weak policy implementation.

The subject matter of this case is an evaluation of the Information Society policy implemented in Southern Italy in the years 2000–06 under the aegis of the Structural Funds of the European Union. A total budget of €1 billion was spent by that program. Implementation of such policies has been taking place under seven-year Framework Programmes 2000–06 and 2007–13. Here, we consider a specific case from the 2000–06 round of funding.

A detailed bottom-up study was conducted that reviewed over 200 tenders and their formulation, coming up with the conclusion that very seldom are the needs specified. Often, they are even part of what is asked of the contractor (i.e. we ask them to tell us what we need). A subjective analysis of tenders was made. Two specific measures were derived that, albeit subjective, can hardly be dismissed in their conceptual foundation: clarity and credibility of tenders' formulation.

Figure 14.1 exemplifies the clarity concept in the formulation of the objective; Figure 14.2 provides further insight into the process of implementation at the regional and local levels – publication dates of tenders have been plotted over time. In the vertical axis the amounts have been plotted. Notice that tendering peaks at the end of the funding period (2006).

No measure of output or outcome is available. Despite the fact that there is a table at the European level that specifies what is meant by 'information society' and lays out indicators whereby the beneficiary countries are also funded, this table is ignored throughout the 'descending' phase of the programming of funds and projects. Never in the programming or the projects are the indicators of what makes an information society recalled. This means it is not possible to make the project at hand consistent with the overall policy and enable the measuring of the effect of funding by the indicators that were used in the first place. Nonetheless, an overall set of country indicators, the 'i2010', was available from 2003 onwards and could profitably be used, but no reference to them whatsoever was made in any stage of the program in Italy or in Europe (Table 14.1).

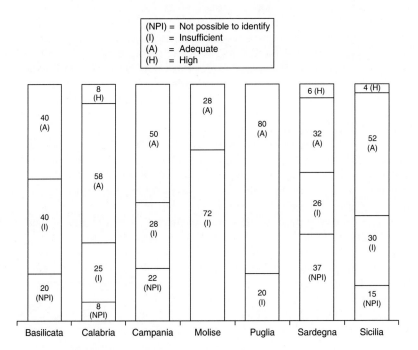

Figure 14.1 Readability of public tenders (%)

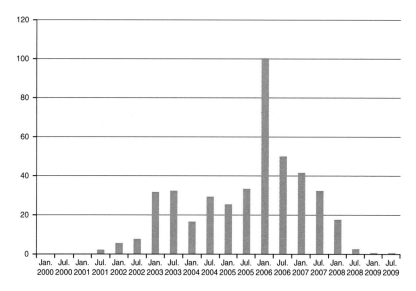

Figure 14.2   Distribution of amounts tendered over time (€ millions per semester)

No measures were developed throughout the whole chain of implementation, which involved the European, the national, the regional and the local levels of implementation. The theory of this goes back to Regina Herzlinger, the American economist and founder of the theory of non-profit organizations in the 1970s. One does not understand how improvement is expected to be achieved. The regional operational plans are vague. Development will, sooner or later, take place. Market forces and general gross national product growth will do their part, but how much of the specific effort will have contributed to this development is wholly questionable.

No quantification is made throughout the line of implementation; neither are specific goals indicated. It is my view that governments at the national, regional and local levels should concentrate their action on indicators and fields aptly monitored by such indicators as are left out by the household and corporate markets for the information society.

Doing so, government could generate projects – and changes – that are measurable, 'monitorable' and defendable, even if they failed to obtain their objectives. What is needed are clearer and stricter frameworks, rather than stricter controls. It would be appropriate to assume a set of indicators and stick to it, deriving from it the projects that would work according to an explicit theory of change (Table 14.2).

The Lisbon policy is a series of statements from the European Union Council of Prime Ministers. Laid out in 2007, it was put into effect in December 2009.

Table 14.1 i2010 indicators for the information society: Italy

	Category	2003	2004	2005	2006	EU25	Rank
1	**Broadband**						
1.1	Total DSL coverage (as % of total population)	82.0	85.0	87.0		87.4	16
1.2	DSL coverage in rural areas (as % of total population)			44.6		65.9	19
1.3	Broadband penetration (as % of total population)	3.2	6.7	10.0	13.6	15.7	13
1.4	DSL penetration (as % of total population)	2.8	6.2	9.4	13.1	12.8	10
1.5	Predominant download speed			0.5–1 Mbps			
1.6	Households having broadband (as % of those having access to the internet at home)			33.6	40.5	62.1	25
1.7	Enterprises with broadband access (%)	31.2	23.3	56.7	69.6	74.5	15
1.8	Number of 3G subscribers per 100 inhabitants			15.3		5.0	2
1.9	Digital television in households			38.7		30.6	5
1.10	Music: number of single downloads per 100 inhabitants			5.5			13
2	**Internet usage**						
2.1	Population who are regular internet users (%)	24.9	25.7	28.3	30.8	46.7	25
3	**Take up of Internet services (as % of population)**						
3.1	Sending emails	–	–	26.5	29.1	43.8	23
3.2	Searching for information about goods and services	–	–	21.2	23.2	42.9	26
3.3	Internet telephoning or videoconferencing	–	–	2.2	3.3	7.1	27
3.4	Playing/downloading games and music	–	–	10.4	10.5	18.2	28
3.5	Listening to the web radio/watching web tv	–	–	4.6	5.3	11.8	27

(continued)

Table 14.1 Continued

	Category	2003	2004	2005	2006	EU25	Rank
3.6	Reading online newspaper/magazines	–	–	12.8	12.8	19.0	24
3.7	Internet banking	–	–	7.6	8.9	22.0	24
4	**Places of access**						
4.1	Home (%)	22.7	21.3	24.2	26.6	42.6	22
4.2	Work (%)	13.6	14.6	15.9	16.7	23.0	23
4.3	Place of education (%)	1.8	4.0	3.8	4.9	8.0	25
4.4	Public Internet access program (%)	0.7	6.0	3.7	4.9	6.8	16
5	**e-Government indicators**						
5.1	Basic public services for citizens fully available online (%)	25.0	27.3	–	36.4	36.8	13
5.2	Basic public services for enterprises fully available online (%)	75.0	87.5	–	87.5	67.8	3
5.3	Population using e-Government services (%)	–	–	14.1	16.1	23.8	20
5.4	of which for returning completed forms (%)	–	–	3.6	5.0	8.1	19
5.5	Enterprises using e-Government services (%)	–	65.0	72.6	86.5	63.7	4
5.6	of which for returning completed forms (%)	34.5	35.4	28.9	49.4	44.8	15
6	**ICT in schools**						
6.1	Number of computers connected per 100 pupils	–	–	–	6.5	9.9	21
6.2	Schools with broadband access (%)	–	–	–	69.0	67.0	17
6.3	Teachers having used the computer in class during the last 12 months (%)	–	–	–	72.4	74.3	14
7	**e-Commerce**						
7.1	e-Commerce as % of total turnover of enterprises	–	–	–	2.0	11.7	20
7.2	Enterprises receiving Internet orders (%)	–	–	–	3.3	13.9	24
7.3	Enterprises purchasing on the Internet (%)	–	–	–	27.1	37.9	12

8	**e-Business (% enterprises)**					
8.1	With integrated internal business processes	11.6	33.1	47.7	46.5	37.3	6
8.2	With integrated external business processes	–	–	–	–	13.5	–
8.3	Security: enterprises using secure servers (%)	34.7	54.7	30.3	39.3	41.0	13
8.4	Using digital signatures for authentication (%)	4.3	10.5	8.8	11.5	14.3	12
9	**Employment and skills**					
9.1	Employees using computers connected to the Internet (%)	24.3	21.5	24.8	28.2	36.1	20
9.2	Persons employed with ICT user skills (%)	22.9	17.6	17.6	19.0	18.5	11
9.3	Persons employed with ICT specialist skills (%)	2.8	2.8	2.9	2.7	3.1	18
10	**Indicators of growth of ICT and R&D**					
10.1	ICT sector share of total GDP	4.8	–	–	–	5.5	15
10.2	ICT sector share of total employment	3.6	–	–	–	4.0	15
10.3	ICT sector growth (constant prices)	1.3	–	–	–	3.6	15
10.4	R&D expenditure in ICT by the business sector, as % of GDP	0.1	–	–	–	0.3	11
10.5	R&D expenditure in ICT by the business sector, as % of total R&D expenditure	22.9	–	–	–	25.7	8

Source: European Commission, i2010, Annual Information Society Report 2007. *A European Information Society for Growth and Employment*, Luxembourg, European Communities, 2007, p. 93.

Table 14.2   Capgemini indicators for e-government

Capgemini indicators
Citizens
1   Income taxes
2   Job search
3   Social Security benefits
4   Personal documents
5   Car registration
6   Application for building permission
7   Declaration to the Police
8   Public libraries
9   Birth and marriage certificates
10 Enrollment in higher education
11 Announcement of moving
12 Health-related service
Businesses
13 Social Contribution for employees
14 Corporate tax
15 VAT
16 Registration of a new company
17 Submission of data to the Statistical Office
18 Customs declaration
19 Environment-related permits
20 Public procurement

Source: Capgemini *et al.* (2006): 4.

Christ stopped at Eboli is the title of the 1945 memoir by Carlo Levi, physician, painter, writer, and communist Jew who, in the years before World War II, was confined by Mussolini near the small village of Eboli, south of Naples, in Italy. The sense of the title of the novel is that civilization never made it to the south of the country. The story is, among other things, one of backwardness and difficult social development.

The sense of this case is that it is very difficult to implement very general and abstract policies. Diligence is required in translating principles into actions. All chains of implementation imply risks that must be factored in the planning phase.

15
Four Fruitful Generalizations: From CSR to Politics

The cases on CSR are actually an analysis in the domain of work

In the previous chapters, we have gained an overview of contemporary work, ranging from large corporations subject to international competition, to local and nationwide monopolies, to private non-profit organizations and, finally, to public administration, government, and the political arena itself. Using the pseudo-aseptic chisel of CSR, we have opened the black box of organizational activities and we have gained a thorough view on work in all its aspects of different economic sectors. In Chapter 1 – on CSR in large international firms – and then in Chapters 11 through 14, we have gained a total view of the economy. Large corporations are often subject to criticism; however, they are subject to each other's competition and, if one does not like Windows, one can always, with some extra effort, turn his own preferences to Linux. Monopolies are harder to control through competition; they are also hard to control through institutions of public administration because it is even more difficult for public administration to lend itself to accountability. The political arena seems to be very competitive but, often, it is competitive within a small set of opportunities and the political class appears as a chaste rather than as a regular set of working people. Private non-profit organizations for their part appear to be subject to competition. We can now draw four fruitful generalizations:

- work evasion exists;
- work evasion includes large proportions of the economy and the work force;
- there is a competitive divide;
- the competitive divide partially explains the contemporary social malaise.

Work evasion exists

Accounting for work is essential in modern society. Our initial hypothesis was that, in CSR, there were some good manners and some philanthropy.

Once we have extended the notion of CSR to all economic sectors of activity in society, however, a deeper picture emerges: good manners do not emerge out of some misinterpretation or misunderstanding about the notion of CSR; they emerge from an inability to work, from the reports and, in the cases from the political arena, the very idea of work comes out blurred, not to mention the measure of work.

We do not know what a good director of a correctional facility looks like; we do not know what a good police precinct chief looks like. Social responsibility reports are empty owing to the absence of communicable matter. We call this phenomenon the 'evasion' of work.

The evasion of work does not exclude the fact that there are a lot of people who do work, and that there are bureaus where a great deal of action takes place. Evasion of work is technical. It is work that is unaccounted for; not measured; potentially, not geared to the needs of society.

Why 'work' and not 'labor'? Because we are speaking of all work: labor has this connotation of blue-collar work and of employee work. We are speaking of all work: self-employed work, entrepreneurial work, executive work. Work. Not labor.

The preceding is not generic disgruntled citizen talk. I have professionalized the discourse here. 'Buck-passing which clients recognize as a symptom of some alleged bureaucratic mentality, is in fact part of the same discourse of accountability, personhood, and superior force. While disgruntled clients blame bureaucrats, the latter blame "the system" and excessively complicated laws' (Herzfeld, 1992).

The theoretical ancestors: Morgenstern, Niskanen *et al.*

The preceding conclusion is very much in accord with the studies of William A. Niskanen (chairman emeritus of the Cato Institute): bureaucracies tend to overproduce and to over-remunerate their production factors. This view is the outcome of the influence of many authors.

This 'weak' theory of CSR reporting is good for the private, public and non-profit sectors. There is no sense in the administrative distinction between the private and public sectors, demonstrated also by the 2009 bail-out of private firms by the public sector. Besides, much of the economy is non-competition-driven, so 'not irresponsibility' reporting is needed. CSR is always present and for everybody: in public, private and non-profit sectors.

Oskar Morgenstern in his 'Thirteen Critical Points' (1972) says that 'the theory of the firm is now solely concerned with physical production and physical output.' Yet, about 60% of the gross national product in the United States arises from non-physical (i.e. service) activities, which are also being organized in firms. How is productivity of an orchestra, a school, a law firm measured? What does 'productivity of a nation' mean under these circumstances? Even within the firms producing physical goods, there are many activities having nothing directly to do with output – conveniently labeled 'overhead' – still further restricting the domain of physical output notions.

In Chapter 9 (p.89), I recalled the theories of Herbert Simon and Harvey Leibenstein. I would like to recall here, specifically, the view of William A. Niskanen (1968), as expressed in his paper 'Non-market decision making – the peculiar economics of bureaucracy'. In this work, and in the numerous subsequent revisions of it, Niskanen devises the economics of the budget maximizing bureaucrat. This hypothesis leads Niskanen to many conclusions that are observed in reality and that, indeed, we have pointed out in our cases. Niskanen also identifies possible corrections, which have been the basis of our case studies in the autarky of public administration, the non-profit sector and irrelevant politics. Bureaucracies tend to overproduce and to cost more than is warranted by their services. Bureaucracies are 'irresponsible', to put it in the language we have adopted here.

Several symptoms of the illnesses of bureaucracy are identified by Niskanen:

- The 'passion of reformers for bureau consolidation': there is an intrinsic motion towards the abolition of competition among bureaus, even by those who are well-meaning in their actions.
- The bureaucrat will not reveal the cost of his or her own operations: when shown, in 2006, the personnel costs we have produced in Chapter 13 (p. 161), the minister responsible for security services said he had tried to obtain the same information himself, but kept getting different answers all the time.
- The politician has a very weak interest in controlling the bureaucrat;
- The bureaucrat has an interest in enhancing demand for his or her own services: this is what gives us 'police day' and other parades.
- Production factors tend to be over-remunerated in bureaucracies: this is what leads to salaries in the public sector being higher – besides being less risky – than in the private sector; also, this is what leads to some government procurement that is costlier than it should be.

The remedies that Niskanen devises are:

- Multiplicity of bureaus; that is, try to implement competition among different bureaus that provide the same product or service – this could be the case of schools or of local health units, whereby the free option of 'clients' would be a surrogate for a market mechanism. The budget of the units should then be proportional, or somehow take into account the freely expressed preferences of the clients; certainly, quality must be controlled and the clients must be informed of the quality of the services they are purchasing, or that they are adopting (in the case of government health programs, for instance) – but, again, these are other tasks of other bureaucracies.

- Mixed budget regime: lump sum and market; that is, have some of the budget of the bureau be earned on the market, so that the value of the part provided by government lump sum funding can easily be assessed.
- A corollary: as we have said, products and services should be measured, assessed and benchmarked. Examples of this kind of work have been provided throughout in the previous chapters.

It is interesting to note that, when speaking of bureaucracies, we tend to identify them with government bureaus. But Niskanen had in mind not only government bureaus, but also all those segments of an organization that are somehow remote from the market. The public relations department is one instance. So, Niskanen's theory is valid for all economic sectors, public and private, monopolistic and competitive. That is why all sectors strive to identify metrics to measure their performance, to obtain guidance in their work and instruments to demonstrate the value of their activity. They 'account for their work'.

Max Weber is the founder of organizational sociology – no question about that. But Max Weber's view of the organizational mechanism is no longer a useful tool with which to predict organizational behavior. Though Weber and his works are quoted as though they were right, and administrative and legal cultures around the world are based on this assumption, common observation shows otherwise.

Work evasion is pandemic

The evasion of work includes large proportions of the economy and the work force. Summarizing all the cases that we have presented in the previous chapters, we can present a taxonomy according to the economic environment whereby work is performed. We can therefore proceed to an example where we run the numbers of the evasion of work, calculating who is and who is not subject to competition in a large Western economy.

In Chapter 5, we presented a taxonomy of organizational sectors as an instrument with which to identify potential irresponsibility on the part of an organization, according to the competitive environment:

- government sector (public non-profit sector);
- regulated for-profit private sector (monopoly or subject to moderate competition);

- non-profit associative private sector (not subject to competition: entrepreneurial associations and trade unions);
- non-profit private sector (subject to competition);
- for-profit private sector (subject to competition);
- SMEs – (small and medium-sized enterprises).

It is interesting here to quantify the number of jobs in the different sectors. Therefore, we present the following case study.

Case study: the prevalence of competition in society

Running the numbers in an economy of 23 million workers

In this case, a detailed example is provided of who is and who is not subject to competition in a relatively large national economy: a list of jobs by category, indicating who is subject to competition and who is not. The idea here is to name all work categories and assign them to one or the other side of the competitive divide: subject/not subject to competition. It is clear that there will be grey areas. Identification of individual numbers is a bottom-up process. However, we reconcile the numbers with top-down statistics from the census bureau (Table 15.1).

From Table 15.1 we get our basic proportions about the head count of jobs:

- more than 25% non-competitive;
- less than 75% competitive.

The sum total of this exercise is that, in an economy with 23 million workers, 17 million are subject to competition and 6 million are not. In public debate, journalists have twice questioned these numbers as 'optimistic'; that is, they thought the workers not subject to competition totaled more than our estimate. That shows our estimate to be conservative, which is a good position for our argument.

An expression of the general sentiment about workers' quantities is to be found in the 2008 French bestselling novel *L'élégance du hérisson* – at some point, the protagonist cannot help exclaiming: 'Too many railway men, too few plumbers!'

There is a competitive divide among workers

Those who are subject to competition do account for their work; those who are not subject to competition must account for their work in other ways; societies can be characterized by the 'competitive divide.' We contend that what really makes a difference in work – and in society as a whole – is the presence and the vivaciousness of a dialectic between workers subject to competition and workers not subject to competition. The competitive divide

Table 15.1 The prevalence of competition in society: running the numbers in an economy of 23 million workers

Synthesis:

1	Agriculture	1,018,000
2	Industry	6,942,000
3	Services	15,040,000
	Total economy	**23,000,000**

	Activity	Detail on services	Detail on services	Subject to competition	Not subject to competition	Total
1	**Agriculture**			1,018,000		1,018,000
2	**Industry**					6,942,000
	Industry			5,000,000		
	Defense and electronic systems conglomerate				90,000	
	Construction			1,852,000		
3	**Services**			8,900,453	6,139,547	15,040,000
	Not subject to competition		6,139,547			
	Banking		340,865			
	Insurance (excluding agents and their employees)		170,433			
3.1.1	Telecom company		85,000			
	Highway company		10,000			
	State television		20,000			
	Air traffic control company		5,000			
	Air traffic oversight agency		5,000			
	State air company		20,000			
	Other companies within state-owned industrial conglomerate		20,000			

State railway company		95,000
State postal service		90,000
State-owned electric power conglomerate		90,000
State-owned oil and power conglomerate		50,000
Muni's – local utility companies, of which		490,181
Electric power	8,994	
Gas	8,415	
Water	23,649	
Sanitation/garbage collection and environmental services	38,376	
Transportation	71,197	
Pharmacies	3,550	
Culture and tourism	6,000	
Housing	7,000	
Health care	323,000	
Other transportation		50,000
Automobile club		10,000
Road vehicle registration agency		5,000
Port authorities, inter-ports, airports		50,000
Pharmacy stores		14,000

(continued)

186

Table 15.1 Continued

	Activity	Detail on services	Detail on services	Subject to competition	Not subject to competition	Total
	Others:		700,000			
	In-house companies of local government					
	Public–private consortia					
	State ICT procurement corporation					
	State ICT corporation					
	Notary publics					
	Journalists					
	Lawyers					
3.1.2	Politicians		179,485			
	Labor union representatives		20,000			
3.1.3	Central and local government employees:		3,619,583			
3.2	**Subject to competition**		**8,900,453**			
	Coffee shop owners		150,000			
	Other small businesses		451,041			
	Shops		2,000,000			
	Street vendors		500,000			
	Insurance (agents and their collaborators)		170,000			
	Micro-enterprises		5,000,000			
3.3	Non-profit sector		629,412			
	TOTAL			16,770,453	6,229,547	23,000,000

is more important than left and right, agent or principal, public or private, or the master–slave class struggle.

These concepts are borrowed from the concept of the dual labor market developed in the 1970s by the MIT economists and philosophers Michael Piore and Charles Sabel.

The theory of a dual labor market divides the economy into primary and secondary sectors. Distinction may also be made between the formal and informal sectors, or between sectors with high/low value-added. The secondary sector is characterized by short-term employment relationships where there is little or no prospect of promotion within the organization, and where wages are primarily determined by market forces. This sector consists primarily of low-skill or unskilled jobs characterized by low earnings, easy entry, impermanent jobs and low returns to education or experience. Labor in the informal economy is often recompensed equally informally – i.e. 'under-the-table,' tending to attract the poor and a disproportionate number of minority group members.

Indeed, the competitive divide leads to an 'accountability divide'. This is a new frontier in the domain of privilege, defining new groups of haves and have-nots: those who do not account for their work and those who do. An issue of equality is at stake here. Equality *vis-à-vis* the basic tenets of constitutions (De Ros, 2010).

What does 'accounting for work' mean? It means performing work that is immersed in an evaluation process, be it a market mechanism or a pseudo-market mechanism (i.e. meritocracy), an evaluation process of its social utility, preferably an international one, when government jobs are implied, as local standards may be entirely out of scale even at a national level.

Accountability is transparency, and being able to respond and justify work actions (Mays, 2010).

We work with rough variables. Accounting for work is a proxy for the social utility of work; the reverse may not be true. This need only be true in the intervals we are considering here.

We call accounting for work as 'good' – maybe 'less bad' would be better; what matters are the differences in the social contribution of different jobs and different positions *vis-à-vis* competition, accounting and dialectics. What is also important is the practical import of those differences, the impact that they have and the existence of an opportunity to amend that state of the economy and of society. So, we are talking tactics, here; implementation, as discussed in Chapter 7.

One way to look at the impact of unaccountability is to look at the World Bank Governance Indicators. The test of this reasoning is its effectiveness in amending situations stigmatized by those indicators.

As there is a 'Stalin's barber' syndrome (i.e. being oblivious to the damage to the social fabric carried out by virtue of one's own work), the reverse is also true: positive social contribution is often made unawares. Adam Smith, the Scottish social philosopher and a pioneer of political economy, came up with the classic case of a brewer who only cares for his profit – but, in so doing, benefits society with a good product, one that people are willing to pay for. So, the opposite of Stalin's barber is Adam Smith's brewer – lack of awareness being their common denominator.

The competitive divide partially explains the contemporary social malaise

The problem of the accountability of work may have something to do with the claimed unsatisfactory nature of contemporary life. In the words of Zygmunt Bauman's *Does Ethics Have a Chance in a World of Consumers?* (2008), human beings despair of a 'final victory' in their quest for making sense out of human existence.

We would like to use for this phenomenon the term "malaise", which US President Jimmy Carter used at the end of the 1970s to describe a general sense of loss in society.

People seem to long for a 'steady state' in their life and in society. Paradoxically, this longing for a steady state appears to be stronger in the wishes of those who are not subject to competition. For example, 'stable work' is often invoked by those who aspire to public sector tenured jobs. In fact, the longing for a steady state is presented by Ludwig Von Mises, the Austrian economist and philosopher, as a characteristic of bureaucratic behavior. Thus, we find the link between malaise and the competitive divide. Social malaise can be a result of non-accountability of work. Those who are subject to competition are not immune from such moral predicament; however, they are distracted from it, being busy working.

From CSR to politics: interdisciplinary work and anti-politics

The undertaking we have been conducting in the previous pages is pervasive. When criticizing an entire political establishment using instruments that are non-conventional, 'life is not easy and the accusation of being anti-political is behind the corner' (Alessandro Ferrara, Italian philosopher, currently Professor of Political Philosophy at the University of Rome Tor Vergata, December 6, 2008).

Anti-politics is when all possibilities are denied for a political class and are liquidated with statements such as: 'They are all corrupt, they only seek their own personal power.' Being anti-political is a mistake, and anti-political arguments are not worth considering; they are dismissed. So, the accusation of being anti-political is a very bad one.

Context specific definitions of anti-politics are Poujadisme (a conservative reactionary movement to protect the interests of small traders) and Know-Nothing.

However, there has to be a way to infer generalities based on facts – to be meaningful, rather than anti-political.

Today's risk of being anti-political nests in a schizophrenia that has us nodding in agreement with the punctual charges made by journalists on the front page of the papers, and then has us plugging our nose and accepting the generic vision of society proposed by our politicians, however badly it reflects our daily routine. It's a sort of post-indifference, if you wish, since the problem isn't just political but, more than anything, cultural. It's an attempt to reconcile being human and thinking in an individual way with the means undertaken to earn a living.

Sometimes, however, 'the accusation of being anti-political is leveled by the vague to those who are specific,' and Ferrara (2008b) acknowledges this may happen in our case. The accusation of anti-politics often springs out at the interface between disciplines. Interdisciplinary work calls for that accusation.

Ours is also a legitimate approach to a political view of society that derives from considerations generated by disciplines other than political science and other human sciences.

Our view is not 'anti-political'. Our belief is that power is like the air: it occupies all available space. When power is not strongly held or democratically held, much worse conditions arise, as we have argued in Chapter 14 (p. 172).

In his new essay on William Niskanen's theory of bureaucracy, uneasiness with the not-so-smooth workings of democracy has been effectively researched and described by Andrea Lapiccirella in the framework of the interrupted triangle of democratic governance. Bureaucracies operate within the framework of the so-called 'broken triangle of governance' (Figure 15.1)

There is no printing error in the diagram: the two-way arrow between the citizens and politics represents a dialectic relationship between the two parties involved. The one-way arrow between the citizens and the bureaucracies

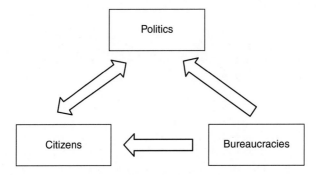

Figure 15.1 The so-called 'broken triangle of governance'

means that the citizens have no way to influence the bureaucracies. The one-way arrow between politics and the bureaucracies means that politicians do not have sufficient incentives to control bureaucracies effectively.

While there is at least a formal dialectic between the citizens and politicians – which takes place at election time, and approves, with the vote of the former, the political program of the latter – there is no control of politicians over the bureaucracies, neither is there control of the citizens, and bureaucracies behave *vis-à-vis* politics (and the citizens) as a perfect monopolist (this key variation was suggested by the American economist Gordon Tullock to William Niskanen). Bureaucracies are virtually independent of both citizens and politicians, who ideally should exert control over them. This model overrides the Max Weber civil servant mystique, which assumed government bureaucracy to be an optimal and rational provider of goods and services.

Reality, however, is still very much Weberian. I observe that administrative law is based on the Max Weber model of rational bureaucracy: when it comes to defining the tasks of bureaucracy, law in general – and administrative law specifically – implicitly assume that bureaucracies will literally implement law and will put forth a *per se* optimal effort; optimal from the point of view of efficient use of resources and effective impact on society as desired by the law itself. A usual consequence of this can be observed when additional tasks are asked of bureaucracies and new resources are needed, revealing that the relevant organization is assumed to be operating on the feasibility frontier.

Sociologists appear to be willing to kill Weber with Weber. In fact – when approaching inequality in our society – there is still the expectation that Weber should work and reality is seen as a deviation from what Weber had said it should be. There is wonder when Weber patently does not work any longer (Bauman, 2008). Also, emphasis on the rules (rather than on work) to ameliorate the quality of the social environment appears to be a post-Weberian approach (Abravanel, 2008).

Stakeholders of what? The cost of non-government

We have already seen the headcount. The prevalence of potential social conflict. What is at stake, however; what are the quantities at stake? Let us measure the quantitative potential of this conflict.

This section presents macro-numbers of an economy that are relevant to our argument: salaries of workers not subject to competition are more relevant than profits of corporations. Work and productivity is a more relevant issue than the labor–capital dialectic.

Table 15.2 and Figure 15.2 present the percentile share of income between labor and capital; then, the share of labor is divided into competitive and non-competitive labor. It is then shown that the extra profit of non-competitive work is quantitatively higher, or at least comparable with, the

Table 15.2 Quantitative example

	Subject to competition (€/billion)	Not subject to competition (€/billion)	Total (€/billion)
GDP			1,300
Capital	100		
Government debt	100		
Government salaries		200	
Monopoly salaries		200	
Salaries earned in the competitive sectors	700		
Proportions of income			
Capital vs. labor:	(100 + 100) = 200 vs. 1,100 = less than 20%		
Non-competitive salaries vs. competitive salaries:	400 vs. 700 = circa 35% vs. 65%		
Proportion of jobs			
Non-competitive: 25%			
Competitive: 75%			

actual profits from capital. Therefore, the battle is better fought against non-competitive work than against over-remunerated capital – which can always fly abroad, whereas labor is going to be much less mobile, especially non-competitive labor. We see that non-competitive work appropriates a share

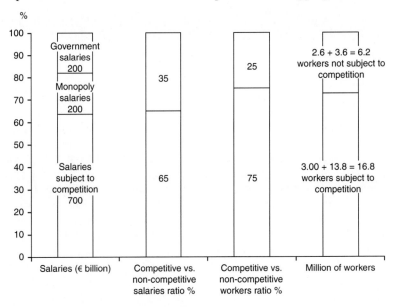

Figure 15.2 Quantitative example, €/billion

of income higher than its head count, 35% vs. 25%, when their pension plans are also taken into account (Parks, 2010). If it were to appropriate its 'fair share' – corresponding to the head count of 25% – it would appropriate about €100 billion less than it appropriates today.

This €100 billion is the extra revenue of non-competitive jobs: this is what Niskanen calls the extra cost of production factors in non-competitive environments.

For those who are subject to competition, then, it appears therefore more fruitful to fight over-remunerated labor than to fight capital. Capital can fly away. Labor can't.

The idea here is not so much for those who are subject to competition to appropriate the extra revenue of those who are not subject to competition as it is to bring to fruition for society the full productivity of work from those who are not subject to competition. Thus, the calculation is a minimum estimate of the social value that is redeemable when competition – or better, accountability – is established within society.

The calculations in the explication of Table 15.2 were income-based. On the other hand, impact-based calculations lead to much larger numbers. It has been estimated that one third of gross domestic product is lost for lack of infrastructure, lack of purpose in government, modest schooling systems, and lack of competition in services (Nardozzi, 2010).

'Communicating vessels'

The statement formulated in the preceding paragraphs appears to be a very crude argument, but it is exactly what is to be found in the words of pundit journalist Eugenio Scalfari, founder of *La Repubblica*, a leftist newspaper in Italy. You do not necessarily have to call it 'competition' to arrive at the point of accounting for work. In July 2010, the pundit writes the following:

> Is there a way to compensate for the loss of welfare of the weak class in the affluent countries? Yes there is and it is the following: make the communicating vessels system work not only at the international level, for international competition, between countries, but also at the national level, within individual countries. Take Italy, an affluent country where there are still enclaves of evident poverty (not only in the South of the country) and intolerable differences in the echelon of incomes and of individual wealth. Between the Italy of the affluent strata of the population and the Italy of the poor, the communicating vessels system is stuck. It does not work. Wealth that is produced is not redistributed. It reflows on itself and feeds the regressive system of making the rich richer and the poor poorer. A policy of common wealth would dismantle this perverse circle spiral and start a virtuous circle. Through a fiscal reform that redistributes welfare.

The case in point is precisely a case of international competition. Justice is seen by the leftist journalist in the 'equalization' among national workers. He uses the image of 'communicating vessels', which is another way to speak about the equalizing effect of competition.

The cure is different; the diagnosis too – the idea of the communicating vessels is the same. I have called it 'competition.' The pundit calls it 'communicating vessels.'

He sees the poor: I see those who are subject to competition. He see the (undefined) rich: I see those who are not subject to competition. He sees fiscal reform: I see more competition; we see accounting for work.

The basic idea is the same: one section of the country walking on the shoulders of another section. The other basic idea is key: this is the only way to fight international competition. This is the only response that is adequate.

16
What Is To Be Done? Developing a Political Agenda for Small and Medium-Sized Enterprises

A latent energy lies at the heart of many economies of the world: that energy is the positive value of competition through which hundreds of millions of people live their daily occupations. Being subject to competition, they are accountable for their work. Competition, then, is a powerful driver of responsibility. Many other workers in the same economies are less accountable to positive social or economic forces: the workers of regulated industries, monopolies and public administration, or government. However, tapping the energy of competition is a difficult task, as competition is a tricky force that is hated by those very people who live with it: in fact, in public and private discourse competition is quite often preceded by a scary adjective: 'cut-throat'. Hence, cut-throat competition. Thus, economic units subject to competition fail to bring that value to bear in the social and political arena, thereby failing to turn their weakness – being subject to competition – into an opportunity (i.e. asking that all workers be subject to a form of competition or accountability). This predicament delivers a deficit of meritocracy in society, a deficit of effectiveness in governments' action, and lack of efficiency in protected and regulated industries. The end result is an overall weakness in the economies affected by such deficit, a competitive disadvantage. I have shown, through cases in capsule form, the differences of accountability in the diverse sectors of the economy; to quantify the potential; to identify the hindrances that prevent the coming of competition as a factor of social and political advancement within each country; and, finally, to reveal those economic actors that could benefit from gaining awareness of being subject to competition, thus questioning the negative aura that pervades the value of competition and turning that value into a positive one.

Competition is lived within the narrow limits of vertical industries and international trade debate. Thus, it is only characterized as a constraint. Competition should be brought to bear horizontally, among different economic sectors, within the boundaries of each country and nation, in order to make governments accountable for their actions and regulated industries efficient in their functioning. When accountable, and therefore on their way to becoming efficient and effective – the governments' equivalent of being subject to competition, governments, infrastructure and monopolies contribute to the competitive advantage of nations. The logic of collective action (i.e. structured self-interest) thus delivers SMEs as a key stakeholder in embracing the value of competition and in its observation by those sectors of the economy and the institutions that today do not observe it. SMEs are too small to be studied, too many to be ignored, too fragmented to be helped. The value of SMEs lies only in their efficiency in the role of a shock absorber in the economy, but this only brings vague statements of principle. Through the force of competition, the representative bodies of SMEs have an opportunity to become full-field stakeholders in the political arena to make governments effective and regulated industries efficient.

Starting from CSR – CSR, analyzing what CSR is, what it is not, and what I'd like it to be, I extend CSR to all organizations in the economy (private businesses and public institutions) and thus I develop the concept of 'accounting for work' as a duty for everybody within society. Such a duty brings to the political and economic foreground the struggle between work subject to competition and work performed under monopoly privilege. Once the political arena is redefined along these lines, SMEs become protagonists in the debate for the advancement of society. There is a potential benefit here for SMEs to harvest, and all they have to do is become aware of the value of the competition/accountability that they already embody. With no extra work, they can gain advancement in society.

In each specific economy, over 25% of the workforce is not subject to competition, and is only subject to very few accountability measures on their work. Nearly 75% of the workforce is neglecting this reality. When such a pervasive criticism is leveled at such a large part of society, the possible causes must be outlined; a perspective must be given of possible change and a reason for collective action must be found. In this section, I report a possible set of causes of such a situation; I then identify such forces in the reality of competition, horizontal competition – as will be explained later – within national states (countries), and I identify the stakeholders of such value (competition) in the representative bodies of SMEs.

Seventeen million working people are subject to competition and are not utilizing this force as a cohesive reason for social and political action. This is hardly a new fact: the situation has always been like this. We are simply revealing a particular and contemporary aspect of it; we are revealing the latency of this potential. Professor Alessandro Ferrara, in: 'Weaknesses of democratic political culture in Italy' (1999), identifies a set of causes for this situation. Here are the four weaknesses:

- the charisma of he who is invested with power as a moral background institution;
- the elitist '*basso continuo*': the general acceptance by a vast and disorganized majority of a small, active and well-organized minority;

- history will be the judge: the elite consider themselves accountable only to history, not the people;
- avoid tough political confrontation for fear of a civil war.

These weaknesses refer to the general problem of democratic political action, and I propose that they are an apt example with which to introduce further explanation of the predicament of workforce inaction. I have identified a small sub-set of democratic weakness: the evasion of work. I look at the evasion of work as an economic problem, a specific economic problem arising from the specific institutional and organizational arrangement of the government and the monopolistic sectors of the economy. So, I am in search of an economic cause that may also have a political import. And I am in search of stakeholders that might be moved by such economic force.

What, then, is the force that will move society towards accountability? Horizontal competition is the answer. This force will be the self-interest and the collective action of those who are subject to vertical competition *vis-à-vis* those who are not. Horizontal competition is the competition between those who are, in their work, subject to vertical competition and those who are not subject to such vertical competition. Horizontal competition is a force more relevant to the economy than the owner–employee, public–private, left–right, labor–capital dialectic. We could call it power struggle, as well. Vertical competition exists because many want to sell to few; horizontal competition exists because social groups – differing by their position *vis-à-vis* competition – still compete with each other to appropriate shares of national income, for instance: public sector workers' salaries are driven by different mechanisms than those regulating the salaries of private sector workers; nonetheless, there is a struggle between private sector workers and public sector workers to increase their own salaries, one at the expense of the other. This is horizontal competition.

One question is always asked about CSR: 'Why bother?' My argument answers this question through horizontal competition: all institutions must account for their work because it is in the self-interest of those who are subject to competition that those who are not subject to competition account for their work as well. This is a 'straw in thy neighbor's eye' approach, noticing that 'virtue is its own reward' does not enjoy good reviews.

The ghost of competition

'Vertical competition' is a driver of accountability. Vertical competition is the struggle among companies engaged within each industry and within the same economic sector. This is the competition we are usually accustomed to think about; the competition that brings producers (but not consumers) unwelcome phenomena such as price cutting, international relocation and imports. Vertical competition is central to the process of accounting for work because vertical competition in and of itself makes work accountable – if not instantly valuable from a social point of view, at least subject to social scrutiny. Vertical competition certifies accountability. It does not guarantee society that the firm or the organization will behave correctly, but it does guarantee society that – having the opportunity to adopt competing goods and services – it can do without the bad company. Competition does not rule out the need for CSR awareness, management and reporting.

There is a lack of awareness of competition: those who are subject to competition are not aware of it and do not 'use' this important value. Competition is, however, prevalent in our societies and economies; as we have seen in one of the largest world economies (in terms of gross domestic product), nearly 75% of the work force and their jobs is subject to competition. Competition is a sort of ghost: it is there, it is prevalent, but nobody sees it; and competition is only evoked for special purposes. The key purpose for evoking competition is 'vertical' competition. What is vertical competition?

Vertical competition

Competition is mostly evoked as 'vertical' competition – that is, competition within a specific industry – when a specific firm has problems competing in its industry, or when an industry in one country has problems keeping up with international competition. In both cases, competition is dubbed as 'cut-throat' competition.

Cut-throat competition: giving competition a name

Cut-throat competition. Unfair competition. The idea of competition evokes Darwinian images of jungles and 'the survival of the fittest' according to the theory of evolution, and Hobbesian fighting (the philosopher Thomas Hobbes described the state of nature as one where man is a wolf to his fellow man – '*homo homini lupus*,' he said in Latin). Competition still resents the twenty-first century culture of social Darwinism: a cut-throat vision of life where progress is linked with the survival of the fittest; whereas a twentieth-century (rather a twenty-first-century) view of society and the economy is that the fittest need the less fit as well. In a world with over six billion people, everyone is much less in relation with nature as they are with one another.

Competition is a social order; it is not only made of rules. Competition is about work and all that lies within the framework of rules. Rules tell us mostly what must not be done. Work is what has to be done. 'Competition' is a difficult term. In fact, students over time have used other terms to mean the same set of economic and social circumstances. Let's study a few examples in order, at the same time, to clarify our interpretation of this word: competition.

Alfred Marshall himself (the founder of neo-classical micro-economics) was shy about using it. In the introduction to his *Principles of Economics* (2010), he proposes Freedom of Industry and Enterprise, or more briefly,

Economic Freedom. Competition seemed somewhat cannibalistic to him, and he wanted to underline the fact that, when and where there is competition, there a great deal of room for cooperation. One hundred and twenty years after the sound doubts of Alfred Marshall, we can say that Economic Freedom appears to us as vague terminology, and that we can profitably use an amended notion of competition: only when there is competition is there room for voluntary – and, therefore, effective – cooperation.

Still on the virtues that competition is supposed to bring about, it has been proposed that, instead of competition, there is need for its opposite: respect of civil servants for their fellow citizens; social cohesion and social capital (Ruggeri, 2010; Micelli, 2010). In one word, the virtues outlined can be summarized in the term 'civicness', proposed by Robert Putnam (1993).

I fully agree with this interpretation; that this is what is needed – irrespective of how we name it. Our proposal to bring about competition where civicness is absent is only due to Niskanen's observations: it is difficult to build civicness where social norm is absent. Competition is one way to bring about social norm where it is absent. Competition is meant to bring about in civil service the same consideration we receive when we enter a coffee shop. To build fair competition into a society has important implications on definitions, norm and values. For instance, competition is a herald of social justice, as is proposed in the following concept of 'communicating vessels.'

Referring to society as 'Communicating vessels' means to look at different classes and social groups as part of a whole: nobody should be left behind; no group should prosper while others are suffering; affluent groups should share their fortune with less well-to-do groups. Communicating vessels: the image is from physics. The level of water in communicating vessels is the same and must be the same for equilibrium to be present; when we pour water into one vessel, water spontaneously flows into the other vessels until the level is the same everywhere and equilibrium is restored. The idea is clear, and it reminds us of another ancient image: the parts and the whole of the human body.

The idea of communicating vessels sounds like a modern revival of the legend about the speech that Menenius Lanatus Agrippa made to the seceded plebs on the Aventine Hill in 494 BC: 'society is like a human body, all sections of society are like the limbs of the human body: they all contribute in the same way to the welfare of society.'

Competition is meant also to be a herald of meritocracy – another synonym. Competition stands for scrutiny, obtained through rules and/or social norm.

'Benchmark' is yet one more synonym for competition. Comparison is the basic method of benchmarking, and comparison is the first step of competition. It may not lead to choosing one supplier instead of another; it may not have immediate economic consequences: we can however affirm that benchmarking as well is a very close approximation of competition.

So far, we have seen alternative terms to competition that are meant to signify exactly what competition is about. There are also instances of pejorative terms used to mean phenomena that might not be seen as negative at all but, rather, fair. Take, for instance, 'international financial speculation,' it is meant to be a pejorative behavior, but one could interpret it as 'the right punishment for peoples and their governments who can't get their act together and can't give themselves some financial discipline, and therefore need someone from outside to remind them'. Those who do not have self-discipline will, sooner or later, get just plain discipline.

Not even on the negative side is competition granted its own role. In fact, deviances from (fair) competition are not identified as such but, rather, are given specific names and are seldom related to the absence of competition. Take the 'conflict of interest' in connection with government officials. This is where a government official also holds meaningful financial interests in the economy that are under his or her potential influence, or a government official is appointed to an oversight job and might also be appointed to the (better paid) job he is supposed to oversee. These are instances of absence of (fair) competition.

An alternative view of competition can also be gained through a view of the absence of competition. We could ask those who are excluded from competing, those who never entered a fair race: the unemployed who are excluded from work by guaranteed laborers, travelers of mass transit who suffer unfair competition from cars that do not bear the full cost of pollution and congestion, and who suffer disservice from the strikes of guaranteed transit drivers; gifted potential immigrants who suffer the measures against illegal immigrants, and the absence of a fair immigration policy and implementation of it; gifted candidates in some pseudo-competitive civil service contest; young professionals having problems accessing closed-shop professions; the citizens themselves who are excluded from the opportunity to propose candidates for general elections. Corruption is the absence of competition, crime is non-competitive. We may conclude that competition is cut-throat when it is absent.

A horizontal view of competition

However, not only vertical competition is at work here, but also 'horizontal competition.' 'Horizontal competition' is the struggle between different industries and sectors of society to appropriate shares of national income (i.e. the objective of vertical competition among individual companies is to prevail on competitor companies and win shares of vertical markets). But competition also takes place (in a less evident way, but with no less impact on income) on an aggregate level, between entire sectors of society: public administration – for instance – vs. private companies. Originally, CSR came into being through the pressure of public institutions on private corporations: this pressure was one instance of 'horizontal competition' between different economic sectors (public institutions forcing private businesses to do something for society, therefore also for the workers of public administration). Once the duty of accountability is extended to all economic sectors (public and private sectors, for-profit and non-profit), horizontal competition between economic sectors becomes the crucial driver of accountability. A reverse process can take place: sectors subject to competition (i.e. private companies) could demand accountability from those sectors that are not subject to vertical competition (i.e. the public sector) with the objective of reaping a benefit from better work and more socially profitable work by the public sector.

I expanded on the notion of vertical competition in order to clarify the notion of horizontal competition, which is the case in point here.

I hypothesize that there is little awareness of horizontal competition in society because this kind of competition has not been formulated in a positive way, under a positive value, such as I propose here: the positive value of competition. Horizontal competition in society has often been framed in a negative way, as class hatred or as social envy, or as class struggle and class conflict.

However, many of the positive definitions of competition given – civicness, meritocracy, communicating vessels – embody within themselves a horizontal view of competition (i.e. a view of competition 'across' industries and economic sectors, just as we have evoked at the beginning of this chapter: a large section of the workforce walking on the shoulders of the others).

So, the competition we want to evoke here is horizontal competition that takes place among different economic sectors of society, just as we have shown in the previous chapters of this book: jobs and workers not subject to competition are subsidized by jobs and workers subject to competition. Nothing is more horizontal than a communicating vessel: they express horizontality between distant objects.

Competition is meritocracy: it is not cheating, it is observance of rules; it is transparency; it is not corruption; it is not favoritism. Competition in the economy is like competition in sports, those who lose are poorer, but do not die: the winners still need someone to play the next time around. In the economy, you always need consumers.

Put like this, it looks like a dream, but it is a dream come true: nearly three quarters of the economy and of the jobs are subject to competition and happen under the fairy-tale rules described. Think of coffee shops; think of department stores; think of car makers where there are no barriers, or 'voluntary restrictions' to imports; think of the infinite number of service jobs where, as consumers, we have the opportunity of changing our supplier. Complaints do happen, cheating does happen – but we can change. Once we are not satisfied with some product or service, we can change. This is the infinite reality of small and medium-sized companies and of large international companies subject to international competition.

A different acceptance than Marshall's

Alfred Marshall introduces the notion of vertical and horizontal competition:

> This competition is primarily 'vertical': it is a struggle for the field of employment between groups of labor belonging to different grades, but engaged in the same branch of production, and enclosed, as it were, between the same vertical walls. But meanwhile 'horizontal' competition is always at work, and by simpler methods: for, firstly, there is great freedom of movement of adults from one business to another within each trade; and secondly, parents can generally introduce their children into almost any other trade of the same grade with their own in their neighborhood. (Marshall, 2010)

These are different interpretations from my accepted understanding of the words 'vertical' and 'horizontal.' In my sense, both of Marshall's 'competitions' would still be included within vertical competition. By horizontal competition I refer to what Marx called 'class struggle;' that is, the struggle between different strata (if you see one above the other) of society, or between different vertically juxtaposed sectors of the economy.

Partitioning the workforce

The workforce in the economy can therefore be partitioned horizontally between that part of it which is subject to vertical competition and that part of it which is not subject to vertical competition. The notion of 'competitive divide' is thus derived: the work of workers, employees and executives who are not subject to vertical competition enjoys a shelter *vis-à-vis* the work of those who are subject to competition. Therefore, those who are not subject to competition must give account of their work through the introduction of vertical competition or through pseudo-market mechanisms, such as CSR reporting and benchmarking. Somehow, the work and the jobs that are not subject to competition must account for the validity of their social contribution, basically through virtual vertical competition (benchmarking) and transparency reporting.

What is accountability? Accountability is responsiveness to demand; it is work effort, transparency, customer sovereignty, reciprocal trust, measure, multiplicity of alternatives, social utility of work. Competition is a driver of accountability.

From an empirical point of view, SMEs and the majority of workers and jobs in the economy are on the competitive side of the 'competitive divide'; monopolistic sectors, such as the government sector, are on the non-competitive side of the competitive divide.

In order to generate inter-sector dynamics, it is useful to gain an overall view of the working population. Figure 16.1 illustrates the basic concept of our proposal: competition drives accountability. Therefore, the different 'work

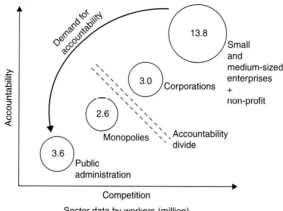

Figure 16.1   Competition drives accountability

groups' that comprise society are set in the competition–accountability plane. The group most subject to competition, SMEs, has self-interest in demanding accountability from the groups located near the origin of the plane.

So, who is the unknown stakeholder of this country-level game? Which is the social class oblivious to the fact that is not getting its fair share of the game?

Doing the numbers is a fertile operation: you 'see' the different categories and potential stakeholders. Specific institutions are identified: the organizations that represent small enterprises. SMEs are subject to competition. So they account for work. It is in the interest of SMEs and of their employees that all workers in the economy account for their work.

I identify a sub-set of the 17 million workers and their jobs that are subject to competition: the small ones, SMEs. In the same economy, out of 17 million jobs subject to competition, there are 8 million VAT codes assigned to either businesses or individuals, meaning entrepreneurial activity at all levels; among these there are 2.6 million small and micro-enterprises under the aegis of traditional representative bodies.

First, let us define the dimensions of SMEs. A 2003 Commission Recommendation of the European Union recognizes micro-enterprises as an economic reality. These are the self-employed. The micro entrepreneurs, with fewer than 10 full-time employees. Medium-sized enterprises have 50 to 249 employees; small enterprises, 10 to 49 employees, and large enterprises over 250 employees:

> Micro, small and medium-sized enterprises are socially and economically important, they represent 99% of an estimated 23 million enterprises in the EU and provide around 75 million jobs representing two-thirds of all employment. SMEs contribute up to 80% of employment in some industrial sectors, such as textiles, construction or furniture. (Commetrics.com)

The small enterprises were not exemplified in the CSR stories in the previous chapters. Did I forget them? Who are the small ones, what does the daily life of a small entrepreneur look like? What is the profile of the small and micro-enterprise? Micro, small and medium-sized enterprises differ from the listed and the large corporations in some important aspects. Let's dwell for a second on micro-enterprises.

Small is not beautiful, but it is useful

The main driver of micro-enterprise is unemployment: you become a micro-entrepreneur – a self-employed person – most probably because of the impossibility of living within a large company (push), rather than by being driven by the mirage of making money or attracted by the economic and human adventure that micro-enterprise nonetheless is (pull). This is the reality of many one-man companies and of owner-operators, for instance. Of the many who become self-employed after receiving a bonus exit payment from a down-sizing corporation. Of the many professionals who want to establish their own practice (e.g. lawyers, accountants). There can be, however, a cultural and ideological positive effect in some regions whereby being an entrepreneur, no matter how self-exploiting, constitutes a positive social value and an element of pride.

Self-exploitation by the entrepreneur is, in fact, a key factor in micro-enterprise: a factor of flexibility, when income is not enough and, conversely, a factor of productivity. Long working hours are a typical lifestyle of the micro-entrepreneur.

The small entrepreneurs are not necessarily nice guys, however. It is interesting to notice the divergence – or the absence of convergence – of nicety with positive social contribution. Saul Bellow's volume *Mosby's Memoirs* provides two interesting examples of this. In 'A Silver Dish', Morris Selbst, as crooked as he is, can pride himself: 'Three people work for me, I meet a payroll.' Selbst is the crooked father of the protagonist of the story, and used to run a laundry business – exploiting others, probably, but on an equal footing, often, with their employees. His egocentricity is also shown in his last name, Selbst, which in German means 'himself' or 'oneself.'

'Competitors are trying to steal my chemist from me. Without him I'll have to fold.' This is from another Bellow character in the same collection of short stories: a middle-aged woman, whose husband died and left her a small factory making plastic bags, is also forced to be a small entrepreneur and hustle around for sales. This is also an example of entrepreneurial activity undertaken out of a push force to earn a living, rather than a pull force into making money.

There is something good in the cheap and lowly, made of traveling salesmen, shopkeepers, farmers, small-time entrepreneurs and their laborers, their technicians, bricklayers – and, of course, the exporting tycoons and the boastful frontier scientists. There is a duty to praise the bad and the ugly: they may carry positive social values.

In micro-enterprises, the owner, the principal and the employee have very similar roles. They typically work in very close contact, sharing the same room – often the only room or store, which constitutes the 'headquarters' of the company.

Micro-entrepreneurs are personally indebted to finance their company. The epitome is Jeff Bezos' mortgaging his house to start up Amazon.com, but this is the standard economic and financing practice in many countries. Micro-entrepreneurs guarantee the bank debt of their companies with their own personal wealth.

In everyday practice, the micro-entrepreneur deals with his or her own bank debt situation, dealing with different short-term financial instruments to leverage their credit towards their customers and obtain cash advances from the bank to pay their own suppliers. When they are in a strong position *vis-à-vis* the banks they do business with, they sort of 'auction' their short-term debt (30–120 days): they will borrow the amount of a collateral invoice from the bank charging the lowest debt rate.

Micro-enterprise is tainted with the stigma of tax evasion. This can take many different roads and many levels, ranging from false invoicing to obtain fake costs to charging private dinners on the company's expense account. One truth is that this is often part of the small company's accumulation process (i.e. the formation of its own capital) and one way through which the entrepreneur obtains a living standard equivalent to that of a corporate employee (he perceives) with his same professional skills.

Micro-entrepreneurs are subject to domestic competition. Often, they are subject to the competition of organizations operating in the non-profit and the government sectors.

We do not believe (as the title of Ernst Schumacher's successful 1973 book has it) that 'small is beautiful'. There are many things that societies can't do other than with large and bureaucratic institutions. However, the circumstance of the existence of a vast area of the economy being run by small institutions, subject to competition, could bring about a very good antidote to the degeneration of bureaucracies: small is not beautiful, but it is useful.

The status of SMEs in the political arena

SMEs need a vision. They are marginal in the political arena, and fight a retroguard battle for 'fiscal reform' to clean up the social stigma of tax evasion – notwithstanding the fact that, at the same time, they pay the income taxes of their employees. They are united under no flag. There is no governing thought to their unity.

'Business and community' is a credo that needs to be elaborated, and their role of 'social shock absorber' can be amplified when appropriately analyzed. These key words are good analytical tools, but they lack charisma and visibility; they lack that sense of scandal and novelty that 'competition' may bring into the political debate.

SMEs exist in the permanent Cinderella state of their fiscal predicament. They are perceived alternately as a weakness or a strength of society and the economy. They do little technological innovation. However, they do make a great deal of effort to serve local communities. And every human being is, ultimately, resident in a local community.

Weaker stakeholders and failed attempts of the past

SMEs may have a Cinderella status in the political arena, but they have the numbers and the stake to count more than other actors that have tried, or are trying, the same feat:

- the Blueguide experience;
- the Minister's attack.

The Blueguide was a publishing initiative that I undertook during the 1990s. The idea was to publish a handbook of government bureaus and the officials managing such bureaus. The value mechanism was based on the hypothesis that a more punctual demand of services by the general public of government officials would stimulate a better response, thereby activating a virtuous spiral of efficiency in government. The initiative lasted a decade (1989–2000), and was terminated as non-profitable.

The Minister's attack was an initiative deployed since 2008 by a Minister for management in the government sector. The basic idea was to link salaries of civil servants to their performance. In order to measure performance, a complex scheme of institutions was devised that would bring about the definition, the quantification and the evaluation of such performance. As of the end of 2010, performance plans of government institutions were in the making and the steady state of reform was expected by 2012. The financial crisis of 2008–10 was seized upon as an opportunity to postpone disbursement of the funds that were meant to be used as incentives to remunerate above-standard performance.

'Why bother?' revised and policy implications

It is not original to propose SMEs as the backbone of the nation (Fox, 2004; Nardozzi, 2010; Paolazzi in Paolazzi and Nardozzi, 2009). However, my argument presents a number of novelties:

- It groups together entrepreneurs and their workers, reaching a massive scale of potential public with this proposal: over half the total workforce.
- It identifies the representative bodies of SMEs as potential leaders, and it identifies specific mechanisms of action, not limiting itself to an exhortation that SMEs 'make themselves leaders of the nation'.
- It identifies specific values: work and competition as an order of culture, of thinking, of lifestyle – not only as rules. Rules are the framework; they

are not the game. No rule will ever teach us how to improve our batting average, or how to score in the game of soccer.
- It looks at society as a whole, to all work, in a comparative fashion; therefore, it includes government and regulated industries.
- It identifies specific theories that explain the gaps, without resorting to *ad hoc* explanations such as national character.
- It is economic because it does not invent new rules to be observed; rather, it appreciates old rules already observed.
- It proposes a vision for SMEs as a collective actor and a full field economic and social stakeholder. The Small Business Act of the European Commission, for instance, does not say what is so good about SMEs that warrants protecting them and fostering them. It is said that SMEs are prevalent in the economy. Cholesterol is also prevalent in people's blood, but we do not try to increase it. My view says why SMEs are good for the economy and society (their being subject to competition, and therefore accountable), and it proposes to disseminate those values more than SMEs *per se*.
- The 'Think Small First' philosophy is good because it observes the basic value of equality as protection for the weak, but the philosophy does not give us the general results for the whole economy that working with values gives us. Certainly, the dynamism of entrepreneurs is to be tapped; however, also tapping dynamism in public sector and monopoly workers is a better story.

SMEs as collective actors and full-field economic and social stakeholders

Developing the message: the social value of competition

At this point, I am in the position to formulate a message and a vision for SMEs on the basis of my argument. A sort of manifesto: 'Accounting for work: the social value of competition.'

Accounting for work. Why?

In a world where everything depends on everything else, in the economy as in the ecology, your welfare depends on my work and vice-versa. This is the ultimate meaning of the 'competitive advantage of nations', and of the concept of country-system: nobody can claim himself to be above scrutiny. This is also the ultimate sense of developing a concept of CSR that is in the core business of the organization, be it a private enterprise or a government institution. All work, public and private, must be accounted for.

  How to account for work. Work that is subject to competition is immersed in an intrinsic mechanism of evaluation and comparison. It is therefore intrinsically accounted for. The free and voluntary transaction between customer and supplier is an instance of accounting for the work of the supplier.

That is the basic building block of social approval for work. Competition is a certifier of accountability. Work subject to competition is accounted for through the mechanism of competitive benchmarking. **Absence of competition generates the risk of 'evasion' of work.** Not all work is necessarily done in a competitive environment. Remoteness of work from voluntary transactions – which measure and socially approve work – increases the possibility that the same work be over-valued, or under-valued – thus opening the way to privilege, and to marginality. Therefore, work not subject to competition is exposed to the risk of being 'evaded,' not accounted for. 'Evasion' of work is an institutional phenomenon; it does not preclude individual workers from doing their work scrupulously.

Work that is not subject to competition must therefore be accounted for through some other mechanism of transparency, evaluation and control – of which we have seen examples in the previous chapters. Where feasible, competition must be introduced. Competition is not privatization. Competition can be introduced into different public institutions. (An empirical demonstration of this argument is contained in the 2002 Report of one of Europe's European National Antitrust Commissions: 'exporting sectors – that are more dependent from sectors that are most problematic from the competition point of view – show lower growth rates than the less dependent sectors'. Evasion of work means holding in fetters those who work and export or efficiently serve the domestic market.)

In some countries evasion of work may recall a similar phenomenon: tax evasion. The question may arise whether those who evade work are the same or are different from those who evade taxes. The two phenomena – when both present – are not to be considered as one sole issue. They are two different issues that must be addressed accordingly.

The competitive divide is pivotal to the economy and society. The real difference of social and economic position (the one that has an impact on the country system; the one having an impact on the quality of the economy and society) is not the contraposition – capital–labor, employer–employee, left–right, public–private. The real difference is in the way a living is earned: whether it is subject to competition or not. That is the competitive divide.

Being subject to competition is therefore a political opportunity. When we acknowledge the competitive divide, a cultural and political opportunity opens for those who are subject to competition: especially the small entrepreneurs and their representative bodies. In the name of competition, SMEs become full-field stakeholders.

A first enlargement of the field is obtained when not only the entrepreneur is represented, but also his or her employees. They are subject to competition as much as their employer. The shopkeeper's Boy Friday has the same social interests as his employer.

At the level of the national arena, once competition is put at the center of the public debate, SMEs have an interest in the government's efforts to evaluate work within the public administration; they have an interest in the functioning and action of the antitrust institutions and all the institutions responsible for vigilance over regulated sectors of the economy. SMEs could ask for structural and organizational reforms that introduce competition among public institutions, shunning the standard argument of eliminating duplication in the awareness that duplication – properly monitored – generates efficiency.

Conclusion

Competition is the divide between useful work and work to be scrutinized.
   Competition is a proof of utility of work.
   Where competition is absent, there is risk of evasion of work. In the name of competition, the small organizations (SMEs) become full-field stakeholders; they can represent their own employees; they can intervene in all government matters.

Agenda

What can the SMEs' representative bodies do operationally to implement the value of competition? The view generated by the competitive divide is not divisive in itself; there is a view onto the outside world – which I emphasized most in the discussion above, but there is also an inside view. In fact, the first thing to do in proposing a specific value is to scrutinize one's own house according to it. So be it for the value of competition.
   Regarding themselves, the representative bodies can:

- run a scan of their own activities and show they are responsible;
- engage employees besides the entrepreneurs;
- help SMEs in their efforts to be responsible by developing a framework that is responsive to the specific needs of SMEs.

Regarding the outside world, the representative bodies can take the following actions:

- be aware of competition on a cultural level;
- strive to understand the role competition has in every issue at hand and what effect a solution would have in terms of competition and accountability of work.

The numerous examples we have given so far have the value of providing points of view on specific issues and ways to think about problems along the lines of the value of competition:

- the representatives of SMEs could act as stakeholders at the local level *vis-à-vis* local and central government:
  - areas that are supposed to be remote from SMEs can be monitored: civil justice, for instance, has a large impact on business; health care costs have a large impact on taxes;
  - the education system can be monitored;
  - money transfer to business can be scrutinized;
  - security and safety;
  - environmental regulations;
- SME representatives could thrive on 'the cost of non-government':
  - publishing a ranking of public administration local branches;
  - inventing a parallel evaluation system based on outcomes, and publishing international data and using them in negotiations with government.

'Business and community' is a key phrase guiding the development of society. Communities. Local communities. What should be the guiding value for business in its interaction with local communities? What does it mean to have relations with local communities? Certainly, personal acquaintance and history and social capital are the variables: civicness. Though, how to prune out – and in the name of what fight against – patronage and personal envy? We believe that competition and its moderate declensions can help:

- awareness of the value of competition is a good acid test with which to define alliances with other organizations;
- on a supra-national level
  - appeal to supra-national bodies to enforce competition in their own countries
  - propose an industrial policy to break-up country-wide monopolies and constitute supra-national competing corporations.

It is not difficult at this point to recognize in the lists above an implementation of Michael Porter and Mark Kramer's 'Strategy and Society "Outside In" look' from society to the business firm.

What is probably new here is the political perspective and the collective action perspective in applying the competitive context diamond. That is, this map is not proposed here from the individual company point of view, but it is proposed from the collective action point of view, as a tool to identify issues to improve and change the competitive context. What is new is the use of the Porter and Kramer model as a tool to generate inter-sector dialectic and dynamics.

The basic idea is that if it is important for an individual firm, when understanding and assessing its competitive context, to figure out – for instance – the degree of enforcement of contracts through an efficient and effective judiciary system, then it is an important item in the agenda for the association of businesses to negotiate with government the improvement of the judiciary system – to ask for the accountability of the judiciary system. In the words of Porter and Kramer, 'transportation infrastructure and honestly enforced regulatory policy affect the company's ability to compete.'

Porter and Kramer assess the 'Social Influences on Competitiveness' through the classical Porter *diamond framework*, which is made of four corners:

1. Context for firm strategy and rivalry: the roles and incentives that govern competition.
2. Local demand conditions: the nature and sophistication of local customer needs.
3. Related and supporting industries: the local availability of supporting industries.
4. Factor (input) conditions: pressure of high-quality, specialized inputs available to firms.

It is not difficult to identify in each of these four domains the role of the non-competitive sector or better yet the role of the sectors of the economy that are less subject to competition. Let's give a few examples:

1. *Context for firm strategy and rivalry*: the quality we have already mentioned, the quality of the judicial system, and we could add the enforcement of competition *per se* (the explicit enforcement of fair competition); the role of government is to prevent and fight corruption, as this make the effectiveness of the police and judiciary system crucial.
2. *Local demand conditions*: the role of government as a leading-edge customer is recognized in the development of innovation.
3. *Related and supporting industries*: the creation of industrial parks is quite often the result of government policy, including land zoning.
4. *Factor (input) conditions*: it is celar that there is a role for government in education and in health care; whether government provides these services directly or not, none the less it is central in defining and implementing the social and economic framework within which such services are provided.

Finally, Porter and Kramer provide a methodology to identify issues and make sure that not only business is minding its own business but that all other parties involved that have an impact on the success of business are minding the business of businesses. When schools and the health care system and the judges are doing their own duty efficiently, they are performing essential – not peripheral, non-fungible – functions of business. We can very well paraphrase Thomas Merton here and say that 'No business is an island.'

Global professional support for sustainability

The Global Alliance for Public Relations and Communication Management – in closing their 2010 6th World Public Relations Forum – approved the Stockholm Accords, a two-year effort to advocate the value of public relations to organizations and society. In the Accords, we read:

> The communicative organization assumes leadership by interpreting sustainability as a transformational opportunity to improve its position within, and contribution to, society by pursuing and constantly reporting on the achievement of its policies and actions across the economic, social and environmental 'triple bottom line.'

What this article of the Accords says is that sustainability is the arena whereby SMEs can bring their values to bear on society as a whole. SMEs could leverage their status, improve their own position in society and contribute their values by pursuing and constantly reporting their policies of sustainability. The Stockholm Accords therefore provide a new framework whereby this transformation of SMEs can be fruitfully deployed.

A research and action project

Who, specifically, will be the social actor of horizontal competition? It is certainly not the individual shopkeeper who will be interested in promoting the social value of competition, but the representatives of those who are subject to competition: the associations of small and medium-sized (and micro) enterprises, micro-enterprises being the self-employed and those small businesses with fewer than 10 employees. The specific incentive for the small business association is tapping the reservoir of social and economic value (being subject to competition) – already embodied in their own fabric – in order to obtain political clout and to negotiate with public sector representatives and governments starting from a vantage point.

I have therefore undertaken a project to take to the local representative bodies of nationwide SME associations the following message: 'You are the embodiment of a positive social and political value: competition; you should make that weigh in your local and national interaction with government and large businesses.'

CSR and its harbinger, competition, confer legitimacy to SMEs as key actors in the political arena. Under the auspices of competition, SMEs become full-field stakeholders in the social and political arena. This is not a 'noble' end; it is an argument of equality of citizens and workers *vis-à-vis* work conditions – accountability being a key condition of work.

The vision I have been outlining can be put to work in practice, in order to see whether it makes sense.

The research and action project is based on field work: delivering the message in order to validate and detail the agenda for SMEs. We have undertaken a research and action project to engage the representatives of SMEs and listen to their observations.

The specific functions we are engaging are those who have responsibility of leadership and content development within the bodies that represent SMEs at local level (a few thousand, less than 10,000, member companies each: the president (who is an entrepreneur), the CEO (who is an employee of the representative body, like the ones that follow), the press officer.

They represent commercial businesses, craftsmen, and actual small industrial outfits.

We are also interested in engaging officers and politicians within public institutions and political parties and trade unions – those who are often the counterparts of SMEs.

The hypothesis is, then, that the representative bodies of SMEs will be sensitive to the message of their being 'positive carriers' of the value of competition. Under the auspices of competition, SMEs become full-field social and political stakeholders. They become interested in seemingly remote fields such as government workers' policy, industrial policy and subsidies, law enforcement and justice.

Our hypothesis will be proven, if the representatives of SMEs will:

- agree to public discussion on the theme of competition as a positive value for them;
- act upon the value of competition, undertaking some of the activities outlined; or identify different or new activities to replace those proposed, modify the message, improve upon it, change it, develop something new, even different from the initial proposal. The idea is to stir the waters of stagnant society.

The resources deployed:

- a team including a sociologist, a journalist and a web engineer;
- a website, started in 2009: www.ilbarbieredistalin.it.

The activities:

- contacting the representatives of SMEs;
- holding local public meetings;
- administering a questionnaire assessing ICT SME position *vis-à-vis* CSR.

Meetings held at Trieste (12 April 2010), Vicenza (6 May 2010), Milan (15 March 2011).

Preliminary findings

Spontaneous and self-initiated activity was not one of our hopes, and experience confirmed that. There are intellectual difficulties as well as energy difficulties: our message is far from straightforward and people are busy doing other things. One preliminary finding is that local SME associations are immersed in vertical competition and, though intrigued, are not ready to act upon the value of horizontal competition. Neither are they very much interested in checking the reality of their own social responsibility (there always being room for improvement). They have practical needs to serve their members, the small entrepreneurs, more than listening to general statements of political intent. They are, however, interested in CSR; and they are interested in developing a consulting formula that allows them to deliver a product or service to their members. Therefore, a CSR concept for SMEs is being developed in partnership with some local associations. A better opportunity seems to exist at the national level, where there are resources devoted to the scouting of new ideas, and analysis of the social and economic environment.

Business leaders. When confronted with the idea of competition, the leaders of SMEs think of the competition they are facing from their own competitors in their own businesses or the competition that the members of their organizations are facing:

- Trieste: large scale distribution vs. small stores;
- Vicenza: price-cutting in specific craft businesses connected to residential and business facilities.

('The problem with competition is unfair competition; they are cutting the prices too much.')

As predicted, people think of vertical competition, and have little awareness or interest in horizontal competition.

Politicians. Local political leaders speak in contrast to the standard talk of their national counterparts (Luigi Copiello, Confederazione Italiana Sindacati dei Lavoratori [Confederation of Workers' Unions] representative in Vicenza). ('The trade unions of civil servants are not doing a service to the nation by overprotecting their members'; he then said 'We must protect all work,' implying 'We must not protect only those workers who are enrolled in our ranks.')

Professionals in the associations:

- are interested in developing services for their business members (e.g. a concept of CSR for SMEs);
- the press office is their penetration point for our proposal; being political institutions, visibility is a key value for them and the press office is a key point of leverage for visibility; our message is an opportunity to gain visibility.

The associations *per se*. In our discussions, we gain an understanding of the associations themselves. They are very political bodies. Important at election time. However, they used to be more tied to political parties than they are in 2010.

Across countries. The focus of SMEs' representative institutions differs from country to country:

- in Germany, they perform personnel training and certification, and export support;
- in Italy, they provide accounting services to their members; credit support; and business promotion.

A European Project

Based on the hypotheses formulated in this book, a specific European Project was approved on July 6, 2011, by the European Commission (DG Employment, Social Affairs and Inclusion), with the following title: 'A new European study to identify and analyse the best practices and strengths of the industrial relations of self-employed workers: representation beyond administrations, the possible leadership of SME.'

A CSR framework for individual SMEs

Business leaders of SMEs – owing to their being subject to competition – are most concerned with their members' satisfaction with the services provided by the association. So, a first result of field work is the cooperative development of a product of CSR for SMEs: developing a business model for proposing the value of competition.

One preliminary finding is that local SME associations, however, being themselves subject to competition, need a business model to receive this message. Professionals in the associations are interested in developing services for their business members (e.g. a concept of CSR for SMEs). This appears to be a somewhat incongruous response to our message about competition, but we have to recall that we came to the concept of competition through the door of responsibility. The representative institutions may be following the same path. Only they are at a different stage than we are.

Notwithstanding all the limitations exposed, a micro-enterprise can be fairly innovative in the domain of accounting for its own work. Awareness of itself, in fact, can be very beneficial and can therefore be an important economic driver. Besides, it may cost very little.

On a CSR framework for SMEs, we can formulate the following statements:

- **Gaining awareness of the company's CSR status is, first and foremost, an internal and confidential operation**. It may seem unnecessary, but specifying that the operation of gaining awareness of the company's CSR status is not necessarily a public and open effort may derive some consensus to the operation itself. There is a benefit in running the initial internal and confidential part of the process. The second part, the communication and the discussion, may never take place, if the entrepreneur sees fit, and yet the benefit of having run it will be there anyway.
- **There is no need for a special report on CSR**. One report, within the current generally accepted accounting procedures, writing everything as

a preface to the financial statements, can be very innovative, along the lines of Robert Eccles' One Report (Eccles and Krzus, 2010).

- **Regarding the specific issues to be documented, nothing succeeds more than being open about the obvious facts of corporate life** (this might be culture-specific):
  - credit quality – the level of actual 'cashability' of credit in the assets and liabilities statement;
  - the saleability of warehouse or WIP (work in progress);
  - CAPEX (capital expenditure) vs. current expenditures – these are choices that are not objective; one can be aware and candid about them;
  - payments to suppliers –the length of time taken to pay debt to suppliers; whether there are debts overdue; a timeline chart may be in order;
  - payments to employees;
  - payments to the principals – no need to state the absolute level of payments, but its variations could be written down;
  - SMEs as 'social shock absorbers' in times of crisis, as they tend not to lay off their employees and to consider them less fungible in the market.

Some touchy issues have to be dealt with, too:

  - fiscal compliance – in order to start a new custom, we have to be soft on the touchy issues of fiscal compliance and employee contracts;
  - no added cost – being in the core business, CSR for SMEs must not add cost to their operations; or better, unjustified cost – meaning cost that does not present a reasonable advantage for business.
- The way data are presented is an important instance of observance of the values of disclosure, implementation, micro-ethics and the unknown stakeholder:
- tables, over time;
- denominators, quantities, so people can understand the importance of the statement at hand.
  Example: If I have €10,000 critical credit, it is important to state whether the total of my credit is €20,000 or €200,000: I would be much more worried in the first instance than in the second.

These are practical ways to express the four values of the USDIME framework: unknown stakeholder, disclosure, implementation and micro-ethics.

CSR questionnaire for SMEs

What SMEs feel and think about CSR is of interest, if competition and accountability have to become their social, political and economic flag.

Assintel is one of two associations that represent ICT businesses in Italy; Assinform is the other. Assintel has three international firms among its members (Oracle, Computer Associates and SAP). Its total membership is over 300, most members being SMEs. In 2010, Assintel decided to sponsor a project with Avis, a non-profit organization in the domain of blood donation. The project is called B2Blood and its scope is that Assintel raises awareness among its members about the opportunity and the benefits of having employees engaged as blood donors. Actual blood donation sessions are then organized with the support of the association and of individual firms that are members of the association.

To probe the state of the level of awareness of SMEs about blood donation and social action in general, we had the opportunity to administer a questionnaire. This questionnaire provides good data with which to identify corporate awareness about customers, social service and so on. We can thus identify companies' real problems, which will be useful in developing a CSR framework for SMEs. We can probe their perception of ethics.

Questionnaire 16.1   CSR questionnaire for SMEs

1	Customer relations do not belong in the social responsibility domain because business relations are not subject to ethics.		
			%
	– Agree	26	22.2
	– Disagree	91	77.1
	– Don't know	1	0.8
2	The real problems of companies are obtaining credit from the banks, delays in receivables, shrinking margins. They do not have time for the rest.		
			%
	– Agree	78	66.1
	– Disagree	40	33.9
	– Don't know	0	0.0
3	Corporate social responsibility is the quest for a relationship between the for-profit and the non-profit sectors; non-profit organizations seek integration with the business world and propose activities that are consistent with the corporate business.		
			%
	– Agree	90	76.3
	– Disagree	28	23.7
	– Don't know	0	0.0

4   The non-profit sector sees the private sector as a 'milk cow' and does not care about business.

		%
– Agree	18	15.3
– Disagree	100	84.7
– Don't know	0	0.0

5   Lacking social cohesion and institutional leadership in our societies, it is (in part) the task of business to build social awareness.

		%
– Agree	99	83.9
– Disagree	19	16.1
– Don't know	0	0.0

6   'Image' is the essence of corporate social responsibility; without communication CSR does not make sense.

		%
– Agree	65	55.1
– Disagree	53	44.9
– Don't know	0	0.0

7   Responsibility is not the same for all companies; rather, there is a ranking which is a function of the specific business the company is engaged in: CSR increases with the critical nature of business (e.g. environmental impact ranks at the top).

		%
– Agree	69	58.5
– Disagree	49	41.5
– Don't know	0	0.0

8   CSR implies gaining awareness of the overall impact of corporate business on society, including those activities that are included in the profit and loss statement.

		%
– Agree	111	94.1
– Disagree	7	5.9
– Don't know	0	0.0

9   CSR means to donate money to charities.

		%
– Agree	26	24.6
– Disagree	89	75.4
– Don't know	0	0.0

10   CSR is to 'give back' to society – in the form of socially responsible activities – part of what the company has received in order to prosper.

		%
– Agree	97	82.2
– Disagree	21	17.8
– Don't know	0	0.0

11   CSR is to cultivate a corporate climate whereby individuals are involved as much as possible, but are also free to express themselves through their own personal experience.

		%
– Agree	112	94.9
– Disagree	6	5.1
– Don't know	0	0.0

12   CSR is not for micro-enterprise (fewer than 10 people).

		%
– Agree	15	12.7
– Disagree	102	86.4
– Don't know	1	0.8

13   Corporate climate, inter-personal relations and individuals' welfare are strictly linked to corporate financial results.

		%
– Agree	88	74.6
– Disagree	30	25.4
– Don't know	0	0.0

14   Employee health is not strictly linked to the corporate core business.

		%
– Agree	43	36.4
– Disagree	75	63.6
– Don't know	0	0.0

15   Employees do not perceive corporate support to health as a meaningful benefit.

		%
– Agree	45	38.1
– Disagree	73	61.9
– Don't know	0	0.0

The questionnaire is reproduced here (answers were supposed to be 'Agree/Disagree/Don't know'). Results are from a sample of 118 answers out of 2000 pieces of e-mail and direct contacts; last update, October 31, 2010.

A first-cut summary of the data in Questionnaire 16.1 delivers a genuine interest in social responsibility in the core business. However, this responsibility is hardly seen from an operational point of view; that is, it is hard to tell what responsibility means with regard to everyday operations. To elicit concrete answers to this question is part of the subject matter of work ahead.

An inter-cultural perspective on economic and social competition

Finally, an effort is also being made to bring the message of competition as a positive value to supra-national and trans-national levels. In fact, the notion of competitive divide is applicable to all economies, if not to the entirety of each specific economy. My notions are confined to that developed part of society that is well above the poverty line. Also, the notion of SMEs is a global one, when taking into account the diverse structure and dimensions of SMEs in each economy. Therefore, a shift by SMEs towards removing the competitive divide appears to be one that all societies and all economies can entertain and profit from. Table 16.1 presents sample data about SMEs from a global perspective. There are differences, but there seems to be no reason why those differences should frustrate my argument.

Interpreting the trans-national level as the European level, exchanging (more than delivering) the message of competition as a positive social, political and economic value to the different countries that comprise the European Union, we may very well obtain a profitable inter-cultural perspective. The following questions may find answers other than the obvious:

Table 16.1 Sample data about SMEs in a global perspective

Country	SMEs per 1,000 people	SME employment as % of total
Brazil	27.1	56.5
China	6.3	78.0
France	41.8	62.7
Germany	36.4	70.4
Italy	77.8	73.0
Netherlands	35.2	58.5
Spain	65.1	76.0
United Kingdom	37.6	56.4
United States	19.6	50.2

Source: Kozak (2007).

- What are the different cultural approaches to the economy and the diverse cultural perspectives on the concept of competition?
- In what way is the economic structure of the enterprise different?

Micro-enterprises in Spain and Italy vs. medium-sized enterprises in Germany; but what about Poland?

- Representative bodies may have a different structure:
  - in Germany: most medium size and manufacturing, less diffused representative bodies; e.g. Dihk, chambers of commerce (Martin Wansleben, leader of Dihk); SMEs: BVMW and Umw;
  - Italy: very pervasive, diffused and (at least at their foundation in the 1950s and 1970s) ideologically constructed and driven;
- Representative bodies may have different roles:
  - e.g. chambers of commerce in Germany mostly implement the European Social Fund for labor training and export.

On a global scale, competition can be framed as an element of civilization, and market economy can be opposed to bureaucratic government or organized crime. Soliciting SMEs' awareness of the positive value of competition (as meritocracy, and solidarity as 'communicating vessels') is one specific way to foster the implementation of economic democracy.

Values and stakeholders: separating the beautiful from the useful

A final summary of propositions and orientation for empirical work is in order. Values and stakeholders: what counts and who counts when the objective function is the common good and the attitude is one of responsibility? What are the things that matter and who are the publics and the social groups that matter? In the current political and social discussion, values are widely flagged, but very vaguely formulated. What do such values mean specifically? Potential stakeholders are not identified and are unaware of their stake. When everything is connected to everything else, the value of your work and your welfare depend on the value of my work. Therefore every worker – laborer or executive, pauper or wealthy – is called upon to be accountable for his or her work. In this framework, values that are hidden in society and the economy become of the essence. Once the whole picture is put together, we may find that the solution is next door and our neighbors own it. Self-interest and so-called 'cutthroat competition' need revising and expanding to the public sector.

The values position

Beyond the values of my process framework (the unknown stakeholder, implementation, disclosure and micro-ethics), other values have been appraised and revealed:

- competition has been shown to generate cut-throat behavior by its absence rather than its presence, as it leaves room for harsher forms of human interaction;
- competition and markets – regulated and properly monitored markets – are drivers of accountability;
- accountability leads to the social utility of work;
- accountability is what counts as a synonym of positive social contribution, and accountability is not necessarily a conscious or voluntary action;
- most accountability in the economy is forced by competition – almost 75 per cent of the working population is accountable, possibly against their will (these are 'the useful');
- we tend to appreciate intellectual and learned people who might not be free from ambiguity and ill will as far as accountability for their work is concerned (these are 'the beautiful');
- work itself has been shown as something different from the administration of work;
- work is a value and stakeholders evaluate it, not forgetting an enthusiasm for technicalities.

CSR has been shown to be a duty of all workers, in the public and private sectors, so the United Nations could perhaps update the Global Compact and make it for all organizations – initially, governments. The abuse of people by their government has been shown to refer not only to dictatorial government, but also to democratic government: a coalition of workers might take advantage of the majority of those who work subject to competition. The basic human value of equality of workers *vis-à-vis* working conditions with regard to markets and the social value of work has been appraised here. The actuality has been viewed as muddling through where the worst is to be avoided; the ideal should be attempting to perfect the imperfect by making improvement where we find something messy and disharmonious.

Other values have been de-emphasized: the value of the future, *per se*, and the stewardship of future generations come out as rhetoric when the value of the present attitude is appraised, and responsibility is not something you do, but something that you are. Even if we were the last generation on Earth, we should put out the lights when we exit the room. Only in the *now* can we seed our future.

Likewise, we should be thinking about our own individual internal moral 'environment' in the same way that we have become accustomed to thinking about the physical external environment. We have been somewhat carried away by self-interest, and are a little too shy to talk about morality and consciousness. Knowledge has been mistaken for being. We are placing our emphasis on the rules, giving too little attention to how we play the game and carry out our own work within those rules. We give too much attention to our identity and too little to how we match up to it in our everyday actions: there is no DNA for organizational behavior. We crave a steady state that is not for us to attain. Likewise, the relevance of universal statements has been limited: what is good here and now may not simultaneously be good elsewhere. Extreme ethical instances may not be relevant to what we should do on Monday morning at work.

The stakeholders' position

There are many people unaware of their social value; they need the protection of reason in lieu of absent collective action:

- SMEs and their workers have a stake in the overall economy and society, but do not behave as though they do;
- we have refocused our attention – not (only) on the poor, but also on the working;
- most workers do not have representation;
- trade unions are self-restricted regarding the administration of work (pay, vacation, benefits, pensions).

There is a role for representatives of SMEs and élites at the national and local levels to monitor government and the quality of the social context. Competition, as we know it, is a vertical economic and sectoral notion: there is also a horizontal competition, among groups of the population that need to be brought into the foreground.

Regarding next steps

We need to separate conventional wisdom acquired through opinion surveys of experts (as in some World Bank and World Economic Forum statistics) from consistently measurable conditions of society:

- we need to measure the amount of over-compensation of monopoly jobs and the cost of non-government;
- we need to analyze the total working population subject to competition;
- integrated reporting in SMEs needs implementing; and
- an intercultural study could be conducted on the diverse views of competition within society.

Sometimes our perspective is blurred by intellectual bias, over-rating awareness and culture over work effort and fatigue. We are underestimating the social contribution of the little people, the ugly, the unlearned, the ignorant and ill-mannered, the often greedy – who are, however, tempered by competition and do their duty, putting forth a great deal of work effort and contributing to the competitiveness of nations. We have before us the task of separating the beautiful from the useful.

Farewell

Dear Economist,

Your critical survey of January 22, 2005 was the best you've ever done on the subject. You backed up a little bit in the 2008 survey, and then came forth again, making fun of Professor Michael Porter and his shared value concept on March 10, 2011. You clarified the limits of CSR: CSR is not philanthropy; if it were strategic philanthropy (i.e. something that gives returns in the long run), then it would only be good management. If CSR wanted to amend the problems of the world, that would not be part of the mission that stockholders agreed with when they bought their shares. That was a neat recap of an introductory economic course, Economics 101. Agreed. Nothing to object to. If CSR is just do-gooding, then it is bullsh*t. However, your approach to capitalism needs a fulcrum that is outside pure egotism. For instance, in the same 2005 survey there is a point where you assert that: 'Managers should think much harder about business ethics'. What then are business ethics? Why should they worry about it, and who would punish them if they did not? Capitalism also obeys Gödel's theorem, then: any system is based on something outside itself; that is, in the case of capitalism, custom and culture – ethics-factors generated outside economic selfishness.

Think, then, of CSR as a new entry on this culture scene. It was not there before; now it is. It was not necessary; however, it exists now and it may stay with us for a while. Its survival – indeed, its development – will be driven by competition among firms, government support and promotion by professionals. Think of CSR as an unpretentious friend of capitalism, a modest usher to it – like its forefather, advertising; a great deal of it is useless, but you do not know what.

What if CSR were extended well beyond the boundaries of patronage, philanthropy and paternalism? As I have tried to set out here, imagine all utilities giving comparable accounts of their quality of service. Imagine Big Pharma voluntarily disseminating data on their trials. Imagine companies and banks giving data on the share of public procurement among their customers, or banks giving data on the risk aversion of their clients compared with the volatility of their portfolio, certified by signed statements instead of informal street-level surveys.

Imagine CSR spreading to where capitalism is yet to be: governments, for one. Accountability of public policy and of the government sector is CSR, too. Imagine a world where you have data on local services across municipalities and countries. I think this would be a more capitalistic world and you'd like it better. Imagine how many *Economist* special surveys you could run on the efficiency and effectiveness of sectoral policies. Imagine freeing public policy from the autarky that governs it. Imagine a European Union that does not foster enterprise by subsidies whose effects are reported in no account. Imagine enterprise fostered through advocacy for an efficient judiciary, trade unions and entrepreneurial associations as whistle-blowers against corruption in government and within businesses. Imagine a market for pointing out the classical foes of capitalism and welfare economics: external effects and missing competition. Unleash your fantasies to a world of lower transaction costs and the correct implementation of capitalism – a dream much dreamt in the developing country from which I am writing.

Imagine all of this and you'll have a CSR report of a new kind: a harbinger of disclosure and dissemination of information. Good friends of capitalism.

Dear Economist, *Imagine* ...

Bibliography

Abbott W.F. and Monsen R.J. (1979) 'On the Measurement of Corporate Social Responsibility: Self Reported Disclosures as a Method of Measuring Corporate Social Involvement,' *Academy of Management Journal*, 22(3): 501–15.

Abravanel, Roger (2008) *Meritocrazia*. Garzanti.

Abravanel, Roger (2010) *Regole*. Garzanti.

AccountAbility (2008) AA1000 Accountability Principles Standard.

Allison, Graham T. (1971) *Essence of Decision – Explaining the Cuban Missile Crisis*. Little Brown.

Allouche, José (2006) *Corporate Social Responsibility, Volume 1 – Concepts, Accountability and Reporting*. Palgrave Macmillan.

Aras, Güler and David Crowther (eds.) (2010) *A Handbook of Corporate Governance and Social Responsibility*, March. Gower.

Aras, Güler and David Crowther (eds.) (2009) *Global Perspectives on Corporate Governance and CSR*. Gower, November.

Aras, Güler and David Crowther (2008) 'Developing sustainable reporting standards,' *Journal of Applied Accounting Research*, 9(1): 4–16. Emerald.

Archibugi, Daniele (2010) *The Global Commonwealth of Citizens. Toward Cosmopolitan Democracy*. Princeton University Press.

Argentieri, Simona (2008) *L'Ambiguità*. Einaudi.

Associazione Liberinsieme (2007) *Dall'idea al brevetto* [From Idea to Patent], Meeting of the Associazione Liberinsieme, Rome, July.

Banerjee, S.B. (2007) *Corporate Social Responsibility: The Good, the Bad and the Ugly*. Edward Elgar.

Barbery, M. (2006) *L'élégance du hérisson*. Gallimard.

Baricco, Alessandro (2002) *Next – Piccolo libro sulla globalizzazione e sul mondo che verrà*. Feltrinelli.

Bassanini, Franco (1996) 'Presentazione', in *La Città più Bella, Guida alle carte dei servizi pubblici*, Cispel, Guidazzurra, Rome: D'Anselmi.

Bauman, Zygmunt (2008) *Does Ethics Have a Chance in a World of Consumers?* Harvard University Press.

Bauman, Zygmunt (2010) 'Le disuguaglianze nel mondo liquido', Public address, Piacenza, 26 September.

Baumol, William J., Robert E. Litan and Carl J. Schramm (2007) *Good Capitalism, Bad Capitalism, and the Economics of Growth and Prosperity*. Yale University Press.

Beckmann, C. Suzanne and Morsing Mette (eds.) (2006) *Strategic CSR Communication*. DJOF Publishing.

Bella, Mariano (2010) 'Società imprenditoriale e sviluppo economico, Confcommercio,' Forum Giovani Imprenditori, I Giovani: *il Futuro del Paese*, Venezia, September 17.

Bellow, S. (1996) *Mosby's Memoirs*. Penguin.

Benkler, Yochai (2006) *The Wealth of Networks: How Social Production Transforms Markets and Freedom*. Strange Fruit. Also available at www.benkler.org.

Berta, Giuseppe (2010) Public address, Turin, February 4.

Bettelheim, Bruno (1987) *A Good Enough Parent: A Book on Child-Rearing*. Knopf.

Bianco, Lucio and Paolo D'Anselmi (1986) 'Strengthening the Management of Public Research Policy in Italy,' *Research Policy*, 15(3), June.

Bonacina, Riccardo (2009) 'Think Negative,' in D'Anselmi *et al.*, 'CSR: la forza del contro-esempio,' *Communitas*, 39, December.

Bonfiglioli, Romano (2011) Leadership e successione – Un'avvincente storia italiana. Franco Angeli.

Bonomi, Aldo (2008) 'Preface,' in P. D'Anselmi, 'Il barbiere di Stalin – Critica del lavoro (ir)responsabile.' Università Bocconi.

Brunetta, Renato (2009) 'Improving the Performance of Public Administration in the Information Society: the Italian Way,' in 'E-Gov. 2.0: Pave the way for e-Participation' Eurospace srl Convegno di Madrid, October 5.

Brunetta, Renato (2008) 'Meeting stakeholders' needs through a more efficient Public Administration,' in 'Improving Performance and Innovation in Public Administration: analyses and research among European e-Government experience,' Eurospace srl Convegno di Sofia, October 1-2.

Caliyurt, Kiymet, and Samuel Idowu (eds.) (2011) *Emerging Fraud: Fraud Cases from Emerging Economics*, Springer.

Calvino, Italo (1993) 'Six Memos for the Next Millennium,' *Charles Eliot Norton Lectures 1985–86*. Vintage International.

Campisi, Domenico and Roberta Costa (2008) *Economia dei sistemi industriali.* Carocci.

Campisi, Domenico, Roberta Costa and Agostino La Bella (1995) *Il governo della spesa pubblica e l'efficienza dei servizi*. Franco Angeli.

Capgemini, Wauters P. and G. Colclough (2006) *Online Availability of Public Services: How is Europe Progressing?* Diegem (Belgium): Capgemini/Ernst & Young.

Carroll, Archie B. (1991) 'The Pyramid of Corporate Social Responsibility: Toward the Moral Management of Organizational Stakeholders,' *Business Horizons*, July–August.

Cnipa–Digit PA (2008) Centro Nazionale per l'Informatica nella Pubblica Amministrazione – Rapporto Finale del POSI PON ATAS (Progetto Operativo sulla Società dell'Informazione, Piano Operativo Nazionale Assistenza Tecnica e Azioni di Sistema), Rome.

commetrics.com/articles/european-commssion-defining-the-term-sme/ [accessed 31 August 2010].

Confcommercio (2010) Censis, Osservatorio su consumi e fiducia, La difficile ripresa, February 24, Mariano Bella, Rome.

Confindustria (2009) *Scenari economici*, 5, June.

Consiglio Nazionale delle Ricerche (2004) 'CNR Report 2003,' Andrea Lapiccirella, Fabrizio Tuzi *et al.*, Rome.

Cormier D., I.M. Gordon and M. Magnan (2004) 'Corporate Environmental Disclosure: Contrasting Management's Perceptions with Reality,' *Journal of Business Ethics*, 49: pp. 143–65.

Crowther, David and Nicolas Capaldi (eds.) (2008), *The Ashgate Research Companion to CSR*. Ashgate.

Crowther, David and Güler Aras (2011) *Governance in the Business Environment*. Emerald.

Cuneo, Gianfilippo (1988) *Italian State Owned Enterprise*, McKinsey Institute, Milan.

Cuneo, Gianfilippo (1997) *Il successo degli altri*. Baldini Castoldi Dalai.

Dahl Rendtorff, Jacob (2009) *Responsibility, Ethics and Legitimacy of Corporations*. Copenhagen Business School Press.

Dahl Rendtorff, Jacob (2010) 'Corporate Citizenship and Republican Business Ethics,' *9th Conference on CSR*, Zagreb, June, Social Responsibility Research Network.

Dal Co, Mario (2007) *La malattia burocratica*, 1, January–February. Il Mulino.

D'Anselmi, Paolo (2008) 'Il barbiere di Stalin – Critica del lavoro (ir)responsabile,' Preface by Aldo Bonomi, Epilog by Toni Muzi Falconi. Università Bocconi.

D'Anselmi, Paolo (1990) 'Cultura dell'attuazione e fine dell'economicismo', in *Una magnifica avventura – Dalla sinistra sommersa alla sinistra dei club*, Edizioni Associate, a cura di G. Francesco Serra.

D'Anselmi, Paolo (1996) 'L'antibiotico concorrenza per l'economia malata', in *Quale capitalismo? L'economia italiana tra crisi dello Stato e globalizzazione*. Atti Liberal.

Das Gupta, Ananda (2010) *Ethics, Business and Society: Managing Responsibly*, Response Books.

Das Gupta, Ananda (2008) *Corporate Citizenship: Perspective in the New Century*, Scholar.

De Luca, Guerrino, personal communications, 2008–11.

De Rita, Giuseppe (2010) Public address at Joint Convention of SME representatives, May 10, Rome.

De Ros, Marina (2010) personal communication.

Del Monaco, Piero (2011) *Qualità della politica e lavoro pubblico*. Caosfera.

Di Vico, Dario (2010) *Piccoli*. Marsilio.

Draghi, Mario (2010) 'Considerazioni Finali, Banca d'Italia – Eurosistema,' Roma, May 31.

Eccles, Robert G. and Michael P. Krzus (2010) 'One Report – Integrated Reporting for a Sustainable Strategy'. Wiley.

Economist, The (2011) 'Oh, Mr. Porter – The new big idea from business's greatest living guru seems a bit undercooked,' Schumpeter column, March 10.

Economist, The (2008) 'In the Stream,' Survey on CSR, January 19.

Economist, The (2006) 'Billanthropy: How to spend money and influence people,' June 29.

Economist, The (2005) 'The Good Company,' Survey on CSR, January 22.

Eliot, T.S. (1936) 'Burnt Norton', *Collected Poems 1909–1935*. Harcourt Brace & Co.

Epstein, Marc J. (2008) *Making Sustainability Work, Best Practices in Managing and Measuring Corporate Social, Environmental, and Economic Impacts*, Forewords by John Elkington and Herman B. 'Dutch' Leonard. Berrett-Koehler.

European Commission (2008a) 'Small Business Act' for Europe, adopted in June.

European Commission (2008b) Communication from the Commission to the Council, the European Parliament, the European Economic and Social Committee and the Committee of the Regions, 'Think Small First,' A 'Small Business Act' for Europe, [SEC(2008) 2101][SEC(2008)2102];, Brussels, 26.6.2008, COM(2008) 394 final.

Ferpi, Federazione Relazioni Pubbliche Italiana, www.ferpi.it.

Ferrara, Alessandro (2008a) *The Force of the Example: Explorations in the Paradigm of Judgment*. University of Columbia University Press.

Ferrara, Alessandro (2008b) Public address, December 6, Rome.

Ferrara, Alessandro (1999 – unpublished) *Alcuni fattori di debolezza della cultura politica democratica in Italia*.

Ferriss, Timothy (2007) *The 4-Hour Work Week*. Crown Publishers.

Fox, Jeffrey J. (2004) *How to make Big Money in Your Own Small Business*. Hyperion.

Frangi, Giuseppe (2009) in D'Anselmi *et al.*, 'CSR: la forza del contro-esempio', *Communitas*, 39, September, Special issue.

Freeman, Edward (2010) *Strategic Management: A Stakeholder Approach*. Cambridge University Press.

Frederick, William C. (2006) *Corporation Be Good! The Story of Corporate Social Responsibility.* Dog Ear Publishing.

Friedman, Milton (1970) 'The Social Responsibility of Business is to Increase its Profits,' *New York Times Magazine,* September 13.

Galbraith, John Kenneth (1958) *The Affluent Society.* Houghton Mifflin.

Galluccio, Caterina (2009) 'La promozione del benessere organizzativo nella pubblica amministrazione: alcuni aspetti teorici,' *Sistemi Intelligenti,* 1, April.

Ghetti, Marco, Isabella Appolloni, Fabia Bergamo (2009) *Leader dentro. Coaching e consapevolezza nel viaggio del leader.* Luiss.

Ghosh Ray, Kamal (2010) *Mergers and Acquisitions: Strategy, Valuation and Integration,* Prentice-Hall of India Learning.

Giannelli, Maria Teresa (2006) *Comunicare in modo etico. Un manuale per costruire relazioni efficacy.* Cortina Raffaello.

Giarda, Piero (2010) Public address, Oscar di Bilancio PA, Rome, Italy, November 17.

Giovannini, Enrico (2010) Public address, Milan, September 29.

Global Alliance for Public Relations and Communication Management (2010) *6th World Public Relations Forum,* Stockholm Accords [accessed November 28, 2010]. http://www.globalalliancepr.org/content/1/1/homepage

Golden, Olivia (2009) *Reforming Child Welfare.* Urban Institute Press.

Görres, Anselm (2010) Green Budget Germany, Personal communication, October 29.

Gramsci, Antonio (2008) *Sotto la Mole (1916–1920).* La Riflessione.

Grunig, James E., David M. Dozier and Larissa A. Grunig (1995) *Manager's Guide to Excellence in Public Relations and Communication Management,* Routledge Communication Series. Erlbaum.

Hennigfeld Judith, Manfred Pohl and Nick Tolhurst (eds.) (2006) *The ICCA Handbook of Corporate Social Responsibility.* John Wiley.

Henriques A. and J. Richardson (2004) *The Triple Bottom Line; Does It All Add Up? Assessing the Sustainability of Business and CSR.* Earthscan.

Herzfeld, Michael (2009) *Evicted from Eternity – The Restructuring of Modern Rome.* University of Chicago Press.

Herzfeld, Michael (1993) *The Social Production of Indifference – Exploring the Symbolic Roots of Western Bureaucracy.* University of Chicago Press.

Herzlinger, Regina and Denise Nitterhouse (1994) *Financial Accounting and Managerial Control for Non-Profit Organizations.* South Western Publishing.

Hesse, Herman (1951) *Siddharta.* Bantam.

Hiatt, Jeff M. and Timothy J. Creasey (2003) *Change Management: The People Side of Change.* Prosci Learning Center Publications.

Hinna, Luciano (2006) *Economia delle aziende pubbliche.* McGraw-Hill.

Hirschman, Albert O. (1970) *Exit, Voice, and Loyalty: Responses to Decline in Firms, Organizations, and States.* Harvard University Press.

Hou, Shengtian, Fu Weihui and Li Xiaosong (2010) 'Achieving Sustainability with a Stakeholder-Based CSR Assessment Model for Foreign Invested Enterprises in China', *Journal of International Business Ethics,* 3(1).

Ichino, Pietro and I Nullafacenti (2008) *Perché e come reagire alla più grave ingiustizia della nostra amministrazione pubblica.* (Oscar argomenti), Mondadori.

Idowu, Samuel O. and Walter Leal Filho (2008) *Global Practices of Corporate Social Responsibility.* Springer.

Idowu, Samuel O. and Walter Leal Filho (2009) *Professionals' Perspectives of Corporate Social Responsibility.* Springer.

Kakabadse Andrew, Kakabadse Nada *et al.* (2007) 'CSR in Practice: Delving Deep', *EABIS – European Academy of Business in Society.* Palgrave Macmillan.

Karnani, Aneel (2010) 'The Case Against CSR', *Wall Street Journal*, August 23.

Kotler, Philip, and Lee Nancy (2005) *CSR – Doing the Most Good for Your Company and Your Cause*. John Wiley.

Kozak, M. (International Finance Corporation, World Bank Group) (2007) 'Micro, Small, and Medium Enterprises: A Collection of Published Data', last update January 26.

KPMG (2008) 'International Survey of Corporate Responsibility Reporting 2008'. http://www.kpmg.com/LU/en/IssuesAndInsights/Articlespublications/Pages/KPMG InternationalSurveyonCorporateResponsibilityReporting2008.aspx.

KPMG (2010) 'Global Compact 2010, United Nations Global Compact: Communication on Progress'. http://www.kpmg.com/Global/en/IssuesAndInsights/ ArticlesPublications/Pages/United-Nations-Global-Compact-Communicationon-Progress-2010.aspx [Accessed January 5, 2011].

Krkac, Kristijan (n.d.) 'Lying by Default,' 9th Symposium 'Contemporary Philosophical Issues,' Rijeka, 2007. Available at www.ffri.uniri.hr/datoteke/9simpozicpi_sazeci.doc

Krkac, Kristijan and Jelena Debeljak (2008) 'Change Management and CSR: An Essay in the Ontology and Business Ethics of Change/Process Management', in David Crowther and Nicolas Capaldi (eds.) (2008), *The Ashgate Research Companion to CSR*. Ashgate.

La Bella, Agostino (2005) *Leadership*. Apogeo.

La Bella, Agostino and Elisa Battistoni (2008) *Economia e organizzazione aziendale*. Apogeo.

Ladzani, Watson, and Jurie van Vuuren (2005) *Entrepreneurship Training for Emerging SMEs in South Africa*, digital, International Council of Small Business.

Lam, Maria (2000) *Working with Chinese Expatriates in Business Negotiations: Portraits, Issues, and Applications*, Praeger.

Lapiccirella, Andrea, Tiziana Micolitti and Elena Battistoni (eds.) (2011) *Economia della pubblica amministrazione, la teoria di William A. Niskanen*. Hoepli.

Leibenstein, Harvey (1978) *General X-Efficiency Theory and Economic Development*. Oxford University Press.

Lennon, John (1971) *Imagine*. Apple/EMI.

Leonard, Herman B., Jane Wei-Skillern *et al.* (2007) *Entrepreneurship in the Social Sector*. Sage.

Leonard, Herman B., Jane Wei-Skillern *et al.* (1992) *By Choice or by Chance? Tracking the Values in Massachusetts Public Spending*. Pioneer Institute for Public Policy Research.

Leonard, Herman B., Jane Wei-Skillern *et al.* (1986) *Checks Unbalanced – The Quiet Side of Public Spending*. Basic Books.

Louche, Céline, and Samuel Idown (eds.) (2011) *Theory and Practice of Corporate Social Responsibility*, Springer.

Lynn, Laurence E. (1991) 'The Budget-Maximizing Bureaucrat: Is There a case?', in André Blais and Stéphanie Dion (eds.), *The Budget-Maximizing Bureaucrat – Appraisal and Evidence*. University of Pittsburgh Press.

Macchitella, Vittorio (2010) Personal communications, September.

Maffettone, Sebastiano (2008) 'Inaugural Address of Academic Year 2008'. Luiss.

Mahbubani, Kishore (2008) *The New Asian Hemisphere: The Irresistible Shift of Global Power to the East*. Public Affairs.

Marcoux, Alexei, and Al Gini (2008) *Case Studies in Business Ethics*. Prentice-Hall.

Marcuse, Herbert (1955) *Eros and Civilization*. Beacon Press.

Marcuse, Herbert (1964) *One-Dimensional Man: Studies in the Ideology of Advanced Industrial Society*. Beacon Press.

Marshall, Alfred (2010) *Principles of Economics*. Cosimo.

Mays, Claire (2010) Personal communication, December.

McKinsey & Co. (2007) 'Shaping the New Rules of Competition: UN Global Compact Participant Mirror', July.

McKinsey Quarterly (2002) 'American Non-Profit Organizations,' 1.

Meadows, Donella H., Dennis L. Meadows, Jorgen Randers and William W. Behrens III (1972) *I limiti dello sviluppo* [*Limits to Growth*], Preface by Aurelio Peccei, System Dynamics Group – MIT and Club di Roma, Mondadori.

Melidco, Nicola (1999) *Bassanini in Comune*, D'Anselmi.

Micelli, Stefano (2010) Public address, May 5, Vicenza.

Micelli, Stefano and Eleonora Di Maria (2004) *On Line Citizenship: Emerging Technologies for European Cities*. Springer.

Monaco, Paolo, CNA Vicenza (2010) Personal communication, May 5.

Morgenstern, Oskar (1972) 'Thirteen Critical Points in Contemporary Economic Theory: An Interpretation,' *Journal of Economic Literature*, 10(4), December: 1184.

Moore, Mark H. (1995) *Creating Public Value Strategic Management in Government*. Harvard University Press.

Moro, Giovanni (2010) Public addresses, June 22, Vicenza; September 29, Milan.

Muzi Falconi, Toni (2011) 'Viaggio in Italia – Towards Integrated Reporting', Spokesperson for the Italian Integrated Reporting Committee, Global Reporting Initiative, Rome, November 25.

Muzi Falconi, Toni (2005) *Governare le Relazioni. Obiettivi, strumenti e modelli delle relazioni pubbliche: Marketing & Comunicazione*. Il Sole 24 Ore Pirola.

Muzi Falconi, Toni (2008) 'Chiacchiere di bottega,' in P. D'Anselmi, 'Il barbiere di Stalin – Critica del lavoro (ir)responsabile.' Università Bocconi.

Nardozzi, Giangiacomo (2010) *Il futuro dell'Italia, Lettera ai piccoli imprenditori*. Laterza.

Nayak, Pulin (1995) *Economic Development and Social Exclusion in India*. International Institute for Labour Studies. ILO.

Nayak, Pulin (2009) 'Anatomy of the Financial Crisis: Between Keynes and Schumpeter,' *Economic and Political Weekly*, Special Issue, Reprinted in Global Economic and Financial Crisis, Sameeksha Trust, Orient Blackswan, Hyderabad.

Nelson, Jane (2008) 'CSR and Public Policy: New Forms of Engagement between Business and Government,' CSR Initiative Working Paper 45, Harvard Kennedy School.

Nelson, Jane (2010) Personal communication, February 12.

Niskanen, William A. (2001) 'Bureaucracy: A Final Perspective', in William A. Shughart and Laura Razzolini (eds.), *The Elgar Companion of Public Choice*. Edward Elgar.

Niskanen, William A. (1968) 'Non-market Decision Making – The Peculiar Economics of Bureaucracy', *American Economic Review*, 58(2).

Nunez Martìn, Antonio (2009) 'Karl Rove, el "arquitecto" de George Bush', *Nueva Rivista*, June–September.

OECD (2010) *Modernising the Public Administration: A Study on Italy*. OECD.

Olson, Mancur (1965) *The Logic of Collective Action: Public Goods and the Theory of Groups*. Harvard University Press.

Osculati, Gianemilio (2008) *Gestire con successo*. Il Sole 24 Ore Pirola.

Osuji, Onyeka (2010) 'Fluidity of Regulation – CSR Nexus and Social Reporting: The Multinational Corporate Corruption Model,' 9th Conference on Corporate Social Responsibility, Zagreb, Croatia, 15–19 June 2010, Social Responsibility Research Network. Available at www.davideacrowther.com/9timetable.html.

Paolazzi, L. and G: Nardozzi (eds.) (2009) *Oltre la crisi. Pmi classe dirigente*. Confindustria.

Paoletich, Monica, Ascom, Gorizia (2010) Personal communication, October 11.

Papoutsy C. (2008) *Ethics, CSR, & Sustainability: An Aristotelian Vision, Mission, And Strategy For the Global Economy and a Sustainable Planet*. Socially Responsible Publishing.

Parks, Paul (2010) Personal communication, December 22.

Perkins, Dwight H., Steven Radelet and David L. Lindauer (2006) *Economics of Development*. Norton.

Perrini, Francesco, Stefano Pogutz and Antonio Tencati (2006) *Developing Corporate Social Responsibility: A European Perspective*. Edward Elgar.

Piermattei, Livia (2010) 'Transformative Innovation towards Integrated Reporting Passes through a Hands-on/Transition Phase and Leads to Real Innovation in Management', in R. G. Eccles, Beiting Cheng, and Daniela Saltzman (eds.), *The Landscape of Integrated Reporting – Reflexions and Next Steps*. Harvard Business School.

Piore, Michael and Charles Sabel (1986) *The Second Industrial Divide: Possibilities For Prosperity*. Basic Books.

Pistella, Fabio (2009) 'Convergenza fra gli obiettivi di riforma del lavoro pubblico e quelli relativi alla realizzazione dell'amministrazione digitale, Cnipa – Centro nazionale per l'informatica nella pubblica amministrazione,' *oggi Digit PA*, Rome, April 21.

Pleines, Heiko, and Andreas Umland (2008) 'Corporate Governance in Postsozialistichen Volkswirtschaften', *Soviet and Post-Soviet Politics and Society*, 75.

Ponti, Marco (2010) *Corruzione: necessarie ma non sufficienti le sanzioni*. Il Fatto.

Popper, Karl, quoted in Caterina Galluccio (2009) 'La promozione del benessere organizzativo nella pubblica amministrazione: alcuni aspetti teorici,' *Sistemi Intelligenti*, 1, April.

Porter, M.E. (1990) *The Competitive Advantage of Nations*. Free Press.

Porter, M.E. and Kramer, R. (2006) 'Strategy and Society: The Link between Competitive Advantage and Corporate Social Responsibility', *Harvard Business Review*, December: 62–78.

Prahalad C.K. and M. Porter (2003) *Harvard Business Review on Corporate Social Responsibility*. Harvard Business School Press.

Pressman, Jeffrey L. and Aaron Wildavsky (1973) *Implementation: How Great Expectations in Washington are Dashed in Oakland*. University of California Press.

Putnam, Robert (1993) *Making Democracy Work: Civic Traditions in Modern Italy*. Princeton University Press.

Rawls John (1971) A Theory of Justice. Harvard University Press.

Rifkin, Jeremy (2005) *The European Dream: How Europe's Vision of the Future Is Quietly Eclipsing the American Dream*. Polity.

Rolando Stefano (2008) Public address, November 11, Milan.

Ruggeri, Tommaso (2010) Public address, May 5, Vicenza.

Ruggie, John (2008) In the Stream, Survey on CSR, *The Economist*, January 19.

Ruggie, John (2010) 'Engaging Business: Addressing Respect for Human Rights,' Keynote Address, U.S. Chamber of Commerce, International Organization of Employers, Hosted by Coca-Cola Company, Atlanta, February 25.

Rusconi, Gianfranco (1988) *Il bilancio sociale d'impresa. Problemi e prospettive*. Giuffrè.

Sachs, Jeffrey D. (2005) *The End of Poverty*. Penguin.

Salvini, Gianpaolo and Luigi Zingales con Salvatore Carrubba (2010) *Il buono dell'economia – Etica e mercato oltre i luoghi comuni*. Università Bocconi.

Schelling, Thomas (1978) Micromotives and Macrobehavior. Norton.

Sehirli, Kubra (2009) 'Corporate Governance in Family Firms: A Comparison between Italy and Turkey,' in Aras and Crowther (eds.), *Global Perspectives on Corporate Governance and CSR*. Gower, November.

Simon, Herbert (1997) *The Administrative Behavior*. Free Press.

Sirilli, Giorgio (2005) *Ricerca & sviluppo: Farsi un'idea*. Il Mulino.

Sirilli, Giorgio and Alberto Silvani (1995) 'R&D Evaluation in Italy: A Science and Technology Policy View,' *Research Evaluation*, 5(1): 69–77, April.

Smith, Vernon (2009) 'We Have Met the Enemy and He is Us,' Istituto Bruno Leoni, Milan, May.

Stein, Gertrude (1922) 'Sacred Emily' (written in 1913), *Geography and Plays*.

Tabellini, Guido (2010) 'Sviluppo economico e capitale sociale,' Public address, November 23, Università Bocconi, Milan.

Tabellini, Guido (2008) *L' Italia in gabbia. Il volto politico della crisi economica*. Università Bocconi.

Tencati, Antonio (2010) 'Corporate Reporting Frameworks,' in Aras and Crowther (eds.), *A Handbook of Corporate Governance and Social Responsibility*. Gower, March.

Tencati A., F. Perrini and S. Pogutz (2004) 'New Tools to Foster Corporate Socially Responsible Behavior', *Journal of Business Ethics*, 53(1–2): 173–90.

Tullock, Gordon, (2005) *Bureaucracy, The Selected Works of Gordon Tullock, Volume 6*. Liberty Fund.

Turi, Roberto and Gruppo di lavoro Bilancio Sociale, with Andrea Gasperini of AIAF (2008) 'Mission Intangibles', Gli Asset Intangibili nel Bilancio Sociale di Italia Lavoro SpA, AIAF.

Tuzi, Fabrizio (2010) *L'Innovazione Dimezzata*. Brioschi.

Tuzi, Fabrizio, Alberto Silvani and Giorgio Sirilli (2005) 'R&D Evaluation in Italy: More Needs to be Done,' *Research Evaluation*, 14(3), December 1: 207–15.

Vacca, Roberto (2000) *The Coming Dark Age (revisited)*. www.printandread.com

Vaute, Monique (2008) 'Roma e i suoi Barbari,' Exhibition Catalog, Venice.

Veblen, Thorstein (1899) *The Theory of the Leisure Class: An Economic Study of Institutions*. Prometheus Books, 1899.

Viale, Riccardo (2010) *La conoscenza nascosta*. Mondadori.

Vignali, Raffaello (2010) Per uno 'Statuto delle imprese,' Una proposta di legge, Norme per la tutela della libertà di impresa. Statuto delle imprese (AC 2754), 2010, Power Point, 15 pages, Camera dei Deputati.

Visser Wayne (2011) *The Age of Responsibility – CSR 2.0 and the new dna of business*. John Wiley.

Visser Wayne, Dick Matten, Manfred Pohl and Nick Tolhurst (2007) *The A to Z of Corporate Social Responsibility: A Complete Reference Guide to Concepts, Codes and Organisations*. John Wiley.

Vogel D. (2006) *The Market for Virtue: The Potential and Limits of Corporate Social Responsibility*. Brookings Institution.

Von Mises, Ludwig (1944) *Bureaucracy*. Yale University Press.

Weber, Max (1976) *The Protestant Ethic and the Spirit of Capitalism*. Scribner.

Weber, Max (1952) 'The Essentials of Bureaucratic Organization: an Ideal-Type Construction', in Robert K. Merton *et al.* (eds.), *Reader in Bureaucracy*. Free Press.

Weber, Sanija (2010) 'Employees "Lost in Translation": From Stakeholder Management to Employee Engagement and Implications for Corporate Social Responsibility (CSR) Practices,' 9th Conference on Corporate Social Responsibility, Zagreb, Croatia, June, Social Responsibility Research Network. Available at www.davideacrowther.com/9timetable.html.

Weiss, Carol H. (1972) *Evaluation Research: Methods for Assessing Program Effectiveness.* Prentice Hall.

Werther W. and D. Chandler (2005) *Strategic Corporate Social Responsibility: Stakeholders in a Global Environment.* Sage Publications.

Williams, Geoffrey (ed.) (2010) *Responsible Management in Asia – Perspectives on CSR.* Palgrave Macmillan.

World Bank, Worldwide Governance Indicators (WGI) project. Available at http://info.worldbank.org/governance/wgi/index.asp.

Wright, Tim (2003) 'Plus ca change, plus c'est la meme chose, The Grand Illusion of Corporate Social Responsibility, Leicester University Management Centre.' timwright@sharp42.demon.co.uk.

Young, Stephen (2010) 'The Case for CSR,' *Wall Street Journal*, August 27.

Zabala, Santiago (ed.) (2007) *Weakening Philosophy: Essays in Honour of Gianni Vattimo.* McGill-Queen's University Press.

Zambon Stefano and Giuseppe Marzo (2007) *Visualising Intangibles: Measuring and Reporting in the Knowledge Economy.* Ashgate.

Zu Liangrong (2008) *Corporate Social Responsibility, Corporate Restructuring and Firm's performance: Empirical Evidence from China.* Springer.

Index

Key: **bold** = extended discussion; f = figure; q = questionnaire; t = table.

240   *Index*